About the Editors

ARTHUR P. DAVIS is professor emeritus of English at Howard University and the author of *From the Dark Tower: Afro-American Writers, 1900–1960*. The late J. SAUNDERS REDDING was Ernest I. White Professor of American Studies and Humane Letters at Cornell University and the author of *To Make a Poet Black*. JOYCE ANN JOYCE is currently a professor of English at Chicago State University and the author of *Native Son: Richard Wright's Art of Tragedy*.

Bantam Classics
Ask your bookseller for classics by these American writers

Louisa May Alcott
L. Frank Baum
Willa Cather
Kate Chopin
James Fenimore Cooper
Stephen Crane
Theodore Dreiser
Frederick Douglass
W. E. B. Du Bois
Ralph Waldo Emerson
Benjamin Franklin
Charlotte Perkins Gilman
Alexander Hamilton
Nathaniel Hawthorne
O. Henry
Harriet A. Jacobs
Henry James
John Jay
James Weldon Johnson
Helen Keller
Abraham Lincoln
Jack London
James Madison
Herman Melville
Edgar Allan Poe
Upton Sinclair
Gertrude Stein
Harriet Beecher Stowe
Henry David Thoreau
Mark Twain
Booker T. Washington
Edith Wharton
Walt Whitman

Selected African American Writing from 1760 to 1910

Edited by

Arthur P. Davis

J. Saunders Redding

Joyce Ann Joyce

BANTAM BOOKS
New York　Toronto　London　Sydney　Auckland

A　B A N T A M　C L A S S I C

SELECTED AFRICAN AMERICAN WRITING FROM 1760 TO 1910

A Bantam Classic Book / published by arrangement with
Howard University Press

PUBLISHING HISTORY
Selected African American Writing from 1760 to 1910 is excerpted from
Chapters 1, 2, and 3 of *The New Cavalcade: African American Writing
from 1760 to the Present*, Volume I, published by
Howard University Press.
(Originally published as *Cavalcade: Negro American Writing from 1760
to the Present*). Copyright © 1971 by Arthur P. Davis and Saunders
Redding) Sixty percent of the specified chapters have been excerpted.
Bantam Classic edition / January 1995

Whittier Preparatory School, Phoebus VA, 1907. Photo credit: James
Van Der Z. Copyright credit by: Donna Mussenden-Van Der Zee.

ISBN 0-553-21435-7

Published simultaneously in the United States and Canada

Bantam Books are published by Bantam Books, a division of Bantam
Doubleday Dell Publishing Group, Inc. Its trademark, consisting of the
words "Bantam Books" and the portrayal of a rooster, is Registered in
U.S. Patent and Trademark Office and in other countries. Marca Registrada.
Bantam Books, 1540 Broadway, New York, New York 10036.

PRINTED IN THE UNITED STATES OF AMERICA

OPM   0 9 8 7 6 5 4 3 2 1

To
J. SAUNDERS REDDING,
scholar, teacher, critic,
and
highly esteemed fellow-editor

Contents

PART 2
Freedom Fighters: 1830–1865

Contents

PART 3
Accommodation and Protest: 1865–1910

General Introduction

Selected African American Writing from 1760 to 1910 is an abridged version of *The New Cavalcade: African American Writing from 1760 to the Present,* Volumes I and II, published by Howard University Press. It is our hope that this Bantam edition will extend the appreciation and understanding of the authors and the works of this period to yet another audience.

The term "African American writing" as used in the title requires an explanation that goes beyond the obvious one of a body of writing by black Americans. Some black writers "write like whites." The entire stock of their referents is white, Anglo-Saxon–American derived. Most black American writers, however, create out of a dual consciousness: African and American. The writers are twin-rooted, and while one root is nourished by the myths, customs, culture, and values traditional in the Western world, the other feeds hungrily on the experiential reality of blackness. These writers have a special vision. They are persuaded by a special mission. In their work they combine the sermon and the liturgy, the reality and the

dream, the *is* and the *ought to be*. Their writing is intended
to appeal as much to the cognitive as to the affective side
of our beings.

The purpose of this anthology is to provide a representative selection of the best prose and poetry written by
African Americans between 1760 and 1910. While it has
been our primary aim to make these choices on the basis
of literary merit, we have also tried to cover as many areas
of black life in America as was consistent with our first
objective. We believe that this collection gives a fairly
comprehensive picture of the black experience in America
from 1760 to 1910.

For the purposes of a historical survey, it seemed sen-
sible to divide the chronology of African American writing into three periods. They are designated and dated:
Pioneer Writers (1760–1830); Freedom Fighters (1830–
1865); Accommodation and Protest (1865–1910). Each
period is prefaced by a critical introduction, which provides, we believe, a background sufficient to give meaning
and perspective to the offerings in each section. For each
author we have provided a brief biobibliographical headnote. The bibliographical data at the end of the headnote
should be helpful to student and teacher alike, serving, we
hope, as springboards for additional study.

Whenever feasible we have given whole works rather
than excerpts. A few entries, however, have been far too
long to include in their entirety, and we have used parts
of the works—parts that we believe can stand alone. In
every case we have seen to it that the selection not only
can stand alone but is fairly representative of the author's
general matter and manner. Whenever we left out short
sections of a work, we have indicated this omission with
the conventional ellipses; for longer omissions we have

used ornaments. When novels or autobiographies have chapter titles, we have used them, noting the work from which the excerpt was taken. When chapter titles do not exist in the original work, we simply note the work from which the selection was taken. In the selections we have exercised discretion in matters of spelling, punctuation, and capitalization in those works that were carelessly printed and edited in the eighteenth century and the early decades of the nineteenth.

In this volume we have faced the issue of what to call ourselves—an issue that has prevailed since Emancipation. The popular name at first was, seemingly, "colored" (as in NAACP); then came "negro" (with a lowercase *n*); then "Negro" (with an uppercase *N*); then "Afro-American"; then "Black" (with a capital *B*); then "black" (with a lowercase *b*); and now "African American."

Until the 1960s *Negro* was still widely accepted, although after the social and literary changes of the sixties *black* gradually became the popular designation. For some older scholars and laypersons, *black* was an ugly term, and they hung on to *Negro* or used *Afro-American*. We the editors have tended to use the term *African American;* however, we felt free to use *Negro, black,* and *Afro-American*. In short, we have no desire to enter into any controversy over what to call ourselves. It is a decision that the people will make, as they have always done.

In preparing this volume we have examined and consulted practically all of the anthologies, collections, and critical works on African American literature extant, and in some ways we are indebted to all of them. We wish, however, to acknowledge a special indebtedness to the following works: *The Negro in Literature and Art* (third edition) and *Early Negro American Writers* by Benjamin Brawley; *To Make a Poet Black* by J. Saunders Redding; *The Negro Author* by Vernon Loggins; *Dictionary of American Negro Biography,* edited by Rayford W. Logan and Michael R. Winston; *Dictionary of Literary Biography,* Volume 33, *Afro-American Fiction Writers After 1955; Dictionary of Literary Biography,* Volume 41, *Afro-American Poets Since 1955; Dictionary of Literary Biography,* Volume 50, *Afro-American Writers Before the Harlem Renaissance; Dictionary of Literary Biography,* Volume 51, *Afro-American Writers from the Harlem Renaissance to 1940,* all of which were edited by Trudier Harris and Thadious M. Davis.

Though we designed this volume primarily as a book for students, we hope it is something more. We hope that students, scholars, and the general public will read this book with pleasure and profit.

Arthur P. Davis
Joyce Ann Joyce

Acknowledgments

Compiling an anthology requires so much bibliographical, critical, and other kinds of help, from colleagues, fellow scholars, and friends, it is practically impossible to thank all of them here. We must, therefore, settle for a chosen few, especially those who have helped to bring out *The New Cavalcade*: among them Fay Acker, senior editor of the Howard University Press, who, through her guidance, made our job easier; Cynthia Lewis and Iris Eaton, also of Howard University Press, who handled the numerous permissions requests for both volumes of *The New Cavalcade;* Janell Walden Agyeman, who researched information for the headnotes; Kamili Anderson, who prepared the bibliographies; Rhonda Williams and Lisa McCullough, who worked on headnotes; Professor Eugene Hammond and Janet Duncan of the University of Maryland; Kathy Johnson and Laurie Wilshusen of the University of Nebraska; and O. Rudolph Aggrey, director of the Howard University Press, who encouraged and supported, in every way possible, this project. We cannot thank individually all of the members of the famous

Moorland-Spingarn Research Center who helped us almost daily for a long period. It is a great library with a highly efficient and helpful staff. We are also deeply indebted to Ethelbert E. Miller, supervisor of Howard University's African American Resource Center, for his help in securing source material for our book.

PART 1

||===||===||===||===||===||

PIONEER WRITERS: 1760–1830

The history of African American writing begins approximately a century and a half after the first black people were landed at Jamestown in the English colony of Virginia in 1619. Whereas the colonial period was marked by cultural and political advancement of the white colonists, leading to their independence, this same period fixed the social position of African Americans, fastened upon them an aggregate of character qualities that were not always reflective of proved attributes, and created for them a repertoire of cultural and social roles that they seemed destined to play forever. Whether free man or slave, the African American was forced into a markedly inferior status which was said to be justified by his "natural" character; and his character was variously and simultaneously described as "savage," "irrepressibly comic," "lecherous," "childish," "sullen," and "without a redeeming human trait."

These attributions and the rationalizations they supported were passionately touted in the South, and the passion increased as such notions were challenged by the

philosophy of the Enlightenment and the political con-
cepts of human equality and the natural rights of man.
Though the characterizations were considered less valid
in the North, they were not rejected there. North and
South, blacks had become stereotyped by the middle of
the eighteenth century.

The stereotype represented an accommodation of religious and moral scruples to the white man's material interests. It was the answer to questions that had troubled
rational men since the beginning of the modern slave era,
and that were—as diaries, letters, and essays of the period
indicate—particularly pervasive in colonial times: How
can slavery be justified? Can black men be excluded from
the brotherhood of Christianity? Is slavery right in the
eyes of God?

Although hundreds of historical incidents document the
fact that blacks responded to the denial of their humanity
in a variety of ways, a careful survey of African American
writing suggests that the variety of responses can be sub-
sumed under three basic attitudes and their corresponding
modes of behavior: accommodation, protest, and escape.
These are the attitudes that were established almost at the
beginning and were structured into the body of myths and
"traditions" that symbolize them. From the first, blacks
had a choice of either accommodating to, protesting
against, or escaping from a way of life that was cruelly
exploitative and inexcusably demeaning. For the illiterate
black man the response was direct and physical. He accommodated by projecting the harmless aspects of the
black stereotype; he protested by committing acts of violence; he escaped by running away.

But responses were not so clear-cut for sophisticated,
literate blacks. Jupiter Hammon was among the first of

those who left records. He accommodated. He said what seemed to be acceptable. In his one extant prose piece, "An Address to the Negroes of the State of New York," he states, "As for myself . . . I do not wish to be free." But when one reads the servant's replies in "A Dialogue Intitled the Kind Master and the Dutiful Servant," one suspects that Hammon is double-talking, and doing it so artfully and with such subtly pointed irony as not only to reduce the masters' admonitions to absurdity but to constitute a statement of protest against them.

Phillis Wheatley, a much better poet than her older contemporary Hammon, seems also to have combined accommodation and protest, especially in such pieces as "To the Right Honorable William, Earl of Dartmouth" and "To the University of Cambridge, in New-England." But again and again she returned to the mode of escape. It was expressed in her frequently implied rejection of the knowledge that the color of her skin determined her experience—that it set bounds and was prescriptive. Escape often lay in pretending that she was like everyone else in the circle of white acquaintances with which the Wheatley family surrounded her and pretending that she was emotionally involved only in their concerns, directed by their biases, and committed to their tastes. And, to an amazing degree, she did absorb their late-Puritan culture: she was intensely moralistic and religious and considered restraint one of the highest of virtues. Wheatley modeled her work after Alexander Pope and used the heroic couplet, classical allusions, neatness, and precision. Vernon Loggins, in *The Negro Author*, states, "[Wheatley's] work is sophisticated rather than primitive, artificial rather than spontaneous, polished rather than crude. . . . It is in spirit and in execution little different from the sentimental poems turned out, both in England and in America, by numerous skillful versifiers of the eighteenth century who knew well the neoclassical rules for writing poetry and who followed them with studied care.''[1]

Until very recently, scholars have believed that Jupiter Hammon's ''An Evening Thought . . .'' (1760) was the first known poetical publication by an American Negro; but, in light of a contemporary discovery, Hammon and the year 1760 must give precedence to Lucy Terry and the year 1746. In that year, she published a broadside, ballad-type poem entitled ''Bars Fight.'' The twenty-eight-line piece describes in starkly realistic and colorful detail a bloody Indian raid on the settlers in Deerfield, Massachusetts, on August 25, 1746. All that we know about Lucy Terry is that she was a slave who belonged to Ebenezer Wells of Deerfield. This is the entire poem:

> August 'twas the twenty-fifth
> Seventeen hundred forty-six
> The Indians did in ambush lay
> Some very valient men to slay
> The names of whom I'll not leave out
> Samuel Allen like a hero fout
> And though he was so brave and bold
> His face no more shall we behold
> Eleazer Hawks was killed outright
> Before he had time to fight
> Before he did the Indians see
> Was shot and killed immediately

---

[1]Vernon Loggins, *The Negro Author: His Development in America* (New York: Columbia University Press, 1931), 16.

Oliver Amsden he was slain
Which caused his friends much grief and pain.
Simeon Amsden they found dead
Not many rods off from his head.
Adonijah Gillet, we do hear
Did lose his life which was so dear
John Saddler fled across the water
And so [sic] excaped the dreadful slaughter
Eunice Allen [sic] see the Indians comeing
And hoped to save herself by running
And had not her petticoats stopt [sic] her
The awful creatures had not cotched [sic] her
And tommyhawked her on the head
And left her on the ground for dead.
Young Samuel Allen, Oh! lack-a-day
Was taken and carried to Canada.

George Moses Horton, the last of the pioneer poets,
was a considerably more complex person and poet than
either Phillis Wheatley or Jupiter Hammon. Scarcely typical of his poetry are the lines from "On Liberty and
Slavery" which first brought him to general notice in
1829.

Alas! and am I born for this,
     To wear this slavish chain?
Deprived of all created bliss,
     Through hardship, toil and pain!

After the publication of *The Hope of Liberty,* from which
he expected to earn enough to buy his freedom and a
passage to Africa, Horton contented himself for more than
thirty years with the place he occupied and the reputation

he acquired in Chapel Hill, North Carolina. His knack for composing verses on a variety of subjects at a moment's notice gave him the status of a "character" at the university, where he fulfilled poetic commissions for the students. "For twenty-five cents he would supply a poem of moderate warmth, but if a gentleman wished to send a young lady an expression of exceptional fervor, fifty cents would be the fee."[2] But not all the commissions were for love verses. Some of his brightest pieces were purely comic, as in "The Creditor to His Proud Debtor."

> My duck bill boots would look as bright,
> Had you in justice served me right.
> Like you, I then could step as light
>   Before a flaunting maid.
> As nicely could I clear my throat,
> And to my tights my eyes devote;
> But I'd leave you bare, without a coat
>   For which you have not paid.

Horton's verses are refreshing after the solemnity of Phillis Wheatley's work and the religious common-meter hymn doggerel of Jupiter Hammon. His rhythms are seldom monotonous, and his verse structure is varied. He was a troubadour, a purveyor of gossip, a maker of quips, with a special penchant for ridicule. He dealt, often lightheartedly, with love, the fickleness of women and fortune, the curse of drink, and the elusiveness of fame. Of the slave poets, Horton was by far the most imaginative and the freest.

[2]Benjamin Brawley, *Early Negro American Writers* (Chapel Hill: University of North Carolina Press, 1935), 110.

As art, early Negro autobiographical writing is less important than early Negro poetry, but as history it is more important and had a larger contemporary audience. After all, autobiographical writing centers on the experiences of "real life," and the mind of eighteenth-century and postcolonial America had a great affinity for the true. It saw little connection between imagination and experience and cared less for imaginative insight than for the surface rendering of reality. Literary "art" was suspect. It was typical that William Lloyd Garrison, the abolitionist, counseled Frederick Douglass to *tell* his story and expressed an impatience with literary and intellectual embellishments.

The author of the first black American autobiography, then, need not have apologized for the "capacities and conditions" of his life, nor for the language in which he sets them forth. *A Narrative of the Uncommon Sufferings and Surprising Deliverance of Briton Hammon, a Negro Man* is a booklet of fourteen pages. Published in Boston in 1760, it describes episodes in Hammon's roundabout journey from New England to Jamaica to the British Isles and back. In the course of his journey Hammon suffers shipwreck, is held captive by Indians in Florida, and is imprisoned by Spaniards. But the telling falls flat. Hammon makes no attempt at description or character delineation and provides no insights. The *Narrative* deserves mention only because it is the first in a genre that by the middle of the nineteenth century became the most popular form of Negro expression.

While Briton Hammon, who lacked intellectual sophistication, owed nothing to tradition, John Marrant did. He most certainly knew *Pilgrim's Progress,* and he was probably acquainted with Jeremy Taylor's *Holy Living and Holy Dying.* Two of Marrant's three works are autobiographical, but only the title of the first reveals the fact that the author was a Negro. A *Narrative of the Lord's Wonderful Dealings with J. Marrant, a Black* (London, 1785) and *Journal of John Marrant* (London, 1789) tell of miraculous conversions followed by equally miraculous escapes (which symbolize God's mercy) from all sorts of natural cataclysms (which symbolize God's power and wrath) and man-created disasters (which symbolize humanity's wickedness). Marrant's third book, *Sermon,* is just that—a long narrative sermon that retells, with wildly imaginative elaborations, the Old Testament.

The most important autobiography of the period was written by an African, Olaudah Equiano, who was only briefly a slave in America. His autobiography, *The Interesting Narrative of the Life of Olaudah Equiano, or Gustavus Vassa, the African* (London, 1789) principally relates his experiences as a slave in foreign lands and is notable for several reasons. It ran to eight editions in five years. It is a great antislavery document and conveys a wealth of firsthand impressions and information about slavery, which, as Vassa makes brilliantly clear, was one thing in Africa, another in England, and something altogether different in America, but an evil everywhere. *The Narrative* is also an absorbing travel book. Vassa was taken to many places, and his descriptions of people, manners, and customs are powerfully evocative of the realities of eighteenth-century life in several parts of the world. No autobiography of the period matches Vassa's for clarity, honesty, and truth.

But most of the autobiographical writings of this time were essays of protest, and the Negro authorship of several of them is questionable. Some dedicated white abolitionists were not above writing "slave narratives" and issuing them as the authentic work of blacks. There is grave doubt, for instance, that "Petition of an African," which was published in an antislavery journal called *American Museum,* was written by a Negro woman as claimed. Similar doubts are attached to "An Essay on Slavery," signed "Othello," which was also printed in *American Museum* in 1788.

Other autobiographical writers are easily identified as Negroes. One of these was Benjamin Banneker. An engineer, mathematician, and astronomer, Banneker served on the commission that laid out the streets of the nation's capital. In a letter of protest to Thomas Jefferson, he cited his own achievements as evidence against the "train of absurd and false ideas which so generally prevail with respect to the Negro." Other blacks, who certainly did not think of themselves as writers, produced pamphlets and tracts, letters, and petitions which were widely circulated. David Walker's *Appeal,* published in 1829, aroused the slaveholding South to such a pitch of anger and fear as to persuade the governor of Virginia to prepare a special legislative message about it, and the mayor of Savannah, Georgia, to request that the mayor of Boston suppress it. Walker stressed the blatant hypocrisy of American Christianity; earlier writers, among them Benjamin Banneker, struck at the national hypocrisy of a government which could wage a war to give whites their freedom from tyranny without considering freedom from slavery for its black "citizens." Even Jupiter Hammon, in his mild accommodationist way, pointed out this inconsistency.

By the end of the period, George Moses Horton was the only generally recognized writer who remained an accommodationist. Escape in the Phillis Wheatley sense was unthinkable. Protest was the mode and the theme. For all the variations in degrees of talent, in intellect, in "ways of seeing," and in style, protest united Briton Hammon and John Marrant, Gustavus Vassa, Benjamin Banneker, and David Walker. Whether they were as optimistic as Hammon or as desperate as Walker, these authors believed that their writing could help change the lives of blacks for the better. This was their commitment—to contribute to an amelioration of the black race's lot. If in their pursuit of this goal they did not produce literary art, they did reaffirm the values and the ideals of freedom, equality, and justice—ideals that blacks were seldom credited with appreciating and understanding.

Phillis Wheatley

(c. 1753–1784)

Practically all that is known of the early life of Phillis Wheatley is found in the following letter, written in 1772 by her master, John Wheatley, and printed in her *Poems on Various Subjects* (1773):

> Phillis was brought from *Africa to America,* in the Year 1761, between Seven and Eight years of age. Without any assistance from School Education, and by only what she was taught in the Family, she, in sixteen Months Time from her Arrival, attained the English Language, to which she was an utter Stranger before, to such a Degree, as to read any, the most difficult Parts of the Sacred Writings, to the great Astonishment of all who heard her.
>
> As to her Writing, her own Curiosity led her to it; and this she learnt in so short a Time, that in the Year 1765, she wrote a letter to the Rev. Mr. Occam, the *Indian* Minister, while in *England.*
>
> She has a great Inclination to learn the Latin Tongue, and has made some Progress in it. This

Relation is given by her Master who bought her, and with whom she now lives.

John Wheatley, a prosperous Boston tailor, purchased the frail little African to be a companion for his wife Susannah. The Wheatleys soon made Phillis a member of the family. Under their instruction, especially that of Mary, Wheatley's daughter, Phillis became not only a well-educated young girl but also something of a local celebrity. By 1766, at the age of twelve or thirteen, she was writing verses. In 1770 she published her first poem, "An Elegiac Poem on the Death of George Whitefield," which "appeared in at least six different editions in Boston, Philadelphia, and New York, within a few months."[1] In 1771 she received an unusual honor for a slave by becoming a "baptized communicant" of Boston's Old South Meeting House.

The high point in Phillis Wheatley's life came in 1773, when the Wheatleys sent her to London for her health. There Phillis met the Countess of Huntingdon, the patroness of George Whitefield and other Methodists, who introduced the girl to many distinguished Londoners. The Lord Mayor gave Phillis a copy of the 1770 folio edition of *Paradise Lost;* the Earl of Dartmouth presented her with a copy of Smollett's 1770 translation of *Don Quixote.* Phillis was urged to stay in England long enough to be presented at Court, but learning that Mrs. Wheatley was ill, she returned to Boston. Before she left London, however, Phillis arranged for the publication of her only

---

[1] Vernon Loggins, *The Negro Author* (New York: Columbia University Press, 1931), 16.

book, *Poems on Various Subjects, Religious and Moral,* which appeared in 1773 with a "Dedication" to the gracious Countess of Huntingdon.

Mrs. Wheatley died in March 1774, Mr. Wheatley died in 1778. In the same year Phillis, now a "free Negro," married a Negro named John Peters. He was a jack-of-all-trades who was apparently not so successful as he was versatile. At various times he supposedly worked as a baker, grocer, lawyer, and physician. Phillis and John Peters had three children, but their marriage seems not to have been a happy one.

In 1776 Phillis Wheatley wrote a poem entitled "To His Excellency General Washington" and sent the general a manuscript copy. The poem was subsequently published in the April 1776 issue of the *Pennsylvania Magazine, or American Monthly Museum.* Washington courteously thanked the black poet in a letter, dated February 28, 1776, and invited her to visit him at Cambridge, where she was graciously received by the general and his fellow officers.

After the Revolution, Phillis Wheatley drew up "Proposals" for another book of poems and published them originally in the October 30, 1779, *Evening Post and General Advertiser.* But the volume itself was never published, and of the items included in her "Proposals" only five are now extant.

Before the winter of 1783–84, Phillis lost her two older children. Her husband was in jail, and she had to earn her living by working in a "cheap boarding house." She died at the age of thirty-two on December 5, 1784. Her last child died soon enough afterward to be buried with her.

Phillis Wheatley left forty-six known poems. Of these, eighteen are elegies, several of them probably written at the request of friends. They are "correct," typical eighteenth-century elegies using the religious imagery common to this type of poem. She wrote six poems inspired by public acts like the repeal of the Stamp Act and Washington's appointment as commander in chief. It is possible that had she lived longer she would have written more of this type of poem. But not all of Phillis Wheatley's poetry is occasional; she created versified selections from the Bible ("Goliath of Gath") and an adaptation from the sixth book of Ovid's *Metamorphoses*. In addition, she composed typically eighteenth-century poems on abstractions like "Imagination," "Recollection," and "Virtue" and wrote companion poems on "Morning" and "Evening" which show Milton's influence. Her poem in blank verse, "To the University of Cambridge, in New-England," probably also was influenced by Milton.

Phillis Wheatley's poetic master was Alexander Pope, and she was second to none of her contemporaries in capturing the music and cadence of her mentor. In an age of imitators of Pope, she was among the best.

For the most recent study of Phillis Wheatley, see John C. Shields, ed., *The Collected Works of Phillis Wheatley* (1988). The entry written by Saunders Redding, in Rayford W. Logan and Michael R. Winston, eds., *Dictionary of American Negro Biography* (1982) provides comprehensive commentary, as does the article by Kenny J. Williams in the *Dictionary of Literary Biography, Volume 50*. The impact of Wheatley's critical reception upon criticism of African American writing produced since the eighteenth century is examined by Henry Louis Gates, Jr., in his *Figures in Black: Words, Signs, and the "Racial" Self* (1987). Other important sources of comment on Wheatley include Julian D. Mason, Jr., ed., *The Poems of Phillis Wheatley* (1966); Benjamin Brawley, *The Negro in Literature and Art* (3rd ed., 1929); Brawley, *Early Negro American Writers* (1935); J. Saunders Redding, *To Make a Poet Black* (1939); and Vernon Loggins, *The Negro Author* (1931). For "interpretive essays on the life and poetry" of Wheatley see *Bid the Vassal Soar* (1974) by Merle A. Richmond; for an excellent anthology of essays and comments, see William H. Robinson, *Critical Essays on Phillis Wheatley* (1982). Jean Wagner, the French critic, comments on Wheatley's life and work in his study *Black Poets of the United States: From Paul Laurence Dunbar to Langston Hughes* (1973), and see June Jordan's excellent essay in *Wild Women in the Whirlwind* (1990).

All of the following poems come from *The Poems of Phillis Wheatley.*

TO THE UNIVERSITY OF
CAMBRIDGE, IN NEW-ENGLAND

While an intrinsic ardor prompts to write,
The muses promise to assist my pen;
'Twas not long since I left my native shore
The land of errors, and *Egyptian* gloom:
Father of mercy, 'twas thy gracious hand
Brought me in safety from those dark abodes.

From *The Poems of Phillis Wheatley* by Julian D. Mason, Jr., editor, © 1966 by the University of North Carolina Press. Annotations appear in the original text.

Students, to you 'tis giv'n to scan the heights
Above, to traverse the ethereal space,
And mark the systems of revolving worlds.
Still more, ye sons of science ye receive
The blissful news by messengers from heav'n,
How *Jesus'* blood for your redemption flows.
See him with hands out-stretcht upon the cross;
Immense compassion in his bosom glows;
He hears revilers, nor resents their scorn;
What matchless mercy in the Son of God!
When the whole human race by sin had fall'n,
He deign'd to die that they might rise again,
And share with him in the sublimest skies,
Life without death, and glory without end.

Improve your privileges while they stay,
Ye pupils, and each hour redeem, that bears
Or good or bad report of you to heav'n.
Let sin, that baneful evil to the soul,
By you be shunn'd, nor once remit your guard;
Suppress the deadly serpent in its egg.

Ye blooming plants of human race devine,
An *Ethiop* tells you 'tis your greatest foe;
Its transient sweetness turns to endless pain,
And in immense perdition sinks the soul.

ON BEING BROUGHT FROM AFRICA
TO AMERICA

'Twas mercy brought me from my *Pagan* land,
Taught my benighted soul to understand
That there's a God, that there's a *Savior* too:

Once I redemption neither sought nor knew.
Some view our sable race with scornful eye,
"Their colour is a diabolic die."
Remember, *Christians, Negroes,* black as *Cain,*
May be refin'd, and join th' angelic train.

ON THE DEATH OF THE REV. MR. GEORGE WHITEFIELD. 1770

Hail, happy saint, on thine immortal throne,
Possest of glory, life, and bliss unknown;
We hear no more the music of thy tongue,
Thy wonted auditories cease to throng.
Thy sermons in unequall'd accents flow'd,
And ev'ry bosom with devotion glow'd;
Thou didst in strains of eloquence refin'd
Inflame the heart, and captivate the mind.
Unhappy we the setting sun deplore,
So glorious once, but ah! it shines no more.

Behold the prophet in his tow'ring flight!
He leaves the earth for heav'ns unmeasur'd height,
And worlds unknown receive him from our sight.
There *Whitefield* wings with rapid course his way,
And sails to *Zion* through vast seas of day.
Thy pray'rs, great saint, and thine incessant cries
Have pierc'd the bosom of thy native skies.
Thou moon hast seen, and all the stars of light,
How he has wrestled with his God by night.
He pray'd that grace in ev'ry heart might dwell,
He long'd to see *America* excel;
He charg'd its youth that ev'ry grace divine

Should with full lustre in their conduct shine;
That Savior, which his soul did first receive,
The greatest gifts that ev'n a God can give,
He freely offer'd to the num'rous throng,
That on his lips with list'ning pleasure hung.

   "Take him, ye wretched, for your only good,
"Take him ye starving sinners, for your food;
"Ye thirsty, come to this life-giving stream,
"Ye preachers, take him for your joyful theme;
"Take him my dear *Americans,* he said,
"Be your complaints on his kind bosom laid:
"Take him, *ye Africans,* he longs for you,
"*Impartial Savior* is his title due:
"Wash'd in the fountain of redeeming blood,
"You shall be sons, and kings, and priests to God."

   Great *Countess,** we *Americans* revere
Thy name, and mingle in thy grief sincere;
New England deeply feels, the *Orphans* mourn,
Their more than father will no more return.

   But, though arrested by the hand of death,
Whitefield no more exerts his lab'ring breath,
Yet let us view him in th' eternal skies,
Let ev'ry heart to this bright vision rise;
While the tomb safe retains its sacred trust,
Till life divine re-animates his dust.

*The Countess of Huntingdon, to whom Mr. Whitefield was chaplain.

AN HYMN TO THE MORNING

Attend my lays, ye ever honour'd nine,
Assist my labours, and my strains refine;
In smoothest numbers pour the notes along,
For bright *Aurora* now demands my song.

   Aurora hail, and all the thousand dies,
Which deck thy progress through the vaulted skies:
The morn awakes, and wide extends her rays,
On ev'ry leaf the gentle zephyr plays;
Harmonious lays the feather'd race resume,
Dart the bright eye, and shake the painted plume.

   Ye shady groves, your verdant gloom display
To shield your poet from the burning day:
Calliope awake the sacred lyre,
While thy fair sisters fan the pleasing fire:
The bow'rs, the gales, the variegated skies
In all their pleasures in my bosom rise.

   See in the east th' illustrious king of day!
His rising radiance drives the shades away—
But Oh! I feel his fervid beams too strong,
And scarce begun, concludes th' abortive song.

AN HYMN TO THE EVENING

Soon as the sun forsook the eastern main
The pealing thunder shook the heav'nly plain;
Majestic grandeur! From the zephyr's wing,
Exhales the incense of the blooming spring,

Soft purl the streams, the birds renew their notes,
And through the air their mingled music floats.

   Through all the heav'ns what beauteous dies are
      spread!
But the west glories in the deepest red;
So may our breasts with ev'ry virtue glow,
The living temples of our God below!

   Fill'd with the praise of him who gives the light;
And draws the sable curtains of the night,
Let placid slumbers sooth each weary mind,
At mourn to wake more heav'nly, more refin'd;
So shall the labours of the day begin
More pure, more guarded from the snares of sin.

   Night's leaden sceptre seals my drousy eyes,
Then cease, my song, till fair *Aurora* rise.

ON IMAGINATION

Thy various works, imperial queen, we see,
How bright their forms! how deck'd with pomp by thee!
Thy wond'rous acts in beauteous order stand,
And all attest how potent is thine hand.

   From *Helicon's* refulgent heights attend,
Ye sacred choir, and my attempts befriend:
To tell her glories with a faithful tongue,
Ye blooming graces, triumph in my song.

   Now here, now there, the roving *Fancy* flies,
Till some lov'd object strikes her wand'ring eyes,

Whose silken fetters all the senses bind,
And soft captivity involves the mind.

   Imagination! who can sing thy force?
Or who describe the swiftness of thy course?
Soaring through air to find the bright abode,
Th' empyreal palace of the thund'ring God,
We on thy pinions can surpass the wind,
And leave the rolling universe behind:
From star to star the mental optics rove,
Measure the skies, and range the realms above.
There in one view we grasp the mighty whole,
Or with new worlds amaze th' unbounded soul.

   Though *Winter* frowns to *Fancy's* raptur'd eyes
The fields may flourish, and gay scenes arise;
The frozen deeps may break their iron bands,
And bid their waters murmur o'er the sands.
Fair *Flora* may resume her fragrant reign,
And with her flow'ry riches deck the plain;
Sylvanus may diffuse his honours round,
And all the forest may with leaves be crown'd:
Show'rs may descend, and dews their gems disclose,
And nectar sparkle on the blooming rose.

   Such is thy pow'r, nor are thine orders vain,
O thou the leader of the mental train:
In full perfection all thy works are wrought,
And thine the sceptre o'er the realms of thought.
Before thy throne the subject-passions bow,
Of subject-passions sov'reign ruler Thou,
At thy command joy rushes on the heart,
And through the glowing veins the spirits dart.

   Fancy might now her silken pinions try
To rise from earth, and sweep th' expanse on high;

From *Tithon's* bed now might *Aurora* rise,
Her cheeks all glowing with celestial dies,
While a pure stream of light o'erflows the skies.
The monarch of the day I might behold,
And all the mountains tipt with radiant gold,
But I reluctant leave the pleasing views,
Which *Fancy* dresses to delight the *Muse;*
Winter austere forbids me to aspire,
And northern tempests damp the rising fire;
They chill the tides of *Fancy's* flowing sea,
Cease then, my song, cease the unequal lay.

TO HIS EXCELLENCY
GENERAL WASHINGTON

The following LETTER *and* VERSES, *were written by the famous* Phillis Wheatley, *The African Poetess, and presented to his Excellency* Gen. Washington.

SIR.

I have taken the freedom to address your Excellency in the enclosed poem, and entreat your acceptance, though I am not insensible of its inaccuracies. Your being appointed by the Grand Continental Congress to be Generalissimo of the armies of North America, together with the fame of your virtues, excite sensations not easy to suppress. Your generosity, therefore, I presume, will pardon the attempt. Wishing your Excellency all possible success in the great cause you are so generously engaged in. I am,

      Your Excellency's most obedient humble servant,
                    PHILLIS WHEATLEY.

Providence, Oct. 26, 1775.
His Excellency Gen. Washington.

Celestial choir! enthron'd in realms of light,
   Columbia's scenes of glorious toils I write.
While freedom's cause her anxious breast alarms,
She flashes dreadful in refulgent arms.
See mother earth her offspring's fate bemoan,
And nations gaze at scenes before unknown!
See the bright beams of heaven's revolving light
Involved in sorrows and the veil of night!

   The goddess comes, she moves divinely fair,
Olive and laurel binds her golden hair:
Wherever shines this native of the skies,
Unnumber'd charms and recent graces rise.

   Muse! bow propitious while my pen relates
How pour her armies through a thousand gates,
As when Eolus heaven's fair face deforms,
Enwrapp'd in tempest and a night of storms;
Astonish'd ocean feels the wild uproar,
The refluent surges beat the sounding shore;
Or thick as leaves in Autumn's golden reign,
Such, and so many, moves the warrior's train.
In bright array they seek the work of war,
Where high unfurl'd the ensign waves in air.
Shall I to Washington their praise recite?
Enough thou know'st them in the fields of fight.
Thee, first in peace and honours,—we demand
The grace and glory of thy martial band.
Fam'd for thy valour, for thy virtues more,
Hear every tongue thy guardian aid implore!

   One century scarce perform'd its destined round,
When Gallic powers Columbia's fury found;

And so may you, whoever dares disgrace
The land of freedom's heaven-defended race!
Fix'd are the eyes of nations on the scales,
For in their hopes Columbia's arm prevails.
Anon Britannia droops the pensive head,
While round increase the rising hills of dead.
Ah! cruel blindness to Columbia's state!
Lament thy thirst of boundless power too late.
　　Proceed, great chief, with virtue on thy side,
Thy ev'ry action let the goddess guide.
A crown, a mansion, and a throne that shine,
With gold unfading, WASHINGTON! be thine.

Jupiter Hammon

(1711–1806)

A slave of the Lloyd family of Lloyd's Neck, Long Island, Jupiter Hammon served three generations of that family. The Lloyds were evidently considerate masters: they helped their talented slave to publish his verses; they also allowed him to get an education sufficient to write pious religious verse and prose tracts, and they seemingly encouraged his activities as a slave preacher. During the American Revolution, Hammon moved with his masters to Hartford, Connecticut, where he remained during the war, publishing there most of his best-known poetical works, including "An Evening Thought: Salvation by Christ with Penitential Cries" (1761); *An Address to Miss Phillis Wheatly* [sic], *Ethiopian Poetess in Boston* (1778); *An Essay on Ten Virgins* (1779)—a work not yet found, but thought to be in verse; "A Poem for Children" (1782); and "The Kind Master and Dutiful Servant" (1782), published as part of a prose work, *An Evening's Improvement*. His prose works published in Hartford include two evangelical tracts: *A Winter Peace* (1782) and *An Evening's Improvement*. In 1786, for "Members of the

African Society in New York," he published *Address to the Negroes of the State of New York.*

The "accommodationist" tone of this last-named work[1] probably accounts for Jupiter Hammon's neglect during the Abolitionist era, when every effort was made to collect evidence of blacks' intellectual ability. Even though Hammon preferred not to "shake the boat," he like other blacks of his generation saw the hypocrisy of a nation fighting a war for its freedom and remaining blind to slavery within its borders.

Oscar Wegelin's *Jupiter Hammon, American Negro Poet* (1915) was among the first works to publicize Hammon's worth. A fuller treatment is found in Stanley A. Ransom, Jr.'s *America's First Negro Poet: The Complete Works of Jupiter Hammon of Long Island* (1970). See also *Early Black American Poets* (1969), edited by William Henry Robinson; William H. Robinson's entry in *Dictionary of American Negro Biography;* and Sondra A. O'Neale's article in *Dictionary of Literary Biography, Volume 51.* There is also a short biography by Benjamin Brawley in *Dictionary of American Biography.* Hammon is a subject in Bernard W. Bell's study "African-American Writers," in *American Literature 1764–1789: The Revoluntionary Years,* ed. Everett Emerson (1977).

The following poems come from *America's First Negro Poet.*

---

[1]See the introduction to Chapter 1.

AN ADDRESS TO
MISS PHILLIS WHEATLY

I

O come you pious youth! adore
   The wisdom of thy God,
In bringing thee from distant shore,
   To learn His holy word.

Eccles. xii.

II

Thou mightst been left behind
   Amidst a dark abode;
God's tender mercy still combin'd,
   Thou hast the holy word.

Psal. cxxxv, 2, 3.

III

Fair wisdom's ways are paths of peace,
   And they that walk therein,
Shall reap the joys that never cease,
   And Christ shall be their king.

Psal. i, 1, 2; Prov. iii, 7.

IV

God's tender mercy brought thee here;
   Tost o'er the raging main;

From *American's First Negro Poet: The Complete Works of Jupiter Hammon of Long Island,* edited and with an introduction by Stanley A(ustin) Ransom, Jr. (Port Washington, New York: Kennikat Press, Ira J. Friedman Division, 1970).

In Christian faith thou hast a share,
Worth all the gold of Spain.

Psal. ciii, 1, 3, 4.

V

While thousands tossed by the sea,
    And others settled down,
God's tender mercy set thee free,
    From dangers that come down.

Death.

VI

That thou a pattern still might be,
    To youth of Boston town,
The blessed Jesus set thee free,
    From every sinful wound.

2 Cor. v, 10.

VII

The blessed Jesus, who came down,
    Unvail'd his sacred face,
To cleanse the soul of every wound,
    And give repenting grace.

Rom. v, 21.

VIII

That we poor sinners may obtain,
    The pardon of our sin;
Dear blessed Jesus now constrain,
    And bring us flocking in.

Psal. xxxiv, 6, 7, 8.

IX

Come you, Phillis, now aspire,
    And seek the living God,

So step by step thou mayst go higher,
　　Till perfect in the word.

　　　　　　　Matth. vii, 7, 8.

X

While thousands mov'd to distant shore,
　　And others left behind,
The blessed Jesus still adore,
　　Implant this in thy mind.

　　　　　　　Psal. lxxxix, 1.

XI

Thou hast left the heathen shore;
　　Thro' mercy of the Lord.
Among the heathen live no more,
　　Come magnify thy God.

　　　　　　　Psal. xxxiv, 1, 2, 3.

XII

I pray the living God may be,
　　The shepherd of thy soul;
His tender mercies still are free,
　　His mysteries to unfold.

　　　　　　　Psal. lxxx, 1, 2, 3.

XIII

Thou, Phillis, when thou hunger hast,
　　Or pantest for thy God;
Jesus Christ is thy relief,
　　Thou hast the holy word.

　　　　　　　Psal. xiii, 1, 2, 3.

XIV

The bounteous mercies of the Lord,
    Are hid beyond the sky,
And holy souls that love His word,
    Shall taste them when they die.

Psal. xvi, 10, 11.

XV

These bounteous mercies are from God,
    The merits of His Son;
The humble soul that loves His word,
    He chooses for his own.

Psal. xxxiv, 15.

XVI

Come, dear Phillis, be advis'd,
    To drink Samaria's flood;
There nothing that shall suffice
    But Christ's redeeming blood.

John iv, 13, 14.

XVII

While thousands muse with earthly toys;
    And range about the street,
Dear Phillis, seek for heaven's joys,
    Where we do hope to meet.

Matth. vi, 33.

XVIII

When God shall send his summons down,
    And number saints together,

Blest angels chant, (triumphant sound),
    Come live with me forever.
                    Psal. cxvi, 15.

XIX

The humble soul shall fly to God,
    And leave the things of time,
Start forth as 'twere at the first word,
    To taste things more divine.
                    Matth. v, 3, 8.

XX

Behold! the soul shall waft away.
    Whene'er we come to die,
And leave its cottage made of clay,
    In twinkling of an eye.
               Cor. xv, 51, 52, 53.

XXI

Now glory be to the Most High,
    United praises given,
By all on earth, incessantly,
    And all the host of heav'n.
                  Psal. cl, 6.

AN ADDRESS TO THE NEGROES OF THE STATE OF NEW YORK

When I am writing to you with a design to say something to you for your good, and with a view to promote your happiness, I can with truth and sincerity join with the apostle Paul, when speaking of his own nation the

Jews, and say that "I have great heaviness and continual sorrow in my heart for my brethren, my kinsmen according to the flesh." Yes my dear brethren, when I think of you, which is very often, and of the poor, despised and miserable state you are in, as to the things of this world, and when I think of your ignorance and stupidity, and the great wickedness of the most of you, I am pained to the heart. It is at times almost too much for human nature to bear, and I am obliged to turn my thoughts from the subject or endeavour to still my mind, by considering that it is permitted thus to be by that God who governs all things, who seteth up one and pulleth down another. While I have been thinking on this subject, I have frequently had great struggles in my own mind, and have been at a loss to know what to do. I have wanted exceedingly to say something to you, to call upon you with the tenderness of a father and friend, and to give you the last, and I may say dying advice, of an old man, who wishes your best good in this world, and in the world to come. But while I have had such desires, a sense of my own ignorance and unfitness to teach others has frequently discouraged me from attempting to say anything to you; yet when I thought of your situation, I could not rest easy.

When I was at Hartford in Connecticut, where I lived during the war, I published several pieces which were well received, not only by those of my own colour, but by a number of the white people, who thought they might do good among their servants. This is one consideration, among others, that emboldens me now to publish what I have written to you. Another is, I think you will be more likely to listen to what is said, when you know it comes from a Negro, one of your own nation and colour, and therefore can have no interest in deceiving you, or in saying anything to you, but what he really thinks is your interest and duty to comply with. My age, I think, gives me some right to speak to you, and reason to expect you will hearken to my advice. I am now upwards of seventy years old, and cannot expect, though I am well, and able to do almost any kind of business, to live much longer. I have passed the common bounds set for man, and must soon go the way of all the earth. I have had more experience in the world than the most of you, and I have seen a great deal of the vanity and wickedness of it. I have great reason to be thankful that my lot has been so much better than most slaves have had. I suppose I have had more advantages and privileges than most of you who are slaves have ever known, and I believe more than many white people have enjoyed, for which I desire to bless God, and pray that he may bless those who have given them to me. I do not, my dear friends, say these things about myself to make you think that I am wiser or better than others; but that you might hearken, without prejudice, to what I have to say to you on the following particulars.

1st. Respecting obedience to masters. Now whether it is right, and lawful, in the sight of God, for them to make slaves of us or not, I am certain that while we are slaves, it is our duty to obey our masters, in all their lawful commands, and mind them unless we are bid to do that which we know to be sin, or forbidden in God's word. The apostle Paul says, ''Servants be obedient to them that are your masters according to the flesh, with fear and trembling in singleness in your heart as unto Christ: Not with eye service, as men pleasers, but as the servants of Christ doing the will of God from the heart: With good will doing service to the Lord, and not to men: knowing that whatever thing a man doeth the same shall he receive of the Lord, whether he be bond or free.''—Here is a plain command of God for us to obey our masters. It may seem hard for us, if we think our masters wrong in holding us slaves, to obey in all things, but who of us dare dispute with God! He has commanded us to obey, and we ought to do it cheerfully, and freely. This should be done by us, not only because God commands, but because our own peace and comfort depend upon it. As we depend upon our masters, for what we eat and drink and wear, and for all our comfortable things in this world, we cannot be happy, unless we please them. This we cannot do without obeying them freely, without muttering or finding fault. If a servant strives to please his master and studies and takes pains to do it, I believe there are but few masters who would use such a servant cruelly. Good servants frequently make good masters. If your master is really hard, unreasonable and cruel, there is no way so likely for you to convince him of it, as always to obey his commands, and try to serve him, and take care of his interest, and try to promote it all in your power. If you are proud and stubborn and always finding fault, your master will think the fault lies wholly on your side, but if you are humble, and meek, and bear all things patiently, your master may think he is wrong, if he does not, his neighbours will be apt to see it, and will befriend you, and try to alter his conduct. If this does not do, you must cry to him, who has the hearts of all men in his hands, and turneth them as the rivers of waters are turned.

2d. The particular I would mention, is honesty and faithfulness. You must suffer me now to deal plainly with you, my dear brethren, for I do not mean to flatter, or omit

speaking the truth, whether it is for you, or against you.
How many of you are there who allow yourselves in stealing from your masters. It is very wicked for you not to
take care of your masters goods, but how much worse is it
to pilfer and steal from them, whenever you think you
shall not be found out. This you must know is very
wicked and provoking to God. There are none of you so
ignorant, but that you must know that this is wrong.
Though you may try to excuse yourselves, by saying that
your masters are unjust to you, and though you may try to
quiet your consciences in this way, yet if you are honest in
owning the truth you must think it is as wicked, and on
some accounts more wicked to steal from your masters,
than from others.

We cannot certainly, have any excuse either for taking anything that belongs to our masters without their
leave, or for being unfaithful in their business. It is our
duty to be faithful, *not with eye service as men pleasers.*
We have no right to stay when we are sent on errands,
any longer than to do the business we were sent upon.
All the time spent idly, is spent wickedly, and is un-
faithfulness to our masters. In these things I must say,
that I think many of you are guilty. I know that many
of you endeavour to excuse yourselves, and say that you
have nothing that you can call your own, and that you
are under great temptations to be unfaithful and take
from your masters. But this will not do, God will certainly punish you for stealing and for being unfaithful.
All that we have to mind is our own duty. If God has
put us in bad circumstances, that is not our fault and he
will not punish us for it. If any are wicked in keeping
us so, we cannot help it, they must answer to God for
it. Nothing will serve as an excuse to us for not doing

our duty. The same God will judge both them and us. Pray then my dear friends, fear to offend in this way, but be faithful to God, to your masters, and to your own souls. . . .

I will conclude what I have to say with a few words to those negroes who have their liberty. The most of what I have said to those who are slaves may be of use to you, but you have more advantages, on some accounts, if you will improve your freedom, as you may do, than they. You have more time to read God's holy word, and to take care of the salvation of your souls. Let me beg of you to spend your time in this way, or it will be better for you, if you had always been slaves. If you think seriously of the matter, you must conclude, that if you do not use your freedom, to promote the salvation of your souls, it will not be of any lasting good to you. Besides all this, if you are idle, and take to bad courses, you will hurt those of your brethren who are slaves, and do all in your power to prevent their being free. One great reason that is given by some for not freeing us, I understand, is that we should not know how to take care of ourselves, and should take to bad courses. That we should be lazy and idle, and get drunk and steal. Now all those of you, who follow any bad courses, and who do not take care to get an honest living by your labour and industry, are doing more to prevent our being free, than anybody else. Let me beg of you then for the sake of your own good and happiness, in time, and for eternity, and for the sake of your poor brethren, who are still in bondage to lead quiet and peaceable lives in all Godliness and honesty, and may God bless you, and bring you to his kingdom, for Christ's sake, Amen.

Gustavus Vassa (Olaudah Equiano)

(c. 1745–1797)

According to his own statement Gustavus Vassa was born in what is now the interior of eastern Nigeria, probably in 1745. His language was Ibo, and his people came under the nominal jurisdiction of the king of Benin. Captured by local raiders when he was about ten or eleven, Vassa was taken to the coast and sold to slavers bound for the West Indies.

After a few days in the islands, he was shipped to Virginia, served as a slave there, and eventually became the property of a Captain Pascal. This man gave him the name Gustavus Vassa, which remained with him the rest of his life. Vassa traveled widely with Captain Pascal, serving under him during Wolfe's campaign in Canada and with Admiral Boscawen in the Mediterranean during the Seven Years' War. On these trips Vassa, an intelligent youngster, learned a great deal, including English. After leaving Pascal he spent some time in England, went to school, and acquired the skills to become a shipping clerk and an amateur navigator.

With his next master, Robert King, a Quaker from

Philadelphia, Vassa traveled often between America and the West Indies. He evidently had a chance to make money on his own, because in 1766 he bought his freedom from Mr. King for £40. Then twenty-one and a free man, Vassa continued his life as a seaman, crossing the Atlantic several more times; on one occasion he went with a scientific expedition to the Arctic.

In the meantime Vassa had been converted to Methodism; he had also become an abolition speaker and traveled through the British Isles lecturing against slavery.

In 1786 Vassa was appointed commissary for Slaves for the Black Poor Going to Sierra Leone, a project to colonize freed slaves in Africa. Because Vassa felt that the men in charge of the mission were both dishonest and prejudiced, he spoke out against them and consequently was relieved of his post as commissary. He later volunteered to go to Africa as a missionary but was rejected.

On April 7, 1792, Gustavus Vassa married Susan (or Susanna) Cullen. The notice of this wedding which appeared in *The Gentleman's Magazine* refers to him as "Gustavus Vassa the African, well known as the champion and advocate for procuring the suppression of the slave trade."

In 1789 Vassa published *The Interesting Narrative of the Life of Olaudah Equiano, or Gustavus Vassa, the African,* a work which became—with good reason—a bestseller of the day. The narrative was a valuable antislavery document and was used by abolition forces on both sides of the Atlantic. It was also a highly readable travel book of the type popular in the eighteenth century. The author includes some wonders—crowing snakes and neighing seahorses—but he never strays too far from common sense.

Most American scholars interested in black literature claim Gustavus Vassa as the first important writer of African American autobiography. Although he did spend some time in Philadelphia, in Virginia, and in other places in this country, he is at best an "honorary" American black writer. Actually he belongs in the eighteenth-century tradition of travel writing, one with which we associate Defoe and Swift. It does no harm, however, to claim him as an autobiographer. He is certainly a worthy addition to early African American literature. According to *The Gentleman's Magazine,* Gustavus Vassa died in London on April 30, 1797. (Other dates have also been given.)

For comment on Gustavus Vassa and an excellent reprint (and abridgment) of his work, see Paul Edwards, ed., *Equiano's Travels* (1967). Edwards also brought out in 1969 a two-volume facsimile reprint of the first edition of Vassa's work. The following volumes contain valuable comments on Vassa: Vernon Loggins, *The Negro Author,* and Benjamin Brawley, *Early Negro American Writers.* See also Marion L. Starkey, *Striving to Make It My Home: The Story of Americans from Africa* (1964) and Arna Bontemps, ed., *Great Slave Narratives* (1969), in which one finds an abridged version of Vassa's autobiography.

More recent commentary on Vassa's achievement may be found in Angelo Constanzo's study, *Olaudah Equiano and the Beginnings of Black Autobiography* (1987). See also *The Journey Back* by Houston Baker, Jr. (1981), *From Behind the Veil: A Study of Afro-American Narrative* by Robert Stepto (1979), and R. Victoria Arana's "Culture Shock and Revolution in Gustavus Vassa's *Narrative,*" *Delos,* 1:2.

The following selections come from chapters 1 and 2 of *Equiano's Travels*.

FROM **EQUIANO'S TRAVELS**

I believe it is difficult for those who publish their own memoirs to escape the imputation of vanity; nor is this the only disadvantage under which they labor: it is also their misfortune that what is uncommon is rarely, if ever, believed, and what is obvious we are apt to turn from with disgust, and to charge the writer with impertinence. People generally think those memoirs only worthy to be read or remembered which abound in great or striking events; those, in short, which in a high degree excite either admiration or pity: all others they consign to contempt and oblivion. It is therefore, I confess, not a little hazardous in a private and obscure individual, and a stranger too, thus to solicit the indulgent attention of the public; especially when I own I offer here the history of neither a saint, a hero, nor a tyrant. I believe there are few events in my life, which have not happened to many: it is true the incidents of it are numerous; and, did I consider myself an European, I might say my sufferings were great: but when I compare my lot with that of most of my countrymen, I regard myself as a *particular favorite of heaven,* and acknowledge the mercies of Providence in every occurrence of my life. If, then, the following narrative does not appear sufficiently interesting to engage general attention, let my motive be some excuse for its publication. I am not so foolishly vain as to expect from it either immortality or literary reputation. If it affords any satisfaction to my numerous friends, at whose request it has been written, or in the smallest degree promotes the interests of humanity, the ends for which it was undertaken will be fully attained, and every wish of my heart gratified. Let it therefore be remembered, that, in wishing to avoid censure, I do not aspire to praise.

That part of Africa, known by the name of Guinea, to which the trade for slaves is carried on, extends along the coast above 3400 miles, from Senegal to Angola, and includes a variety of kingdoms. Of these the most considerable is the kingdom of Benin, both as to extent and wealth, the richness and cultivation of the soil, the power of its king, and the number and warlike disposition of the inhabitants. It is situated nearly under the line, and extends along the coast about 170 miles, but runs back into the interior part of Africa to a distance hitherto, I believe, unexplored by any traveller; and seems only terminated at length by the empire of Abyssinia, near 1500 miles from its beginning. This kingdom is divided into many provinces or districts: in one of the most remote and fertile of which, I was born, in the year 1745, situated in a charming fruitful vale, named Essala. The distance of this province from the capital of Benin and the sea coast must be very considerable: for I had never heard of white men or Europeans, nor of the sea; and our subjection to the king of Benin was little more than nominal; for every transaction of the government, as far as my slender observation extended, was conducted by the chief or elders of the place. The manners and government of a people who have little commerce with other countries, are generally very simple; and the history of what passes in one family or village, may serve as a specimen of the whole nation. My father was one of those elders or chiefs I have spoken of, and was styled Embrenche; a term, as I remember, importing the highest distinction, and signifying in our language a *mark* of grandeur. This mark is conferred on the person entitled to it, by cutting the skin across at the top of the forehead, and drawing it down to the eyebrows: and while it is in this situation applying a warm hand, and rubbing it until it shrinks up into a thick *weal* across the lower part of the forehead. Most of the judges and senators were thus marked; my father had long borne it: I had seen it conferred on one of my brothers, and I also was *destined* to receive it by my parents. Those Embrenche or chief men, decided disputes and punished crimes; for which purpose they always assembled together. The proceedings were generally short: and in most cases the law of retaliation prevailed. I remember a man was brought before my father, and the other judges, for kidnapping a boy; and, although he was the son of a chief or senator, he was condemned to make recompense by a man or woman slave. Adultery, however, was sometimes punished with slavery or death; a punishment which I believe is inflicted on it throughout most of the nation of Africa: so sacred among them is the honor of the marriage bed, and so jealous are they of the fidelity of their wives. Of this I recollect an instance—a woman was convicted before the judges of adultery, and delivered over, as the custom was, to her husband, to be punished. Accordingly he determined to put her to death: but it being found, just before her execution, that she had an infant at her breast; and no woman being prevailed on to perform the part of a nurse, she was spared on account of the child. The men, however, do not preserve the same constancy to their wives, which they expect from them; for they indulge in a plurality, though seldom in more than two. Their mode of marriage is thus:—both parties are usually betrothed when young by their parents (though I have known the males to betroth themselves.) On this occasion a feast is prepared, and the bride and bridegroom stand up in the midst of all their friends, who are assembled for the purpose, while he declares she is henceforth to be looked upon as his wife, and that no other person is to pay any addresses to her. This is also immediately proclaimed in the vicinity, on which the bride retires from the assembly. Some time after, she is brought home to her husband, and then another feast is made, to which the relations of both parties are invited: her parents then deliver her to the bridegroom, accompanied with a number of blessings, and at the same time they tie round her waist a cotton string of the thickness of a goose-quill, which none but married women are permitted to wear: she is now considered as completely his wife; and at this time the dowry is given to the new married pair, which generally consists of portions of land, slaves, and cattle, household goods, and implements of husbandry. These are offered by the friends of both parties; besides which the parents of the bridegroom present gifts to those of the bride, whose property she is looked upon before marriage; but after it she is esteemed the sole property of her husband. The ceremony being now ended, the festival begins, which is celebrated with bonfires, and loud acclamations of joy, accompanied with music and dancing. . . .

As we live in a country where nature is prodigal of her favors, our wants are few and easily supplied; of course we have few manufactures. They consist for the

most part of calicoes, earthen ware, ornaments, and instruments of war and husbandry.—But these make no
part of our commerce, the principal articles of which, as
I have observed, are provisions. In such a state, money
is of little use; however, we have some small pieces of
coin, if I may call them such. They are made something
like an anchor, but I do not remember either their value
or denomination. We have also markets, at which I have
been frequently with my mother. These are sometimes
visited by stout mahogany-colored men from the southwest of us: we call them *Oye-Eboe,* which term signifies
red men living at a distance.—They generally bring us
fire-arms, gunpowder, hats, beads, and dried fish. The
last we esteemed a great rarity, as our waters were only
brooks and springs. These articles they barter with us
for odoriferous woods and earth, and our salt of wood
ashes. They always carry slaves through our land; but
the strictest account is exacted of their manner of procuring them before they are suffered to pass. Sometimes
indeed, we sold slaves to them, but they were only prisoners of war, or such among us as had been convicted
of kidnapping, or adultery, and some other crimes,
which we esteemed heinous. This practice of kidnapping
induces me to think, that, notwithstanding all our strict-
ness, their principal business among us was to trepan
our people. I remember too, they carried great sacks
along with them, which not long after, I had an opportunity of fatally seeing applied to that infamous purpose.

Our land is uncommonly rich and fruitful, and pro-
duces all kinds of vegetables in great abundance.—We
have plenty of Indian corn, and vast quantities of cotton
and tobacco. Our pine apples grow without culture; they
are about the size of the largest sugarloaf, and finely fla-

vored. We have also spices of different kinds, particularly pepper; and a variety of delicious fruits which I have never seen in Europe; together with gums of various kinds, and honey in abundance. All our industry is exerted to improve these blessings of nature. Agriculture is our chief employment; and every one, even the children and women, are engaged in it. Thus we are all habituated to labor from our earliest years. Every one contributes something to the common stock; and, as we are unacquainted with idleness, we have no beggars. The benefits of such a mode of living are obvious. The West India planters prefer the slaves of Benin or Eboe, to those of any other part of Guinea, for their hardiness, intelligence, integrity, and zeal. Those benefits are felt by us in the general healthiness of the people, and in their vigor and activity; I might have added, too, in their comeliness. Deformity is indeed unknown amongst us, I mean that of shape. Numbers of the natives of Eboe now in London, might be brought in support of this assertion: for, in regard to complexion, ideas of beauty are wholly relative. I remember while in Africa to have seen three negro children who were tawny, and another quite white, who were universally regarded by myself, and the natives in general, as far as related to their complexions, as deformed.—Our women, too, were in my eye at least, uncommonly graceful, alert, and modest to a degree of bashfulness; nor do I remember to have heard of an instance of incontinence amongst them before marriage.—They are also remarkably cheerful. Indeed, cheerfulness and affability are two of the leading characteristics of our nation.

Our tillage is exercised in a large plain or common, some hours' walk from our dwellings, and all the neighbors resort thither in a body. They use no beasts of husbandry; and their only instruments are hoes, axes, shovels, and beaks, or pointed iron, to dig with. Sometimes we are visited by locusts, which come in large clouds, so as to darken the air, and destroy our harvest. This, however, happens rarely, but when it does, a famine is produced by it. I remember an instance or two wherein this happened. This common is often the theatre of war; and therefore when our people go out to till their land, they not only go in a body, but generally take their arms with them for fear of a surprise; and when they apprehend an invasion, they guard the avenues to their dwellings, by driving sticks into the ground, which are so sharp at one end as to pierce the foot, and are generally dipt in poison. From what I can recollect of these battles, they appear to have been irruptions of one little state or district on the other, to obtain prisoners or booty. Perhaps they were incited to this, by those traders who brought the European goods I mentioned, amongst us. Such a mode of obtaining slaves in Africa is common; and I believe more are procured this way, and by kidnapping, than any other. When a trader wants slaves, he applies to a chief for them, and tempts him with his wares. It is not extraordinary, if on this occasion he yields to the temptation with as little firmness, and accepts the price of his fellow creatures' liberty, with as little reluctance as the enlightened merchant.—Accordingly he falls on his neighbors, and a desperate battle ensues. If he prevails and takes prisoners, he gratifies his avarice by selling them; but, if his party be vanquished, and he falls into the hands of the enemy, he is put to death; for, as he has been known to foment their quarrels, it is thought dangerous to let him survive, and no ransom can save him, though all other prisoners may be redeemed. We have fire-arms, bows and arrows, broad two-edged swords and javelins: we have shields also which cover a man from head to foot. All are taught the use of these weapons; even our women are warriors, and march boldly out to fight along with the men.—Our whole district is a kind of militia: on a certain signal given, such as the firing of a gun at night, they all rise in arms and rush upon their enemy. It is perhaps something remarkable, that when our people march to the field a red flag or banner is borne before them. I was once a witness to a battle in our common. We had been all at work in it one day as usual, when our people were suddenly attacked. I climbed a tree at some distance, from which I beheld the fight. There were many women as well as men on both sides; among others my mother was there, and armed with a broad sword. After fighting for a considerable time with great fury, and many had been killed, our people obtained the victory, and took their enemy's Chief a prisoner. He was carried off in great triumph, and, though he offered a large ransom for his life, he was put to death. A virgin of note among our enemies, had been slain in the battle, and her arm was exposed in our marketplace, where our trophies were always exhibited.—The spoils were divided according to the merit of the warriors. Those prisoners which were not sold or redeemed, we kept as slaves: but how different was their condition from that of the slaves in the West Indies! With us, they do no more work than other members of the community, even their master; their food, clothing and lodging were nearly the same as theirs, (except that they were not permitted to eat with those who were free-born;) and there was scarce any other difference between them, than a superior degree of importance which the head of a family possesses in our state, and that authority which, as such, he exercises over every part of his household. Some of these slaves have even slaves under them as their own property, and for their own use.

As to religion, the natives believe that there is one Creator of all things, and that he lives in the sun, and is girted round with a belt that he may never eat or drink; but, according to some he smokes a pipe, which is our own favorite luxury. They believe he governs events, especially our deaths or captivity; but, as for the doctrine of eternity, I do not remember to have ever heard of it: some, however, believe in the transmigration of souls in a certain degree. Those spirits, which are not transmigrated, such as their dear friends or relations, they believe always attend them, and guard them from the bad spirits or their foes. For this reason they always before eating, as I have observed, put some small portion of the meat, and pour some of their drink, on the ground for them; and they often make oblations of the blood of beasts or fowls at their graves. I was very fond of my mother, and almost constantly with her. When she went to make these oblations at her mother's tomb, which was a kind of small solitary thatched house, I sometimes attended her.—There she made her libations, and spent most of the night in cries and lamentations. I have been often extremely terrified on these occasions. The loneliness of the place, the darkness of the night, and the ceremony of libation, naturally awful and gloomy, were heightened by my mother's lamentations; and these concurring with the doleful cries of birds, by which these places were frequented, gave an inexpressible terror to the scene.

▮▬▬▬▮

... The first object which saluted my eyes when I arrived on the coast, was the sea, and a slave ship, which was then riding at anchor, and waiting for its cargo. These filled me with astonishment, which was soon converted into terror, when I was carried on board. I was immediately handled, and tossed up to see if I were sound, by some of the crew; and I was now persuaded that I had gotten into a world of bad spirits, and that they were going to kill me. Their complexions, too, differing so much from ours, their long hair, and the language they spoke, (which was very different from any I had ever heard) united to confirm me in this belief. Indeed, such were the horrors of my views and fears at the moment, that, if ten thousand worlds had been my own, I would have freely parted with them all to have exchanged my condition with that of the meanest slave in my own country. When I looked round the ship too, and saw a large furnace of copper boiling, and a multitude of black people of every description chained together, every one of their countenances expressing dejection and sorrow, I no longer doubted of my fate; and, quite overpowered with horror and anguish, I fell motionless on the deck and fainted. When I recovered a little, I found some black people about me, who I believed were some of those who had brought me on board, and had been receiving their pay; they talked to me in order to cheer me, but all in vain. I asked them if we were not to be eaten by those white men with horrible looks, red faces, and long hair. They told me I was not: and one of the crew brought me a small portion of spiritous liquor in a wine glass, but, being afraid of him, I would not take it out of his hand. One of the blacks therefore, took it from him and gave it to me, and I took a little down my palate, which, instead of reviving me, as they thought it would, threw me into the greatest consternation at the strange feeling it produced, having never tasted any such liquor before. Soon after this, the blacks who brought me on board went off, and left me abandoned to despair.

I now saw myself deprived of all chance of returning to my native country, or even the least glimpse of hope of gaining the shore, which I now considered as friendly; and I even wished for my former slavery in preference to my present situation, which was filled with horrors of every kind, still heightened by my ignorance of what I was to undergo. I was not long suffered to indulge my grief; I was soon put down under the decks, and there I received such a salutation in my nostrils as I had never experienced in my life; so that, with the loathsomeness of the stench, and crying together, I became so sick and low that I was not able to eat, nor had I the least desire to taste any thing. I now wished for the last friend, death, to relieve me; but soon, to my grief, two of the white men offered me eatables; and, on my refusing to eat, one of them held me fast by the hands and laid me across, I think the windlass, and tied my feet, while the other flogged me severely. I had never experienced any thing of this kind before, and although not being used to the water, I naturally feared that element the first time I saw it, yet, nevertheless, could I have got over the nettings, I would have jumped over the side, but I could not; and besides, the crew used to watch us very closely who were not chained down to the decks, lest we should leap into the water; and I have seen some of these poor African prisoners most severely cut, for attempting to do so, and hourly whipped for not eating. This indeed was often the case with myself. In a little time after, amongst the poor chained men, I found some of my own nation, which in a small degree gave ease to my mind. I inquired of these what was to be done with us? they gave me to understand, we were to be carried to these white people's country to work for them. I then was a little revived, and thought, if it were no worse than working, my situation was not so desperate; but still I feared I should be put to death, the white people looked and acted, as I thought, in so savage a manner; for I had never seen among any people such instances of brutal cruelty; and this not only shown towards us blacks, but also to some of the whites themselves. One white man in particular I saw, when we were permitted to be on deck, flogged so unmercifully with a large rope near the foremast, that he died in consequence of it; and they tossed him over the side as they would have done a brute. This made me fear these people the more; and I expected nothing less than to be treated in the same manner. I could not help expressing my fears and apprehensions to some of my countrymen; I asked them if these people had no country, but lived in this hollow place? (the ship) they told me they did not, but came from a distant one. 'Then,' said I, 'how comes it in all our country we never heard of them?' They told me because they lived so very far off. I then asked where were their women? had they any like themselves? I was told they had. 'And why,' said I, 'do we not see them?' They answered, because they were left behind. I asked how the vessel could go? they told me they could not tell; but that there was cloth put upon the masts by help of the ropes I saw, and then the vessel went on; and the white men had some spell or magic they put in the water when they liked, in order to stop the vessel. I was exceedingly amazed at this account, and really thought they were spirits. I therefore wished much to be from amongst them, for I expected they would sacrifice me; but my wishes were vain—for we were so quartered that it was impossible for any of us to make our escape.

While we stayed on the coast I was mostly on deck; and one day, to my great astonishment, I saw one of these vessels coming in with the sails up. As soon as the whites saw it, they gave a great shout, at which we were amazed; and the more so, as the vessel appeared larger by approaching nearer. At last, she came to an anchor in my sight, and when the anchor was let go, I and my countrymen who saw it, were lost in astonishment to observe the vessel stop—and were now convinced it was done by magic. Soon after this the other ship got her boats out, and they came on board of us, and the people of both ships seemed very glad to see each other.—Several of the strangers also shook hands with us black people, and made motions with their hands, signifying I suppose, we were to go to their country, but we did not understand them.

At last, when the ship we were in, had got in all her cargo, they made ready with many fearful noises, and we were all put under deck, so that we could not see how they managed the vessel. But this disappointment was the least of my sorrow. The stench of the hold while we were on the coast was so intolerably loathsome, that it was dangerous to remain there for any time, and some of us had been permitted to stay on the deck for the fresh air; but now that the whole ship's cargo were confined together, it became absolutely pestilential. The closeness of the place, and the heat of the climate, added to the number in the ship, which was so crowded that each had scarcely room to turn himself, almost suffocated us. This produced copious perspirations, so that the air soon became unfit for respiration, from a variety of loathsome smells, and brought on a sickness among the slaves, of which many died—thus falling victims to the improvident avarice, as I may call it, of their purchasers. This wretched situation was again aggravated by the galling of the chains, now became insupportable; and the filth of the necessary tubs, into which the children often fell, and were almost suffocated. The shrieks of the women, and the groans of the dying, rendered the whole a scene of horror almost inconceivable. Happily perhaps, for myself, I was soon reduced so low here that it was thought necessary to keep me always on deck; and from my extreme youth I was not put in fetters. In this situation I expected every hour to share the fate of my companions, some of whom were almost daily brought upon deck at the point of death, which I began to hope would soon put an end to my miseries. Often did I think many of the inhabitants of the deep much more happy than myself. I envied them the freedom they enjoyed, and as often wished I could change my condition for theirs. Every circumstance I met with, served only to render my state more painful, and heightened my apprehensions, and my opinion of the cruelty of the whites.

One day they had taken a number of fishes; and

when they had killed and satisfied themselves with as many as they thought fit, to our astonishment who were on deck, rather than give any of them to us to eat, as we expected, they tossed the remaining fish into the sea again, although we begged and prayed for some as well as we could, but in vain; and some of my countrymen, being pressed by hunger, took an opportunity, when they thought no one saw them, of trying to get a little privately; but they were discovered, and the attempt procured them some very severe floggings. One day, when we had a smooth sea and moderate wind, two of my wearied countrymen who were chained together, (I was near them at the time,) preferring death to such a life of misery, somehow made through the nettings and jumped into the sea; immediately, another quite dejected fellow, who, on account of his illness, was suffered to be out of irons, also followed their example; and I believe many more would very soon have done the same, if they had not been prevented by the ship's crew, who were instantly alarmed. Those of us that were the most active, were in a moment put down under the deck, and there was such a noise and confusion amongst the people of the ship as I never heard before, to stop her, and get the boat out to go after the slaves. However two of the wretches were drowned, but they got the other, and afterwards flogged him unmercifully, for thus attempting to prefer death to slavery. In this manner we continued to undergo more hardships than I can now relate, hardships which are inseparable from this accursed trade. Many a time we were near suffocation from the want of fresh air, which we were often without for whole days together. This, and the stench of the necessary tubs, carried off many.

During our passage, I first saw flying fishes, which surprised me very much; they used frequently to fly across the ship, and many of them fell on the deck. I also now first saw the use of the quadrant; I had often with astonishment seen the mariners make observations with it, and I could not think what it meant. They at last took notice of my surprise; and one of them, willing to increase it, as well as to gratify my curiosity, made me one day look through it. The clouds appeared to me to be land, which disappeared as they passed along. This heightened my wonder; and I was now more persuaded than ever, that I was in another world, and that every thing about me was magic. At last, we came in sight of the island of Barbadoes, at which the whites on board gave a great shout, and made many signs of joy to us. We did not know what to think of this; but as the vessel drew nearer, we plainly saw the harbor, and other ships of different kinds and sizes, and we soon anchored amongst them, off Bridgetown. Many merchants and planters now came on board, though it was in the evening. They put us in separate parcels, and examined us attentively. They also made us jump, and pointed to the land, signifying we were to go there. We thought by this, we should be eaten by these ugly men, as they appeared to us; and, when soon after we were all put down under the deck again, there was much dread and trembling among us, and nothing but bitter cries to be heard all the night from these apprehensions, insomuch, that at last the white people got some old slaves from the land to pacify us. They told us we were not to be eaten, but to work, and were soon to go on land, where we should see many of our country people. This report eased us much. And sure enough, soon after we were landed, there came to us Africans of all languages.

We were conducted immediately to the merchant's yard, where we were all pent up together, like so many sheep in a fold, without regard to sex or age. As every object was new to me, every thing I saw filled me with surprise. What struck me first, was, that the houses were built with bricks and stories, and in every other respect different from those I had seen in Africa; but I was still more astonished on seeing people on horseback. I did not know what this could mean; and, indeed, I thought these people were full of nothing but magical arts. While I was in this astonishment, one of my fellow-prisoners spoke to a countryman of his, about the horses, who said they were the same kind they had in their country. I understood them, though they were from a distant part of Africa; and I thought it odd I had not seen any horses there; but afterwards, when I came to converse with different Africans, I found they had many horses amongst them, and much larger than those I then saw.

We were not many days in the merchant's custody, before we were sold after their usual manner, which is this:—On a signal given, (as the beat of a drum,) the buyers rush at once into the yard where the slaves are confined, and make choice of that parcel they like best. The noise and clamor with which this is attended, and the eagerness visible in the countenances of the buyers, serve not a little to increase the apprehension of terrified Africans, who may well be supposed to consider them as the ministers of that destruction to which they think themselves devoted. In this manner, without scruple, are relations and friends separated, most of them never to see each other again. I remember, in the vessel in which I was brought over, in the men's apartment, there were several brothers, who, in the sale, were sold in different lots; and it was very moving on this occasion, to see and hear their cries at parting. O, ye nominal Christians! might not an African ask you—Learned you this from your God, who says unto you, Do unto all men as you would men should do unto you? Is it not enough that we are torn from our country and friends, to toil for your luxury and lust of gain? Must every tender feeling be likewise sacrificed to your avarice? Are the dearest friends and relations, now rendered more dear by their separation from their kindred, still to be parted from each other, and thus prevented from cheering the gloom of slavery, with the small comfort of being together, and mingling their sufferings and sorrows? Why are parents to lose their children, brothers their sisters, or husbands their wives? Surely, this is a new refinement in cruelty, which, while it has no advantage to atone for it, thus aggravates distress, and adds fresh horrors even to the wretchedness of slavery.

George Moses Horton

(1797–c. 1883)

Born in Northampton County, North Carolina, probably in 1797 (slaves rarely knew the exact date of their birth), George Moses was the property of a family of small plantation owners named Horton. When George was a few years old, the master moved to another plantation near the University of North Carolina at Chapel Hill. Here George Moses Horton grew up and became locally famous as a poet.

In an autobiographical sketch written in 1845, Horton tells us that while working as a cowboy, he decided that he would learn to read. By having school children tell him letters, he accomplished this task and read well before he learned to write. Moved by reading "Wesley's old hymns and other pieces of poetry from various authors," the slave boy then decided that he would be a poet.

During his late teens, Horton began visiting the campus of the University of North Carolina on his free time, taking farm products to sell to the students. Soon, however, he began peddling not farm produce but acrostics and love poems (usual charge, 25¢) for undergraduates to send to their girlfriends. At first Horton had to dictate the verses, not yet knowing how to write. Eventually he was allowed to give up all farm work and "hire himself out" for fifty cents a day, an arrangement often made for slaves who had skills that were in demand. He became a "comic" campus orator, a writer of love letters as well as verses for the students, and, for several generations of North Carolina students, a kind of legend in his own time.

Aided by Caroline Hentz, the Yankee wife of one of the university's professors, Horton "achieved" his first publication in 1828. On April 8 of that year, Mrs. Hentz had two of his poems printed in her hometown paper, the *Lancaster* (Massachusetts) *Gazette.* Later she persuaded the *Raleigh Register* to publish a few of Horton's poems with a short biography of the slave. These verses were reprinted by other southern papers and by northern periodicals like *Freedom's Journal* and Garrison's *Liberator.* Some of Horton's verses also appeared in *The Southern Literary Messenger.*

In the meantime, the poet's southern friends attempted to secure Horton's freedom by compiling and selling a book of his poems, called *The Hope of Liberty,* which was printed in 1829 in Raleigh. The plan was not successful, for the book did not sell well, and not enough money came from it. But *The Hope of Liberty* made its way to Cincinnati, where it was read by an abolitionist who had it reprinted in 1837 under the title *Poems by a Slave.* (A third reprint was appended in 1838 to *A Memoir and Poems of Phillis Wheatley.*) The next volume of Horton's poems was underwritten by the president, faculty, students, and the poet's friends at the University of North Carolina. Printed in 1845 in Hillsborough, North Carolina, it was entitled *The Poetical Works of George M. Horton, the Colored Bard of North Carolina.* Horton wrote an autobiographical sketch to serve as a preface to the work.

Perhaps before this last publication, George married a slave belonging to a local farmer. The couple had two children, but from the evidence of several of his poems on the subject, the marriage was not successful.

The Yankees came to Horton's section of North Carolina in 1865, and the poet found a new friend and enthusiastic sponsor in twenty-eight-year-old Captain Will H. S. Banks of the Ninth Michigan Cavalry Volunteers. Under Captain Banks's guidance and editorship, Horton published his last work, *Naked Genius,* in 1865 in Raleigh. There were 132 poems in this volume (42 of them, however, came from *The Poetical Works,* 1845). Many of the new poems, probably suggested by Banks, dealt with Civil War incidents and Civil War heroes like Grant, Sherman, and Lincoln.

Last records of George Moses Horton find him in Philadelphia in 1866. He probably died there in the year 1883.

Horton was a prolific and facile versifier, one who was willing to write about anything—no matter how sublime or trivial—that touched him. One is struck by his range of reading (he knew Milton, Byron, and other English poets), and by his mastery of several poetic forms. He freely uses the ode, blank verse, the heroic couplet, and various stanzaic patterns. Although his subject matter ranges far and wide, Horton had certain themes which he tended to overwork, among them the varieties of love, the transitoriness of life, and the woes of marriage. He must have had a very disagreeable time with his wife, because he never tires of describing the troubles a bad wife can cause. In his later poems he admonishes free blacks to make the most of their newly acquired liberty, to be honest and industrious. Understandably, he retained his love for North Carolina and wrote several touching poems about his regret at leaving his native land; in fact, George Moses Horton never became actually anti-South.

Like many poets of his generation, Horton too often wrote on abstract themes like "Memory," "Prosperity," and "Liberty"; he attempted too many noble flights; and he used mythological characters far too often. But he could handle the language realistically and make humorous folk comparisons. Unfortunately, he did so all too rarely.

For an account of the life and works of George Moses Horton, see Richard Walser's *The Black Poet* (1966); see also William Carroll's University of North Carolina dissertation and book, *Naked Genius: The Poetry of George Moses Horton* (1977) and M. A. Richmond's *Bid the Vassal Soar* (1974). W. Edward Farrison's article "George Moses Horton: Poet for Freedom," *CLA Journal* (March 1971), James A. Emanuel's entry in *Dictionary of Negro Biography,* and William Carroll's entry in *Dictionary of Literary Biography, Volume 50,* should be consulted.

AN ACROSTIC
FOR JULIA SHEPARD

Joy, like the morning, breaks from one divine—
Unveiling streams which cannot fail to shine.
Long have I strove to magnify her name
Imperial, floating on the breeze of fame.

Attracting beauty must delight afford,
Sought of the world and of the Bards adored;
Her grace of form and heart-alluring powers
Express her more than fair, the queen of flowers.

Pleasure, fond nature's stream, from beauty sprung,
And was the softest strain the Muses sung,
Reverting sorrows into speechless Joys,
Dispelling gloom which human peace destroys.

THE CREDITOR TO
HIS PROUD DEBTOR

Ha! tott'ring Johnny strut and boast,
But think of what your feathers cost;
Your crowing days are short at most,
   You bloom but soon to fade.
Surely you could not stand so wide,
If strictly to the bottom tried [sic];
The wind would blow your plume aside,
   If half your debts were paid.

Then boast and bear the crack,
With the Sheriff at your back,
Huzza for dandy Jack,
My jolly fop, my Jo—

The blue smoke from your segar flies,
Offensive to my nose and eyes,
The most of people would be wise,
   Your presence to evade.
Your pockets jingle loud with cash,
And thus you cut a foppish dash,
But alas! dear boy, you would be trash,
   If your accounts were paid.
     Then boast and bear the crack, &c.

My duck bill boots would look as bright,
Had you in justice served me right,
Like you, I then could step as light,
   Before a flaunting maid.
As nicely could I clear my throat,
And to my tights, my eyes devote;
But I'd leave you bare, without a coat,
   For which you have not paid.
     Then boast and bear the crack, &c.

I'd toss myself with a scornful air,
And to a poor man pay no care,
I could rock cross-legged in my chair,

Within the cloister shade.
I'd gird my neck with a light cravat,
And creaming wear my bell-crown hat;
But away my down would fly at that,
    If once my debts were paid.
        Then boast and bear the crack,
        With the Sheriff at your back,
        Huzza for dandy Jack,
        My jolly fop, my Jo—

GEORGE MOSES HORTON, MYSELF

I feel myself in need
    Of the inspiring strains of ancient lore,
My heart to lift, my empty mind to feed,
    And all the world explore.

I know that I am old
    And never can recover what is past,
But for the future may some light unfold
    And soar from ages blast.

I feel resolved to try,
    My wish to prove, my calling to pursue,
Or mount up from the earth into the sky,
    To show what Heaven can do.

My genius from a boy,
    Has fluttered like a bird within my heart;
But could not thus confined her powers employ,
    Impatient to depart.

She like a restless bird,
    Would spread her wings, her power to be

unfurl'd,
And let her songs be loudly heard,
   And dart from world to world.

ON LIBERTY AND SLAVERY

Alas! and am I born for this,
   To wear this slavish chain?
Deprived of all created bliss,
   Through hardship, toil and pain!

How long have I in bondage lain,
   And languished to be free!
Alas! and must I still complain—
   Deprived of liberty.

Oh, Heaven! and is there no relief
   This side the silent grave—
To soothe the pain—to quell the grief
   And anguish of a slave?

Come Liberty, thou cheerful sound,
   Roll through my ravished ears!
Come, let my grief in joys be drowned,
   And drive away my fears.

Say unto foul oppression, Cease:
   Ye tyrants rage no more,
And let the joyful trump of peace,
   Now bid the vassal soar.

Soar on the pinions of that dove
   Which long has cooed for thee,
And breathed her notes from Afric's grove,
   The sound of Liberty.

Oh, Liberty! thou golden prize,
   So often sought by blood—
We crave thy sacred sun to rise,
   The gift of nature's God!

Bid Slavery hide her haggard face,
   And barbarism fly:
I scorn to see the sad disgrace
   In which enslaved I lie.

Dear Liberty! upon thy breast,
   I languish to respire;
And like the Swan unto her nest,
   I'd to thy smiles retire.

Oh, blest asylum—heavenly balm!
   Unto thy boughs I flee—
And in thy shades the storm shall calm,
   With songs of Liberty!

TO ELIZA

Eliza, tell thy lover why
Or what induced thee to deceive me?
   Fare thee well—away I fly—
I shun the lass who thus will grieve me.

Eliza, still thou art my song,
Although by force I may forsake thee;
   Fare thee well, for I was wrong
To woo thee while another take thee.

Eliza, pause and think awhile—
Sweet lass! I shall forget thee never:

Fare thee well! although I smile,
I grieve to give thee up for ever.

Eliza, I shall think of thee—
My heart shall ever twine about thee;
    Fare thee well—but think of me,
Compell'd to live and die without thee.
    "Fare thee well!—and if for ever,
Still for ever fare thee well!"

JEFFERSON IN A TIGHT PLACE
The Fox Is Caught

The blood hounds, long upon the trail,
Have rambled faithful, hill and dale;
But mind, such creatures never fail,
    To run the rebel down.
His fears forbid him long to stop,
Altho' he gains the mountain top,
He soon is made his tail to drop,
    And fleets to leave the hounds.

Alas! he speeds from place to place,
Such is the fox upon the chase;
To him the mud is no disgrace,
    No lair his cause defends.
He leaves a law and seeks a dell,
And where to fly 'tis hard to tell;
He fears before to meet with hell,
    Behind he has no friends.

But who can pity such a fox,
Though buried among the rocks;

He's a nuisance among the flocks,
   And sucks the blood of geese.
He takes advantage of the sheep,
His nature is at night to creep,
And rob the flocks while the herdsmen sleep,
   When dogs can have no peace.

But he is now brought to a bay,
However fast he run away,
He knows he has not long to stay,
   And assumes a raccoon's dress.
Found in a hole, he veils his face,
And fain would take a lady's place,
But fails, for he has run his race.
   And falls into distress.

The fox is captured in his den,
The martial troops of Michigan,
May hence be known the fleetest men,
   For Davis is their prey.
Great Babylon has fallen down,
A King is left without a crown,
Stripped of honors and renown,
   The evening ends the day.

THE SLAVE

What right divine has mortal man received,
   To domineer with uncontroll'd command?
What philosophic wight has thus believed
   That Heaven entailed on him the weaker band?

If Africa was fraught with weaker light,
   Whilst to the tribes of Europe more was given,

Does this impart to them a lawful right
    To counterfeit the golden rule of Heaven?

Did sovereign justice give to robbery birth,
    And bid the fools to theft their rights betray,
To spread the seeds of slavery o'er the earth,
    That you should hold them as your lawful prey?

Why did Almighty God the land divide
    And bid each nation to maintain her own,
Rolling between the deep, the wind and tide,
    With all their rage to make this order known?

The sad phylactory bound on rebel Cain,
    For killing Abel is in blood reveal'd,
For which the soldier falls among the slain,
    A victim on the sanguinary field.

Thus, in the cause of vile and sordid gain,
    To gratify their lust is all the plea;
Like Cain you've your consanguine brother slain,
    And robbed him of his birthright—Liberty.

Why do ye not the Ishmaelites enslave,
    Or artful red man in his rude attire,
As well as with the Black man, split the wave,
    And to his progeny with rage aspire?

Because the brood-sow's left side pigs were black,
    Whose sable tincture was by nature struck,
Are you by justice bound to pull them back
    And leave the sandy colored pigs to suck?

Or can you deem that God does not intend
    His kingdom through creation to display,
The sacred right of nature to defend,
    And show to mortals who shall bear the sway?

Then suffer Heaven to vindicate the cause,
　　The wrong abolish and the right restore;
To make a sacrifice of cruel laws,
　　And slavish murmurs will be heard no more.

SLAVERY

Slavery, thou peace-disturbing thief,
　　We can't but look with frowns on thee,
Without the balm which gives relief,
　　The balm of birthright—Liberty.

Thy wing has been for ages furl'd,
　　Thy vessel toss'd from wave to wave,
By stormy winds 'mid billows hurl'd—
　　Such is the fate of every slave.

A loathesome burden we are to bear,
　　Through sultry bogs we trudging go;
Thy rusty chains we frown to wear,
　　Without one inch of wealth to show.

Our fathers from their native land
　　Were dragged across the brackish deep,
Bound fast together, hand in hand,
　　O! did the God of nature sleep?

When sadly thro' the almond grove
　　The pirate dragged them o'er the sod,
Devoid of pity and of love,
　　They seemed as left without a God.

Are we not men as well as they,
　　Born to enjoy the good of earth,

Brought in creation from the clay,
    To reap a blessing from our birth?

Alas! how can such rebels thrive,
    Who take our lives and wealth away,
Since all were placed on earth to live
    And prosper by the light of day?

The maledictions of our God
    Pervade the dwindling world we see;
He hurls the vengeance with his rod,
    And thunders, let the slave be free!

SNAPS FOR DINNER,
SNAPS FOR BREAKFAST
AND SNAPS FOR SUPPER

Come in to dinner, squalls the dame,
    You need it now perhaps;
But hear the husband's loud exclaim,
    I do not like your snaps;
'Tis snaps when at your breakfast meal,
    And snaps when at your spinning wheel,
Too many by a devilish deal,
    For all your words are snaps.

Why do you tarry, tell me why?
    The chamber door she taps;
Eat by yourself, my dear, for I

Snaps: Stringbeans; the pun-filled relationship between the wife's words and the vegetable she serves is exploited fully by the poet. [Carroll's note]

Am surfeited with snaps;
For if I cough it is the cry,
    You always snap at supper time,
I'd rather lave in vats of lime,
    Than face you with your snaps.

How gladly would I be a book,
    To your long pocket flaps,
That you my face may read and look,
And learn the worth of snaps;
I'm sorry that I learning lack
    To turn you to an almanac;
Next year I'll hang you on the rack,
    And end the date of snaps.

LETTER TO MR. HORACE GREELEY

Sept. 11, 1852
Chapel Hill, N.C.

TO MR. GREELEY

Sir,

   From the information of the president of the University of North Carolina, to wit, the honorable D. L. Swain, who is willing to aid me himself, I learn that you are a gentleman of philanthropic feeling. I therefore thought it essential to apply to your beneficent hand for some assistance to remove the burden of hard servitude. Notwithstanding, sir, there are many in my native section of country who wish to bring me out, and there are

"Letter to Mr. Horace Greeley." Title supplied by editors.

others far too penurious which renders it somewhat du-
bious with regard to my extrication. It is evident that
you have heard of me by the fame of my work in poetry, much of which I am now too closely confined to
carry out and which I feel a warm interest to do; and,
sir, by favoring me with a bounty of 175 dollars, I will
endeavor to reward your generosity with my productions
as soon as possible. I am the only public or recognized
poet of color in my native state or perhaps in the union,
born in slavery but yet craving that scope and expression whereby my literary labor of the night may be circulated throughout the whole world. Then I forbid that
my productions should ever fall to the ground, but
rather soar as an eagle above the towering mountains
and thus return as a triumphing spirit to the bosom of
its God who gave it birth, though now confined in these
loathsome fetters. Please assist the lowering vassal arise
and live a glad denizen the remnant of his days and as
one of active utility.

Yours respect.
George M. Horton
of color

PART 2

FREEDOM FIGHTERS: 1830–1865

The years covered in this section were the most crucial in the history of our country—crucial for black and white alike. They saw a great nation bitterly divided into two camps over the issue of slavery. They were tense and explosive years that ended in a civil war which united the nation and gave nominal freedom to slaves.

In this prelude to the Civil War, the South began to become alarmed at the restlessness of its great slave population. Slaves increasingly showed their deep resentment through escape (often via the Underground Railroad); through their slave narratives, written by them or dictated after they reached the North; through their fiery and incendiary pamphlets; and through violence in the form of insurrections. Although we make token use of the best known of these uprisings—those led by Denmark Vesey, Gabriel Prosser, and Nat Turner—there were many others, a great many others as Herbert Aptheker showed in his study *American Negro Slave Revolts* (1943, 1969). These attacks on the "peculiar institution" brought from southern slaveholders increased harshness in the treatment of the chattel.

The troubles of the South were augmented during the 1830s by the proliferation of abolition forces in the North and to a limited extent in the South. Some of America's ablest and best-known literary, journalistic, religious, and humanitarian leaders became active in the Abolition movement and did yeoman service in it. A case could be made for the movement as the high point in America's moral history. Among the leaders of this great liberal and humanitarian revolution were William Lloyd Garrison (whose *Liberator* was the strongest voice of the movement), Harriet Beecher Stowe (whose *Uncle Tom's Cabin* crystallized the antislavery sentiment of the nation), John Greenleaf Whittier (whose verses helped to popularize the abolitionist position), Charles G. Finney (who was the moving spirit of the religious revival that swept the North and whose efforts enlisted the help of Theodore D. Weld and the Tappan brothers), and John Brown (whose martyrdom at Harpers Ferry symbolized the extent to which the moral and humanitarian elements in the North would go to rid the country of slavery). Negroes, too, were a vital part of this great movement. All of the authors in this chapter wrote against slavery, and one of Abolition's great leaders—and in all probability one of the movement's greatest speakers—was Frederick Douglass.

From the 1830s to the Civil War, American blacks lived with the overriding condition of slavery. It was the reality that bound even those who were born free and lived in the North. Black writers of this period were, as might be expected, especially responsive to this reality, and in much of their work argument takes precedence over art, again as to be expected. Very few writers avoided racial involvement; Daniel A. Payne's little poetic work *Pleasures and Other Miscellaneous Poems* is one of the exceptions. These men and women were primarily preachers, teachers, and activists whose concept of duty was "uplifting a down-trodden race." They organized conventions and addressed them; they established schools and taught in them; they founded churches and preached in them; and a number of them used creative literature as an instrument in their job of uplifting a race.

Among the few poets of this era, we find George B. Vashon, a teacher, who left two major poems: "Vincent Oge," an ambitious piece, celebrating the life and death of a Haitian, and "A Life-Day," telling the tragic story of the marriage of a white man to a beautiful mulatto girl who had been his slave. We also find James M. Whitfield, who published a thin book of verse, *America and Other Poems*. The title poem—and a few others—are of such high quality that his early death was, in retrospect, a real loss to American poetry.

Among the early novelists, William Wells Brown was more dedicated to a literary career than were any of his black contemporaries. Brown produced one of the first novels written by an American Negro, the first Negro play, and the first Negro book of travel. He also published three volumes of history, and a book of autobiographical sketches. Up until quite recently, scholars claimed that Brown's *Clotel* (1853) was the first novel by an American Negro; but after the research and discoveries made by Professor Henry Louis Gates, Jr., and his associates at Yale University, Brown's position has been clarified. Professor Gates discovered, among other documents, a hitherto unknown novel by a Negro woman, entitled *Our Nig* (1859), written by one Harriet E. Wilson. The date makes it the first novel so far by a black woman and the first to be published in America. Brown's *Clotel* and Frank J. Webb's *The Garies and Their Friends* (1857) were both published in London. *Our Nig* was republished in 1983 with a fascinating fifty-five page introduction by Gates (see the headnote for Harriet Wilson.)

Two other novelists of the period concern us here. The first is Frank J. Webb, mentioned previously. His *The Garies and Their Friends* (London, 1857) deals with Negro life in the North, mainly in Philadelphia. Technically a better novel than *Clotel,* it contains an unusual number of "firsts" in Negro fiction (see Webb's headnote). The second novelist, Martin R. Delany, is far better known for activities other than fiction writing. His unfinished novel, *Blake: or; The Huts of America,* appeared serially in the 1859 *Anglo-African Magazine.* A precursor of later militant and nationalistic works by black authors, *Blake* tells the story of a "heroic slave" trying to organize his fellow bondsmen.

Because most of the speeches and sermons of this period were extemporaneous, few have come down to us. Contemporary opinion, however, suggests that the oratory of Henry Highland Garnet, Josiah Henson, and Samuel Ringgold Ward was as eloquent and moving as the white antislavery oratory of Wendell Phillips, the editorials of William Lloyd Garrison, and the poetry of John Greenleaf Whittier. We also know that of the countless antislavery pamphlets written and published during the era none was as incendiary as Garnet's *An Address to the Slaves of the United States of America.*

With the exception of James M. Whitfield, all the black authors of this period either wrote autobiographies or were the subjects of biographical works, and some of these—

particularly Daniel Payne's autobiography—make very interesting reading. But none achieves the literary stature of Frederick Douglass's autobiographical writings. Judged by all acknowledged standards, *Narrative of the Life of Frederick Douglass, My Bondage and My Freedom,* and *Life and Times* are classics of American autobiographical writing.

No one knows when Negro folk literature began to develop, but it had become a separate great body of expression by the middle years of the nineteenth century. Undoubtedly some of it, like the animal tales, derives from Africa, but a large portion originated in the American South. Scholars have shown that many verses found in the spirituals may be traced to the late eighteenth-century Watts-Wesley hymns of the period. Musicologists have pointed out that some of the music of the spirituals may be traced to European origins. Other commentators have insisted that the spirituals have a predominantly West African origin. The controversy over the makeup of the spirituals has been with us since Thomas Wentworth Higginson, greatly impressed by the singing of the black soldiers in his regiment, recorded several spirituals for an article in the *Atlantic Monthly* (1867); and the problem is far too complex to consider here in any depth. Suffice it to say that any one who has heard Negro spirituals *sung by Negroes* knows that, whatever the mixture of original elements, "the black and unknown bards of long ago" transformed these elements into an original and unique contribution to American culture and to world music. Most present-day scholars agree on this, just as they agree on the *American* rather than the *all-black* origins of jazz.

In *Scenes in the Life of Harriet Tubman* (1869), the biography of a runaway slave who became a conductor on the Underground Railroad, we notice an early use of folk material. Sarah H. Bradford, a proper Yankee writer, tells us that Harriet often ''created'' spirituals to inform potential runaways of her presence and her plans. The use of this folk literature as secret communication among slaves was crucial to their survival. The rhetoric, the idioms, and the images it employs are distinctly black American.

Most folk literature was probably the result of group or community effort, and the variety of versions of any one folk piece is probably a consequence of faulty memory and oral transmission. These factors certainly account for the differing versions of folk pieces of the post–Civil War period and the period of tremendous urbanization (1885–1900), when the ''John Henry'' ballad, ''Frankie and Johnnie,'' and countless other urban folk songs and sayings came into being. The original composers, whether individuals or groups, were illiterate and could not record their compositions.

Although Negro folk songs and sayings are, like the sophisticated writings of the period, invariably race conscious and evoke the hard realities of the special black experience, and although they too are coded, in a kind of ''thieves' jargon,'' they achieve universal relevance. The materials of Negro folk literature—myth, legend, belief—are allegoric and parabolic. They illustrate attitudes, emotional states, and experiences that are common to all people.

William Wells Brown

(c. 1816–1884)

William Wells Brown—one of the first African Americans to write a novel, the first to write a play, the first to write a book of travels, and among the first to write history—was born near Lexington, Kentucky. The son of a white father and a mulatto mother, he was one of seven children. According to rumor, Brown's mother was the daughter of Daniel Boone, and his father was thought to be a relative of their master.

Serving under several masters, William Wells Brown did many kinds of work, some of it unusual for a slave. At one time he was hired out to Elijah P. Lovejoy's newspaper office in St. Louis. Under his last master, a riverboat captain, Brown traveled up and down the Ohio and Mississippi rivers. He tried twice to escape. The first time, he took his mother with him, and although the two reached Illinois they were captured and returned to the master. As punishment Brown's mother was sold "down South"; the incident was a terrible blow to the young boy, who felt that he was responsible. His second escape attempt was successful. Having been taken by his master to Cincinnati,

Brown simply walked away. On his way north he was helped by a Quaker named Wells Brown, whose name he adopted.

As a free man Brown worked on steamboats on Lake Erie and was able to help many fugitive slaves to their freedom. He finally settled in Buffalo, brushed up on the "letters" he had somehow learned earlier, and improved remarkably his facility with the language. In 1847 Brown was invited to join the Massachusetts Anti-Slavery Society. Although he lacked the genius of Frederick Douglass, William Wells Brown became a faithful and effective speaker and writer for abolition both here and in England, and for the temperance cause, prison reform, and women's suffrage.

A prolific author, Brown produced the following major works: *Narrative of William W. Brown, a Fugitive Slave* (1847; revised 1848 and 1849); *Three Years in Europe; or, Places I Have Seen and People I Have Met* (London, 1852; enlarged and reprinted in 1855 as *The American Fugitive in Europe*); *Clotel; or, The President's Daughter: A Narrative of Slave Life in the United States* (London, 1853; revised and reprinted under different names in 1860–61, 1864, and 1867); *The Escape; or, A Leap for Freedom: A Drama in Five Acts* (1858); *The Black Man: His Antecedents, His Genius, and His Achievements* (1863); *The Negro in the American Rebellion: His Heroism and His Fidelity* (1867); *The Rising Son; or, The Antecedents and the Advancement of the Colored Race* (1874); and *My Southern Home; or, The South and Its People* (1880).

Brown's *Clotel* is still thought to be the first novel published by an African American. *Clotel* was published in London in 1853. The first novel to be published in

America (also the first to be published by a Negro woman), we now believe, is *Our Nig* (1859), by Harriet E. Wilson (see the headnote for Wilson).

The monumental and definitive *William Wells Brown, Author and Reformer* (1969) by W. Edward Farrison is an outstanding achievement in American scholarship. Farrison's introduction to and annotations in Brown's *The Negro in the American Rebellion: His Heroism and His Fidelity* (1867) and Farrison's entry in *Dictionary of American Negro Biography* are both valuable additions to the scholarship on William Wells Brown. So are the comments in *The Negro Author* by Vernon Loggins and in J. Noel Heermance's *William Wells Brown and "Clotelle": A Portrait of the Artist in the First Negro Novel* (with an introduction by Arthur P. Davis), published in 1969. Brown's contributions are also examined in *The Afro-American Novel* by Bernard W. Bell (1987). See also Josephine Brown's *Biography of an American Bondman, By His Daughter* (1856).

The novel selections come from chapters 1 and 2 of *Clotelle* (1867 version). The selection from *My Southern Home* comes from the 1880 publication.

FROM **CLOTELLE**

With the growing population in the Southern States, the increase of mulattoes has been very great. Society does not frown upon the man who sits with his half-white child upon his knee whilst the mother stands, a slave, behind his chair. In nearly all the cities and towns of the Slave States, the real negro, or clear black, does not amount to more than one in four of the slave population. This fact is of itself the best evidence of the degraded and immoral condition of the relation of master and slave. Throughout the Southern States, there is a class of slaves who, in most of the towns, are permitted to hire their time from their owners, and who are always expected to pay a high price. This class is the mulatto women, distinguished for their fascinating beauty. The handsomest of these usually pay the greatest amount for their time. Many of these women are the favorites of men of property and standing, who furnish them with the means of compensating their owners, and not a few are dressed in the most extravagant manner.

When we take into consideration the fact that no safeguard is thrown around virtue, and no inducement held out to slave-women to be pure and chaste, we will not be surprised when told that immorality and vice pervade the cities and towns of the South to an extent unknown in the Northern States. Indeed, many of the slave-women have no higher aspiration than that of becoming the finely-dressed mistress of some white man. At negro balls and parties, this class of women usually make the most splendid appearance, and are eagerly sought after in the dance, or to entertain in the drawing-room or at the table.

A few years ago, among the many slave-women in Richmond, Virginia, who hired their time of their masters, was Agnes, a mulatto owned by John Graves, Esq., and who might be heard boasting that she was the daughter of an American Senator. Although nearly forty years of age at the time of which we write, Agnes was still exceedingly handsome. More than half white, with long black hair and deep blue eyes, no one felt like disputing with her when she urged her claim to her relationship with the Anglo-Saxon.

In her younger days, Agnes had been a housekeeper for a young slave-holder, and in sustaining this relation had become the mother of two daughters. After being cast aside by this young man, the slave-woman betook herself to the business of a laundress, and was considered to be the most tasteful woman in Richmond at her vocation.

Isabella and Marion, the two daughters of Agnes, resided with their mother, and gave her what aid they could in her business. The mother, however, was very choice of her daughters, and would allow them to perform no labor that would militate against their lady-like appearance. Agnes early resolved to bring up her daughters as ladies, as she termed it.

As the girls grew older, the mother had to pay a stipulated price for them per month. Her notoriety as a laundress of the first class enabled her to put an extra charge upon the linen that passed through her hands; and although she imposed little or no work upon her daughters, she was enabled to live in comparative luxury and have her daughters dressed to attract attention, especially at the negro balls and parties.

Although the term "negro ball" is applied to these gatherings, yet a large portion of the men who attend them are whites. Negro balls and parties in the Southern States, especially in the cities and towns, are usually made up of quadroon women, a few negro men, and any number of white gentlemen. These are gatherings of the most democratic character. Bankers, merchants, lawyers, doctors, and their clerks and students, all take part in these social assemblies upon terms of perfect equality. The father and son not unfrequently meet and dance *vis à vis* at a negro ball.

It was at one of these parties that Henry Linwood, the son of a wealthy and retired gentleman of Richmond, was first introduced to Isabella, the oldest daughter of Agnes. The young man had just returned from Harvard College, where he had spent the previous five years. Isabella was in her eighteenth year, and was admitted by all who knew her to be the handsomest girl, colored or white, in the city. On this occasion, she was attired in a sky-blue silk dress, with deep black lace flounces, and bertha of the same. On her well-moulded arms she wore massive gold bracelets, while her rich black hair was arranged at the back in broad basket plaits, ornamented with pearls, and the front in the French style (*a la Imperatrice*), which suited her classic face to perfection.

Marion was scarcely less richly dressed than her sister.

Henry Linwood paid great attention to Isabella, which was looked upon with gratification by her mother, and became a matter of general conversation with all present. Of course, the young man escorted the beautiful quadroon home that evening, and became the favorite visitor at the house of Agnes.

It was on a beautiful moonlight night in the month of August, when all who reside in tropical climates are eagerly gasping for a breath of fresh air, that Henry Linwood was in the garden which surrounded Agnes' cottage, with the young quadroon by his side. He drew from his pocket a newspaper wet from the press, and read the following advertisement:—

NOTICE.—Seventy-nine negroes will be offered for sale on Monday, September 10, at 12 o'clock, being the entire stock of the late John Graves. The negroes are in excellent condition, and all warranted against the common vices. Among them are several mechanics, able-bodied field-hands, plough-boys, and women with children, some of them very prolific, affording a rare opportunity for any one who wishes to raise a strong and healthy lot of servants for their own use. Also several mulatto girls of rare personal qualities,—two of these very superior.

Among the above slaves advertised for sale were Agnes and her two daughters. Ere young Linwood left the quadroon that evening, he promised her that he would become her purchaser, and make her free and her own mistress.

Mr. Graves had long been considered not only an excellent and upright citizen of the first standing among the whites, but even the slaves regarded him as one of the kindest of masters. Having inherited his slaves with the rest of his property, he became possessed of them without any consultation or wish of his own. He would neither buy nor sell slaves, and was exceedingly careful, in letting them out, that they did not find oppressive and tyrannical masters. No slave speculator ever dared to cross the threshold of this planter of the Old Dominion. He was a constant attendant upon religious worship, and was noted for his general benevolence. The American Bible Society, the American Tract Society, and the cause of Foreign Missions, found in him a liberal friend. He was always anxious that his slaves should appear well on the Sabbath, and have an opportunity of hearing the word of God.

║══║

As might have been expected, the day of sale brought an unusually large number together to compete for the property to be sold. Farmers, who make a business of raising slaves for the market, were there, and slave-traders, who make a business of buying human beings in the slave-raising States and taking them to the far South, were also in attendance. Men and women, too, who wished to purchase for their own use, had found their way to the slave sale.

In the midst of the throng was one who felt a deeper interest in the result of the sale than any other of the bystanders. This was young Linwood. True to his promise, he was there with a blank bank-check in his pocket, awaiting with impatience to enter the list as a bidder for the beautiful slave.

It was indeed a heart-rending scene to witness the lamentations of these slaves, all of whom had grown up together on the old homestead of Mr. Graves, and who had been treated with great kindness by that gentleman, during his life. Now they were to be separated, and form new relations and companions. Such is the precarious condition of the slave. Even when with a good master, there is no certainty of his happiness in the future.

The less valuable slaves were first placed upon the auction-block, one after another, and sold to the highest bidder. Husbands and wives were separated with a degree of indifference that is unknown in any other relation in life. Brothers and sisters were torn from each other, and mothers saw their children for the last time on earth.

It was late in the day, and when the greatest number of persons were thought to be present, when Agnes and her daughters were brought out to the place of sale. The mother was first put upon the auction-block, and sold to a noted negro trader named Jennings. Marion was next ordered to ascend the stand, which she did with a trembling step, and was sold for $1200.

All eyes were now turned on Isabella, as she was led forward by the auctioneer. The appearance of the handsome quadroon caused a deep sensation among the crowd. There she stood, with a skin as fair as most white women, her features as beautifully regular as any of her sex of pure Anglo-Saxon blood, her long black hair done up in the neatest manner, her form tall and graceful, and her whole appearance indicating one superior to her condition.

The auctioneer commenced by saying that Miss Isabella was fit to deck the drawing-room of the finest mansion in Virginia.

"How much, gentlemen, for this real Albino!—fit fancy-girl for any one! She enjoys good health, and has a sweet temper. How much do you say?"

"Five hundred dollars."

"Only five hundred for such a girl as this? Gentlemen, she is worth a deal more than that sum. You certainly do not know the value of the article you are bidding on. Here, gentlemen, I hold in my hand a paper certifying that she has a good moral character."

"Seven hundred."

"Ah, gentlemen, that is something like. This paper also states that she is very intelligent."

"Eight hundred."

"She was first sprinkled, then immersed, and is now warranted to be a devoted Christian, and perfectly trustworthy."

"Nine hundred dollars."

"Nine hundred and fifty."

"One thousand."

"Eleven hundred."

Here the bidding came to a dead stand. The auctioneer stopped, looked around, and began in a rough manner to relate some anecdote connected with the sale of slaves, which he said had come under his own observation.

At this juncture the scene was indeed a most striking one. The laughing, joking, swearing, smoking, spitting, and talking, kept up a continual hum and confusion among the crowd, while the slave-girl stood with tearful eyes, looking alternately at her mother and sister and toward the young man whom she hoped would become her purchaser.

"The chastity of this girl," now continued the auctioneer, "is pure. She has never been from under her mother's care. She is virtuous, and as gentle as a dove."

The bids here took a fresh start, and went on until $1800 was reached. The auctioneer once more resorted to his jokes, and concluded by assuring the company that Isabella was not only pious, but that she could make an excellent prayer.

"Nineteen hundred dollars."

"Two thousand."

This was the last bid, and the quadroon girl was struck off, and became the property of Henry Linwood.

This was a Virginia slave-auction, at which the bones, sinews, blood, and nerves of a young girl of eighteen were sold for $500; her moral character for $200; her superior intellect for $100; the benefits supposed to accrue from her having been sprinkled and immersed, together with a warranty of her devoted Christianity, for $300; her ability to make a good prayer for $200; and her chastity for $700 more. This, too, in a city thronged with churches, whose tall spires look like so many signals pointing to heaven, but whose ministers preach that slavery is a God-ordained institution!

The slaves were speedily separated, and taken along by their respective masters. Jennings, the slave-speculator, who had purchased Agnes and her daughter Marion, with several of the other slaves, took them to the county prison, where he usually kept his human cattle after purchasing them, previous to starting for the New Orleans market.

Linwood had already provided a place for Isabella, to which she was taken. The most trying moment for her was when she took leave of her mother and sister. The "Good-by" of the slave is unlike that of any other class in the community. It is indeed a farewell forever. With tears streaming down their cheeks, they embraced and commended each other to God, who is no respecter of persons, and before whom master and slave must one day appear.

FROM **MY SOUTHERN HOME**

Paying a flying visit to Tennessee, I halted at Columbia, the capital of Maury County. At Redgerford Creek, five miles distant from Columbia, lives Joe Budge, a man with one hundred children. Never having met one with such a family, I resolved to make a call on the gentleman and satisfy my own curiosity.

This distinguished individual is seventy-one years old, large frame, of unadulterated blood, and spent his life in slavery up to the close of the war.

"How many children have you, Mr. Budge?" I asked.

"One hundred, ser," was the quick response.

"Are they all living?"

"No, ser."

"How many wives had you?"

"Thirteen, ser."

"Had you more than one wife living at any time?"

"O, yes, ser, nearly all of dem ware livin' when de war broke out."

"How was this, did the law allow you to have more than one wife at a time?"

"Well, yer see, boss, I waren't under de law, I ware under marser."

"Were you married to all of your wives by a minister?"

"No, ser, only five by de preacher."

"How did you marry the others?"

"Ober de broomstick an' under de blanket."

"How was that performed?"

"Wel, yer see, ser, dey all 'sembles in de quarters, an' a man takes hold of one en' of de broom an' a 'oman takes hole of tudder en', an' dey holes up de broom, an' de man an' de 'oman dats gwine to get married jumps ober an' den slips under a blanket, dey put out de light an' all goes out an' leabs em dar."

"How near together were your wives?"

"Marser had fore plantations, an' dey live 'bout on 'em, dem dat warn't sold."

"Did your master sell some of your wives?"

"O! yes, ser, when dey got too ole to bare children. You see, marser raised slaves fer de market, an' my stock ware called mighty good, kase I ware very strong, an' could do a heap of work."

"Were your children sold away from you?"

"Yes, ser, I see three of 'em sole one day fer two thousand dollars a-piece; yer see dey ware men grown up."

"Did you select your wives?"

"Dunno what you mean by dat word."

"Did you pick out the women that you wanted?"

"O! no, ser, I had nuthin ter say 'bout dat. Marser allers get 'em, an' pick out strong, hearty young women. Dat's de reason dat de planters wanted to get my children, kase dey ware so helty."

"Did you never feel that it was wrong to get married in such a light manner?"

"No, ser, kase yer see I toted de witness wid me."

"What do you mean by that?"

"Why, ser, I had religion, an' dat made me feel dat all ware right."

"What was the witness that you spoke of?"

"De change of heart, ser, is de witness dat I totes in my bosom; an' when a man's got dat, he fears nuthin, not eben de debble himsef."

"Then you know that you've got the witness?"

"Yes, ser, I totes it right here." And at this point, Mr. Budge put his hand on his heart, and looked up to heaven.

"I presume your master made no profession of religion?"

"O! yes, ser, you bet he had religion. He ware de fustest man in de church, an' he ware called mighty powerful in prayer."

"Do any of your wives live near you now, except the one that you are living with?"

"Yes, ser dar's five in dis county, but dey's all married now to udder men."

"Have you many grand-children?"

"Yes, ser, when my 'lations am all tergedder, dey numbers 'bout fore hundred, near as I ken get at it."

"Do you know of any other men that have got as many children as you?"

"No, ser, dey calls me de boss daddy in dis part of de State."

Having satisfied my curiosity, I bade Mr. Budge "good-day."

Harriet E. Wilson

(1827 or 1828–?)

Most of what we now know about Harriet E. Wilson, the author of *Our Nig,* is to be found in the 1983 landmark edition of this work, a work "resurrected" and edited by Henry Louis Gates, Jr. Because of its thoroughness and its distinction as a model of present-day literary scholarship, this edition should be consulted by the reader interested in Harriet E. Wilson and her novel. The title of this book, originally published in 1859, is indeed a full title: *Our Nig; or, Sketches from the Life of a Free Black, in a Two-Story White House, North. Showing that Slavery's Shadows Fall Even There*—by "Our Nig."

Our Nig, which has all of the tear-jerking qualities of nineteenth-century sentimental fiction, is—among other things—a strong statement on the anti-black attitude found all too often in the North. By no means a literary masterpiece, the novel is important. To it can be attributed two "firsts"—the first novel by an American black to be *published* in America; the first to be written and published by a black woman. See the headnotes in this volume for William Wells Brown and for Frank J. Webb.

For additional critical comment on Wilson's pioneering work see Henry L. Gates's article on Wilson in *Dictionary of Literary Biography, Volume 50.* See also the following studies for further comment on Wilson's achievement: Bernard W. Bell's *The Afro-American Novel and Its Tradition* (1987); Hazel V. Carby's *Reconstructing Womanhood: The Emergence of the Afro-American Woman Novelist* (1987); and Gates's *Figures in Black* (1987).

The selections that follow are from chapter 2 of *Our Nig,* in which Frado (Nig), the central character, is abandoned and left in the hands of a cruel mistress, and chapter 6, which gives examples of Frado's brutal treatment. Frado, incidentally, is the offspring of a racially mixed marriage.

MY FATHER'S DEATH

> *Misery! we have known each other,*
> *Like a sister and a brother,*
> *Living in the same lone home*
> *Many years—we must live some*
> *Hours or ages yet to come.*
>
> SHELLEY

Jim, proud of his treasure,—a white wife,—tried hard to fulfill his promises; and furnished her with a more comfortable dwelling, diet, and apparel. It was comparatively a comfortable winter she passed after her marriage. When Jim could work, all went on well. Industrious, and fond of Mag, he was determined she should not regret her union to him. Time levied an additional charge upon him, in the form of two pretty mulat-

tos, whose infantile pranks amply repaid the additional
toil. A few years, and a severe cough and pain in his
side compelled him to be an idler for weeks together,
and Mag had thus a reminder of by-gones. She cared
for him only as a means to subserve her own comfort;
yet she nursed him faithfully and true to marriage vows
till death released her. He became the victim of con-
sumption. He loved Mag to the last. So long as life continued, he stifled his sensibility to pain, and toiled for
her sustenance long after he was able to do so.

A few expressive wishes for her welfare; a hope of
better days for her; an anxiety lest they should not all
go to the "good place;" brief advice about their children; a hope expressed that Mag would not be neglected
as she used to be; the manifestation of Christian patience; these were *all* the legacy of miserable Mag. A
feeling of cold desolation came over her, as she turned
from the grave of one who had been truly faithful to
her.

She was now expelled from companionship with
white people; this last step—her union with a black—
was the climax of repulsion.

Seth Shipley, a partner in Jim's business, wished her
to remain in her present home; but she declined, and returned to her hovel again, with obstacles threefold more
insurmountable than before. Seth accompanied her, giving her a weekly allowance which furnished most of the
food necessary for the four inmates. After a time, work
failed; their means were reduced.

How Mag toiled and suffered, yielding to fits of desperation, bursts of anger, and uttering curses too fearful
to repeat. When both were supplied with work, they
prospered; if idle, they were hungry together. In this

way their interests became united; they planned for the future together. Mag had lived an outcast for years. She had ceased to feel the gushings of penitence; she had crushed the sharp agonies of an awakened conscience. She had no longings for a purer heart, a better life. Far easier to descend lower. She entered the darkness of perpetual infamy. She asked not the rite of civilization or Christianity. Her will made her the wife of Seth. Soon followed scenes familiar and trying.

"It's no use," said Seth one day; "we must give the children away, and try to get work in some other place."

"Who'll take the black devils?" snarled Mag.

"They're none of mine," said Seth; "what you growling about?"

"Nobody will want any thing of mine, or yours either," she replied.

"We'll make 'em, p'r'aps," he said. "There's Frado's six years old, and pretty, if she is yours, and white folks'll say so. She'd be a prize somewhere," he continued, tipping his chair back against the wall, and placing his feet upon the rounds, as if he had much more to say when in the right position.

Frado, as they called one of Mag's children, was a beautiful mulatto, with long, curly black hair, and handsome, roguish eyes, sparkling with an exuberance of spirit almost beyond restraint.

Hearing her name mentioned, she looked up from her play, to see what Seth had to say of her.

"Wouldn't the Bellmonts take her?" asked Seth.

"Bellmonts?" shouted Mag. "His wife is a right she-devil! and if—"

"Hadn't they better be all together?" interrupted

Seth, reminding her of a like epithet used in reference to her little ones.

Without seeming to notice him, she continued, "She can't keep a girl in the house over a week; and Mr. Bellmont wants to hire a boy to work for him, but he can't find one that will live in the house with her; she's so ugly, they can't."

"Well, we've got to make a move soon," answered Seth; "if you go with me, we shall go right off. Had you rather spare the other one?" asked Seth, after a short pause.

"One's as bad as t' other," replied Mag. "Frado is such a wild, frolicky thing, and means to do jest as she's a mind to; she won't go if she don't want to. I don't want to tell her she is to be given away."

"I will," said Seth. "Come here, Frado?"

The child seemed to have some dim foreshadowing of evil, and declined.

"Come here," he continued; "I want to tell you something."

She came reluctantly. He took her hand and said: "We're going to move, by-'m-bye; will you go?"

"No!" screamed she; and giving a sudden jerk which destroyed Seth's equilibrium, left him sprawling on the floor, while she escaped through the open door.

"She's a hard one," said Seth, brushing his patched coat sleeve. "I'd risk her at Bellmont's."

They discussed the expediency of a speedy departure. Seth would first seek employment, and then return for Mag. They would take with them what they could carry, and leave the rest with Pete Greene, and come for them when they were wanted. They were long in arranging affairs satisfactorily, and were not a little startled at the close of their conference to find Frado missing. They thought approaching night would bring her. Twilight passed into darkness, and she did not come. They thought she had understood their plans, and had, perhaps, permanently withdrawn. They could not rest without making some effort to ascertain her retreat. Seth went in pursuit, and returned without her. They rallied others when they discovered that another little colored girl was missing, a favorite playmate of Frado's. All effort proved unavailing. Mag felt sure her fears were realized, and that she might never see her again. Before her anxieties became realities, both were safely returned, and from them and their attendant they learned that they went to walk, and not minding the direction soon found themselves lost. They had climbed fences and walls, passed through thickets and marshes, and when night approached selected a thick cluster of shrubbery as a covert for the night. They were discovered by the person who now restored them, chatting of their prospects, Frado attempting to banish the childish fears of her companion. As they were some miles from home, they were kindly cared for until morning. Mag was relieved to know her child was not driven to desperation by their intentions to relieve themselves of her, and she was inclined to think severe restraint would be healthful.

The removal was all arranged; the few days necessary for such migrations passed quickly, and one bright summer morning they bade farewell to their Singleton hovel, and with budgets and bundles commenced their weary march. As they neared the village, they heard the merry shouts of children gathered around the school-room, awaiting the coming of their teacher.

"Halloo!" screamed one, "Black, white and yeller!" "Black, white and yeller," echoed a dozen voices.

It did not grate so harshly on poor Mag as once it would. She did not even turn her head to look at them. She had passed into an insensibility no childish taunt could penetrate, else she would have reproached herself as she passed familiar scenes, for extending the separation once so easily annihilated by steadfast integrity. Two miles beyond lived the Bellmonts, in a large, old fashioned, two-story white house, environed by fruitful acres, and embellished by shrubbery and shade trees. Years ago a youthful couple consecrated it as home; and after many little feet had worn paths to favorite fruit trees, and over its green hills, and mingled at last with brother man in the race which belongs neither to the swift or strong, the sire became grey-haired and decrepid, and went to his last repose. His aged consort soon followed him. The old homestead thus passed into the hands of a son, to whose wife Mag had applied the epithet "she-devil," as may be remembered. John, the son, had not in his family arrangements departed from the example of the father. The pastimes of his boyhood were ever freshly revived by witnessing the games of his own sons as they rallied about the same goal his youthful feet had often won; as well as by the amusements of his daughters in their imitations of maternal duties.

At the time we introduce them, however, John is wearing the badge of age. Most of his children were from home; some seeking employment; some were already settled in homes of their own. A maiden sister shared with him the estate on which he resided, and occupied a portion of the house.

Within sight of the house, Seth seated himself with his bundles and the child he had been leading, while Mag walked onward to the house leading Frado. A knock at the door brought Mrs. Bellmont, and Mag asked if she would be willing to let that child stop there while she went to the Reed's house to wash, and when she came back she would call and get her. It seemed a novel request, but she consented. Why the impetuous child entered the house, we cannot tell; the door closed, and Mag hastily departed. Frado waited for the close of day, which was to bring back her mother. Alas! it never came. It was the last time she ever saw or heard of her mother.

VARIETIES

"Hard are life's early steps; and but
that youth is buoyant, confident, and
strong in hope, men would behold
its threshold and despair."

The sorrow of Frado was very great for her pet, and Mr. Bellmont by great exertion obtained it again, much to the relief of the child. To be thus deprived of all her sources of pleasure was a sure way to exalt their worth, and Fido became, in her estimation, a more valuable presence than the human beings who surrounded her.

James had now been married a number of years, and frequent requests for a visit from the family were at last accepted, and Mrs. Bellmont made great preparations for a fall sojourn in Baltimore. Mary was installed house-keeper—in name merely, for Nig was the only moving power in the house. Although suffering from their joint severity, she felt safer than to be thrown wholly upon an ardent, passionate, unrestrained young lady, whom she always hated and felt it hard to be obliged to obey. The trial she must meet. Were Jack or Jane at home she would have some refuge; one only remained; good Aunt Abby was still in the house.

She saw the fast receding coach which conveyed her master and mistress with regret, and begged for one favor only, that James would send for her when they returned, a hope she had confidently cherished all these five years.

She was now able to do all the washing, ironing, baking, and the common *et cetera* of house-hold duties, though but fourteen. Mary left all for her to do, though she affected great responsibility. She would show herself in the kitchen long enough to relieve herself of some command, better withheld; or insist upon some compliance to her wishes in some department which she was very imperfectly acquainted with, very much less than the person she was addressing; and so impetuous till her orders were obeyed, that to escape the turmoil, Nig would often go contrary to her own knowledge to gain a respite.

Nig was taken sick! What could be done? The *work,* certainly, but not by Miss Mary. So Nig would work while she could remain erect, then sink down upon the floor, or a chair, till she could rally for a fresh effort. Mary would look in upon her, chide her for her laziness, threaten to tell mother when she came home, and so forth.

"Nig!" screamed Mary, one of her sickest days, "come here, and sweep these threads from the carpet."

She attempted to drag her weary limbs along, using the broom as support. Impatient of delay, she called again, but with a different request. "Bring me some wood, you lazy jade, quick." Nig rested the broom against the wall, and started on the fresh behest.

Too long gone. Flushed with anger, she rose and greeted her with, "What are you gone so long for? Bring it in quick, I say."

"I am coming as quick as I can," she replied, entering the door.

"Saucy, impudent nigger, you! is this the way you answer me?" and taking a large carving knife from the table, she hurled it, in her rage, at the defenceless girl.

Dodging quickly, it fastened in the ceiling a few inches from where she stood. There rushed on Mary's mental vision a picture of bloodshed, in which she was the perpetrator, and the sad consequences of what was so nearly an actual occurrence.

"Tell anybody of this, if you dare. If you tell Aunt Abby, I'll certainly kill you," said she, terrified. She returned to her room, brushed her threads herself; was for a day or two more guarded, and so escaped deserved and merited penalty.

Oh, how long the weeks seemed which held Nig in subjection to Mary; but they passed like all earth's sorrow and joys. Mr. and Mrs. B. returned delighted with their visit, and laden with rich presents for Mary. No word of hope for Nig. James was quite unwell, and would come home the next spring for a visit.

This, thought Nig, will be my time of release. I shall go back with him.

From early dawn until after all were retired, was she toiling, overworked, disheartened, longing for relief.

Exposure from heat to cold, or the reverse, often destroyed her health for short intervals. She wore no shoes until after frost, and snow even, appeared; and bared her feet again before the last vestige of winter disappeared. These sudden changes she was so illy guarded against, nearly conquered her physical system. Any word of complaint was severely repulsed or cruelly punished.

She was told she had much more than she deserved. So that manual labor was not in reality her only burden; but such an incessant torrent of scolding and boxing and threatening, was enough to deter one of maturer years from remaining within sound of the strife.

It is impossible to give an impression of the manifest enjoyment of Mrs. B in these kitchen scenes. It was her favorite exercise to enter the apartment noisily, vociferate orders, give a few sudden blows to quicken Nig's pace, then return to the sitting room with *such* a satisfied expression, congratulating herself upon her thorough house-keeping qualities.

She usually rose in the morning at the ringing of the bell for breakfast; if she were heard stirring before that time, Nig knew well there was an extra amount of scolding to be borne.

No one now stood between herself and Frado, but Aunt Abby. And if *she* dared to interfere in the least, she was ordered back to her "own quarters." Nig would creep slyly into her room, learn what she could of her regarding the absent, and thus gain some light in the thick gloom of care and toil and sorrow in which she was immersed.

The first of spring a letter came from James, announcing declining health. He must try northern air as a restorative; so Frado joyfully prepared for this agreeable increase of the family, this addition to her cares.

He arrived feeble, lame, from his disease, so changed Frado wept at his appearance, fearing he would be removed from her forever. He kindly greeted her, took her to the parlor to see his wife and child, and said many things to kindle smiles on her sad face.

Frado felt so happy in his presence, so safe from maltreatment! He was to her a shelter. He observed, silently, the ways of the house a few days; Nig still took her meals in the same manner as formerly, having the same allowance of food. He, one day, bade her not remove the food, but sit down to the table and eat.

"She *will,* mother," said he, calmly, but imperatively; "I'm determined; she works hard; I've watched her. Now, while I stay, she is going to sit down *here,* and eat such food as we eat."

A few sparks from the mother's black eyes were the only reply; she feared to oppose where she knew she could not prevail. So Nig's standing attitude, and selected diet vanished.

Her clothing was yet poor and scanty; she was not blessed with a Sunday attire; for she was never permitted to attend church with her mistress. "Religion was not meant for niggers," *she* said; when the husband and brothers were absent, she would drive Mrs. B. and Mary there, then return, and go for them at the close of the service, but never remain. Aunt Abby would take her to evening meetings, held in the neighborhood, which Mrs. B. never attended; and impart to her lessons of truth and grace as they walked to the place of prayer.

Many of less piety would scorn to present so doleful a figure; Mrs. B. had shaved her glossy ringlets; and, in

her coarse cloth gown and ancient bonnet, she was anything but an enticing object. But Aunt Abby looked
within. She saw a soul to save, an immortality of happiness to secure.

These evenings were eagerly anticipated by Nig; it
was such a pleasant release from labor.

Such perfect contrast in the melody and prayers of
these good people to the harsh tones which fell on her
ears during the day.

Soon she had all their sacred songs at command, and
enlivened her toil by accompanying it with this melody.

James encouraged his aunt in her efforts. He had
found the *Saviour,* he wished to have Frado's desolate
heart gladdened, quieted, sustained, by *His* presence. He
felt sure there were elements in her heart which, transformed and purified by the gospel, would make her
worthy the esteem and friendship of the world. A kind,
affectionate heart, native wit, and common sense, and
the pertness she sometimes exhibited, he felt if re-
strained properly, might become useful in originating a
self-reliance which would be of service to her in after
years.

Yet it was not possible to compass all this, while she
remained where she was. He wished to be cautious
about pressing too closely her claims on his mother, as
it would increase the burdened one he so anxiously
wished to relieve. He cheered her on with the hope of
returning with his family, when he recovered sufficiently.

Nig seemed awakened to new hopes and aspirations,
and realized a longing for the future, hitherto unknown.

To complete Nig's enjoyment, Jack arrived unexpectedly. His greeting was as hearty to herself as to any of the family.

"Where are your curls, Fra?" asked Jack, after the usual salutation.

"Your mother cut them off."

"Thought you were getting handsome, did she? Same old story, is it; knocks and bumps? Better times coming; never fear, Nig."

How different this appellative sounded from him; he said it in such a tone, with such a rogueish look!

She laughed, and replied that he had better take her West for a housekeeper.

Jack was pleased with James's innovations of table discipline, and would often tarry in the dining-room, to see Nig in her new place at the family table. As he was thus sitting one day, after the family had finished dinner, Frado seated herself in her mistress' chair, and was just reaching for a clean dessert plate which was on the table, when her mistress entered.

"Put that plate down; you shall not have a clean one; eat from mine," continued she. Nig hesitated. To eat after James, his wife or Jack, would have been pleasant; but to be commanded to do what was disagreeable by her mistress, *because* it was disagreeable, was trying. Quickly looking about, she took the plate, called Fido to wash it, which he did to the best of his ability; then, wiping her knife and fork on the cloth, she proceed to eat her dinner.

Nig never looked toward her mistress during the process. She had Jack near; she did not fear her now.

Insulted, full of rage, Mrs. Bellmont rushed to her husband, and commanded him to notice this insult; to whip that child; if he would not do it, James ought.

James came to hear the kitchen version of the affair. Jack was boiling over with laughter. He related all the circumstances to James, and pulling a bright, silver half-dollar from his pocket, he threw it at Nig, saying, "There, take that; 't was worth paying for."

James sought his mother; told her he "would not excuse or palliate Nig's impudence; but she should not be whipped or be punished at all. You have not treated her, mother, so as to gain her love; she is only exhibiting your remissness in this matter."

She only smothered her resentment until a convenient opportunity offered. The first time she was left alone with Nig, she gave her a thorough beating, to bring up arrearages; and threatened, if she ever exposed her to James, she would "cut her tongue out."

James found her, upon his return, sobbing; but fearful of revenge, she dared not answer his queries. He guessed their cause, and longed for returning health to take her under his protection.

Frank J. Webb

(Dates Unknown)

We do not know very much about the life of Frank J. Webb, the author of *The Garies and Their Friends,* the second novel by an American black. The first, *Clotel* by William Wells Brown, was published in 1853; Webb's work came out in 1857, and like Brown's was published in London. Henry Louis Gates's discovery of earlier fiction and the resurrection of Harriet E. Wilson's *Our Nig,* originally published in 1859, have forced us to be more careful about designating "firsts" in African American fiction. Since *Our Nig* was published in America, we now say it was the first novel published by a Negro in America; also the first by a black woman.

The little that we know about Webb comes from one main source: the preface to *The Garies and Their Friends,* written by Harriet Beecher Stowe. She states that Webb was "a coloured young man" born and reared in Philadelphia, adding that "the incidents related [in the novel] are mostly true ones," and that "the majority are faithfully drawn from real life." Mrs. Stowe liked the novel and considered it an example of "what the *free people do attain,* and what they can do in spite of all social obstacles.''

The Garies and Their Friends is a better-written work than Brown's pioneering *Clotel,* and it may be credited with several literary ''firsts.'' It is the first fictional work to treat seriously the ''mixed marriage'' problem; it was among the first African American novels to include a lynch mob; among the first to treat ironically (as Charles Chesnutt was to do later) the problems of the ''color line''; and among the first to make ''passing for white'' a major theme, as several novelists were to do during the New Negro (Harlem) Renaissance of the 1920s. A fascinating and in some ways an unusual novel, Webb's work should be better known than it is. In two respects *The Garies* is closer in content to *Our Nig* than to *Clotel.* Both deal with Negroes in the North and the prejudice they found there; both deal with interracial or ''mixed'' marriages.

For critical comment on *The Garies and Their Friends* and on Webb, see Vernon Loggins, *The Negro Author;* Benjamin Brawley, *Early Negro American Writers* (1935); Hugh M. Gloster, *Negro Voices in Fiction* (1948); and the 1969 Arno Press and *The New York Times* edition of *The Garies and Their Friends,* with an introduction by Arthur P. Davis and a preface by Harriet Beecher Stowe. The entry by Gregory L. Candela in *Dictionary of Literary Biography, Volume 50*, and *The Afro-American Novel and Its Tradition* (1987) by Bernard W. Bell should also be examined.

The selection that follows comes from Chapter XIII of *The Garies and Their Friends,* Arno Press and *The New York Times* edition, 1969.

HOPES CONSUMMATED

To Emily Winston we have always accorded the title of Mrs. Garie; whilst, in reality, she had no legal claim to it whatever.

Previous to their emigration from Georgia, Mr. Garie had, on one or two occasions, attempted, but without success, to make her legally his wife.

He ascertained that, even if he could have found a clergyman willing to expose himself to persecution by marrying them, the ceremony itself would have no legal weight, as a marriage between a white and a mulatto was not recognized as valid by the laws of the state; and he had, therefore, been compelled to dismiss the matter from his mind, until an opportunity should offer for the accomplishment of their wishes.

Now, however, that they had removed to the north, where they would have no legal difficulties to encounter, he determined to put his former intention into execution. Although Emily had always maintained a studied silence on the subject, he knew that it was the darling wish of her heart to be legally united to him; so he unhesitatingly proceeded to arrange matters for the consummation of what he felt assured would promote the happiness of both. He therefore wrote to Dr. Blackly, a distinguished clergyman of the city, requesting him to perform the ceremony, and received from him an assurance that he would be present at the appointed time.

Matters having progressed thus far, he thought it time to inform Emily of what he had done. On the evening succeeding the receipt of an answer from the Rev. Dr. Blackly—after the children had been sent to bed—he called her to him, and, taking her hand, sat down beside her on the sofa.

"Emily," said he, as he drew her closer to him, "my dear, faithful Emily! I am about to do you an act of justice—one, too, that I feel will increase the happiness of us both. I am going to marry you, my darling! I am about to give you a lawful claim to what you have already won by your faithfulness and devotion. You know I tried, more than once, whilst in the south, to accomplish this, but, owing to the cruel and unjust laws existing there, I was unsuccessful. But now, love, no such difficulty exists; and here," continued he, "is an answer to the note I have written to Dr. Blackly, asking him to come next Wednesday night, and perform the ceremony.—You are willing, are you not, Emily?" he asked.

"Willing!" she exclaimed, in a voice tremulous with emotion—"willing! Oh, God! if you only knew how I have longed for it! It has been my earnest desire for years!" and, bursting into tears, she leaned, sobbing, on his shoulder.

After a few moments she raised her head, and, looking searchingly in his face, she asked: "But do you do this after full reflection on the consequences to ensue? Are you willing to sustain all the odium, to endure all the contumely, to which your acknowledged union with one of my unfortunate race will subject you? Clarence! it will be a severe trial—a greater one than any you have yet endured for me—and one for which I fear my love will prove but a poor recompense! I have thought more of these things lately; I am older now in years and experience. There was a time when I was vain enough to think that my affection was all that was necessary for your happiness; but men, I know, require more to fill their cup of content than the undivided affection of a woman, no matter how fervently beloved. You have talents, and, I have sometimes thought, ambition. Oh, Clarence! how it would grieve me, in after-years, to know that you regretted that for me you had sacrificed all those views and hopes that are cherished by the generality of your sex! Have you weighed it well?"

"Yes, Emily—well," replied Mr. Garie; "and you know the conclusion. My past should be a guarantee for the future. I had the world before me, and chose you— and with you I am contented to share my lot; and feel that I receive, in your affection, a full reward for any of the so-called sacrifices I may make. So, dry your tears, my dear," concluded he, "and let us hope for nothing but an increase of happiness as the result."

After a few moments of silence, he resumed: "It will be necessary, Emily, to have a couple of witnesses. Now, whom would you prefer? I would suggest Mrs. Ellis and her husband. They are old friends, and persons on whose prudence we can rely. It would not do to have the matter talked about, as it would expose us to disagreeable comments."

Mrs. Garie agreed perfectly with him as to the selection of Mr. and Mrs. Ellis; and immediately despatched a note to Mrs. Ellis, asking her to call at their house on the morrow.

When she came, Emily informed her, with some confusion of manner, of the intended marriage, and asked her attendance as witness, at the same time informing her of the high opinion her husband entertained of their prudence in any future discussion of the matter.

"I am really glad he is going to marry you, Emily," replied Mrs. Ellis, "and depend upon it we will do all in our power to aid it. Only yesterday, that inquisitive Mrs. Tiddy was at our house, and, in conversation respecting you, asked if I knew you to be married to Mr. Garie. I turned the conversation somehow, without giving her a direct answer. Mr. Garie, I must say, does act nobly towards you. He must love you, Emily, for not one white man in a thousand would make such a sacrifice for a coloured woman. You can't tell how we all like him— he is so amiable, so kind in his manner, and makes everyone so much at ease in his company. It's real good in him, I declare, and I shall begin to have some faith in white folks, after all.—Wednesday night," continued she; "very well—we shall be here, if the Lord spare us;" and, kissing Emily, she hurried off, to impart the joyful intelligence to her husband.

The anxiously looked for Wednesday evening at last arrived, and Emily arrayed herself in a plain white dress for the occasion. Her long black hair had been arranged in ringlets by Mrs. Ellis, who stood by, gazing admiringly at her.

"How sweet you look, Emily—you only want a wreath of orange blossoms to complete your appearance. Don't you feel a little nervous?" asked her friend.

"A little excited," she answered, and her hand shook as she put back one of the curls that had fallen across her face. Just then a loud ringing at the door announced the arrival of Dr. Blackly, who was shown into the front parlour.

Emily and Mrs. Ellis came down into the room where Mr. Garie was waiting for them, whilst Mr. Ellis brought in Dr. Blackly. The reverend gentleman gazed

with some surprise at the party assembled. Mr. Garie
was so thoroughly Saxon in appearance, that no one
could doubt to what race he belonged, and it was
equally evident that Emily, Mrs. Ellis, and her husband,
were coloured persons.

Dr. Blackly looked from one to the other with evident embarrassment, and then said to Mr. Garie, in a
low, hesitating tone:—

"I think there has been some mistake here—will you
do me the favour to step into another room?"

Mr. Garie mechanically complied, and stood waiting
to learn the cause of Dr. Blackly's strange conduct.

"You are a white man, I believe?" at last stammered
forth the doctor.

"Yes, sir; I presume my appearance is a sufficient
guarantee of that," answered Mr. Garie.

"Oh yes, I do not doubt it, and for that reason you
must not be surprised if I decline to proceed with the
ceremony."

"I do not see how my being a white man can act as
a barrier to its performance," remarked Mr. Garie in reply.

"It would not, sir, if all the parties were of one complexion; but I do not believe in the propriety of amalga-
mation, and on no consideration could I be induced to
assist in the union of a white man or woman with a person who has the slightest infusion of African blood in
their veins. I believe the negro race," he continued, "to
be marked out by the hand of God for servitude; and
you must pardon me if I express my surprise that a gentleman of your evident intelligence should seek such a
connection—you must be labouring under some horrible
infatuation."

"Enough, sir," replied Mr. Garie, proudly; "I only regret that I did not know it was necessary to relate every circumstance of appearance, complexion, &c. I wished to obtain a marriage certificate, not a passport. I mistook you for a *Christian minister,* which mistake you will please to consider as my apology for having troubled you;" and thus speaking, he bowed Dr. Blackly out of the house. Mr. Garie stepped back to the door of the parlour and called out Mr. Ellis.

"We are placed in a very difficult dilemma," said he, as he was joined by the latter. "Would you believe it? that prejudiced old sinner has actually refused to marry us."

"It is no more than you might have expected of him—he's a thorough nigger-hater—keeps a pew behind the organ of his church for coloured people, and will not permit them to receive the sacrament until all the white members of his congregation are served. Why, I don't see what on earth induced you to send for him."

"I knew nothing of his sentiments respecting coloured people. I did not for a moment have an idea that he would hesitate to marry us. There is no law here that forbids it. What can we do?" said Mr. Garie, despairingly.

"I know a minister who will marry you with pleasure, if I can only catch him at home; he is so much engaged in visiting the sick and other pastoral duties."

"Do go—hunt him up, Ellis. It will be a great favour to me, if you can induce him to come. Poor Emily—what a disappointment this will be to her," said he, as he entered the room where she was sitting.

"What is the matter, dear?" she asked, as she observed Garie's anxious face. "I hope there is no new difficulty."

Mr. Garie briefly explained what had just occurred, and informed her, in addition, of Mr. Ellis having gone to see if he could get Father Banks, as the venerable old minister was called.

"It seems, dear," said she, despondingly, "as if Providence looked unfavourably on our design; for every time you have attempted it, we have in some way thwarted;" and the tears chased one another down her face, which had grown pale in the excitement of the moment.

"Oh, don't grieve about it, dear; it is only a temporary disappointment. I can't think all the clergymen in the city are like Dr. Blackly. Some one amongst them will certainly oblige us. We won't despair; at least not until Ellis comes back."

They had not very long to wait; for soon after this conversation footsteps were heard in the garden, and Mr. Ellis entered, followed by the clergyman.

In a very short space of time they were united by Father Banks, who seemed much affected as he pronounced his blessing upon them.

"My children," he said, tremulously, "you are entering upon a path which, to the most favoured, is full of disappointment, care, and anxieties; but to you who have come together under such peculiar circumstances, in the face of so many difficulties, and in direct opposition to the prejudices of society, it will be fraught with more danger, and open to more annoyances, than if you were both of one race. But if men revile you, revile not again; bear it patiently for the sake of Him who has

borne so much for you. God bless you, my children,"
said he, and after shaking hands with them all, he departed.

Mr. and Mrs. Ellis took their leave soon after, and
then Mrs. Garie stole upstairs alone into the room where
the children were sleeping. It seemed to her that night
that they were more beautiful than ever, as they lay in
their little beds quietly slumbering. She knelt beside
them, and earnestly prayed their heavenly Father that
the union which had just been consummated in the face
of so many difficulties might prove a boon to them all.

"Where have you been, you runaway?" exclaimed
her husband as she re-entered the parlour. "You stayed
away so long, I began to have all sorts of frightful
ideas—I thought of the 'mistletoe hung in the castle
hall,' and of old oak chests, and all kind of terrible
things. I've been sitting here alone ever since the Ellises
went: where have you been?"

"Oh, I've been upstairs looking at the children. Bless
their young hearts! they looked so sweet and happy—
and how they grow! Clarence is getting to be quite a little man; don't you think it time, dear, that he was sent
to school? I have so much more to occupy my mind
here than I had in Georgia, so many household duties to
attend to, that I am unable to give that attention to his
lessons which I feel is requisite. Besides, being so much
at home, he has associated with that wretched boy of
the Stevens's, and is growing rude and noisy; don't you
think he had better be sent to school?"

"Oh yes, Emily, if you wish it," was Mr. Garie's reply. "I will search out a school to-morrow, or next
day;" and taking out his watch, he continued, "it is

near twelve o'clock—how the night has flown away—
we must be off to bed. After the excitement of the evening, and your exertions of to-day, I fear that you will
be indisposed to-morrow.''

Clarence, although over nine years old, was so backward in learning, that they were obliged to send him to
a small primary school which had recently been opened
in the neighbourhood; and as it was one for children of
both sexes, it was deemed advisable to send little Em
with him.

"I do so dislike to have her go," said her mother, as
her husband proposed that she should accompany Clarence; "she seems so small to be sent to school. I'm
afraid she won't be happy.''

"Oh! don't give yourself the least uneasiness about
her not being happy there, for a more cheerful set of little folks I never beheld. You would be astonished to see
how exceedingly young some of them are.''

"What kind of a person is the teacher?" asked Mrs.
Garie.

"Oh! she's a charming little creature; the very em-
bodiment of cheerfulness and good humour. She has
sparkling black eyes, a round rosy face, and can't be
more than sixteen, if she is that old. Had I had such a
teacher when a boy, I should have got on charmingly;
but mine was a cross old widow, who wore spectacles
and took an amazing quantity of snuff, and used to flog
upon the slightest pretense. I went into her presence
with fear and trembling. I could never learn anything
from her, and that must be my excuse for my present
literary short-comings. But you need have no fear respecting Em getting on with Miss Jordan: I don't be-

lieve she could be unkind to any one, least of all to our little darling.''

''Then you will take them down in the morning,'' suggested Mrs. Garie; ''but on no account leave Emily unless she wishes to stay.''

James Monroe Whitfield

(1822–1871)

Not a great deal is known about the life of James Monroe Whitfield. Earlier scholars say that he was born in Massachusetts, one specifies Boston; but Joan R. Sherman, writing in 1974, claims that he was born in New Hampshire in 1822. These scholars and Sherman also differ on Whitfield's terminal date, but they and Sherman agree that Whitfield as a young man moved to Buffalo, New York, where he worked as a barber. Outside of barbering, the work by which he made his living, Whitfield pursued three major activities: writing poetry, working with the Prince Hall Masons in California and Nevada, and promoting colonization as a ''way out'' for the African American.

In 1853 Whitfield published his best-known work, *America and Other Poems,* which he dedicated to Martin R. Delany. Like Delany, Whitfield was seemingly an investigator for the colonization movement. Delany went to Africa, looking for suitable sites on which to plant colonies of American blacks; Whitfield, we believe, as commissioner went to Central America in 1859 for the same purpose, staying for two years. Before leaving the country, Whitfield had contributed many poems to Douglass's *North Star* and *Frederick Douglass' Paper.* He had also written a brilliant series of letters espousing and defending colonization against Douglass and others who opposed it.

Returning to the West Coast in 1861, Whitfield took up once more his barbering trade, worked with the California Prince Hall Masons as grand master, joined in political debates, and wrote poems. If Whitfield were alive today, he would be called an "activist." His "America" and other works which appeared in abolition papers like Douglass's *North Star* are strong and well-written statements of protest, surprisingly so when one considers his lack of formal education. As Joan R. Sherman has said, he "became a major propagandist for black independence and racial retributive justice. . . .Whitfield's poetry of protest and despair are among the most robust and convincing of his time."[1]

For biographical information, one will find Vernon Loggins's *The Negro Author* helpful. Joan R. Sherman's *Invisible Poets* (1974) has a documented biography, critical comments on Whitfield's works, and a bibliography. See also Sherman's article on Whitfield in *Dictionary of American Negro Biography* and Doris L. Laryea's entry in *Dictionary of Literary Biography, Volume 50.*

"America," "How Long?," and "The North Star" are found originally in *America and Other Poems* (1853), and later found in Benjamin Brawley's *Early Negro American Writers.*

---

[1]Rayford W. Logan and Michael R. Winston, *Dictionary of American Negro Biography* (New York: W. W. Norton and Company, 1982), 650.

AMERICA

America, it is to thee,
Thou boasted land of liberty,—
It is to thee I raise my song,
Thou land of blood, and crime, and wrong.
It is to thee, my native land,
From which has issued many a band
To tear the black man from his soil,
And force him here to delve and toil;
Chained on your blood-bemoistened sod,
Cringing beneath a tyrant's rod,
Stripped of those rights which Nature's God
　　Bequeathed to all the human race,
Bound to a petty tyrant's nod,
　　Because he wears a paler face.
Was it for this that freedom's fires
Were kindled by your patriot sires?
Was it for this they shed their blood,
On hill and plain, on field and flood?
Was it for this that wealth and life
Were staked upon that desperate strife,
Which drenched this land for seven long years
With blood of men, and women's tears?
When black and white fought side by side,
　　Upon the well-contested field,—
Turned back the fierce opposing tide,
　　And made the proud invader yield—
When, wounded, side by side they lay,
　　And heard with joy the proud hurrah
From their victorious comrades say
　　That they had waged successful war,

The thought ne'er entered in their brains
That they endured those toils and pains,
To forge fresh fetters, heavier chains
For their own children, in whose veins
Should flow that patriotic blood,
So freely shed on field and flood.
Oh, no; they fought, as they believed,
   For the inherent rights of man;
But mark, how they have been deceived
   By slavery's accursed plan.
They never thought, when thus they shed
   Their heart's best blood, in freedom's cause,
That their own sons would live in dread,
   Under unjust, oppressive laws:
That those who quietly enjoyed
   The rights for which they fought and fell,
Could be the framers of a code,
   That would disgrace the fiends of hell!
Could they have looked, with prophet's ken,
   Down to the present evil time,
   Seen free-born men, uncharged with crime,
Consigned unto a slaver's pen,—
Or thrust into a prison cell,
With thieves and murderers to dwell—
While that same flag whose stripes and stars
Had been their guide through freedom's wars
As proudly waved above the pen
Of dealers in the souls of men!
Or could the shades of all the dead,
   Who fell beneath that starry flag,
Visit the scenes where they once bled,
   On hill and plain, on vale and crag,

By peaceful brook, or ocean's strand,
   By inland lake, or dark green wood,
Where'er the soil of this wide land
   Was moistened by their patriot blood,—
And then survey the country o'er,
   From north to south, from east to west,
And hear the agonizing cry
Ascending up to God on high,
From western wilds to ocean's shore,
   The fervent prayer of the oppressed;
The cry of helpless infancy
   Torn from the parent's fond caress
By some base tool of tyranny,
   And doomed to woe and wretchedness;
The indignant wail of fiery youth,
   Its noble aspirations crushed,
Its generous zeal, its love of truth,
   Trampled by tyrants in the dust;
The aerial piles which fancy reared,
   And hopes too bright to be enjoyed,
Have passed and left his young heart seared,
   And all its dreams of bliss destroyed.
The shriek of virgin purity,
Doomed to some libertine's embrace,
Should rouse the strongest sympathy
   Of each one of the human race;
And weak old age, oppressed with care,
   As he reviews the scene of strife,
Puts up to God a fervent prayer,
   To close his dark and troubled life,
The cry of fathers, mothers, wives,
   Severed from all their hearts hold dear,
And doomed to spend their wretched lives

In gloom, and doubt, and hate, and fear;
And manhood, too, with soul of fire,
And arm of strength, and smothered ire,
Stands pondering with brow of gloom,
Upon his dark unhappy doom,
Whether to plunge in battle's strife,
And buy his freedom with his life,
And with stout heart and weapon strong,
Pay back the tyrant wrong for wrong
Or wait the promised time of God,
    When his Almighty ire shall wake,
And smite the oppressor in his wrath,
And hurl red ruin in his path,
And with the terrors of his rod,
    Cause adamantine hearts to quake.
Here Christian writhes in bondage still,
    Beneath his brother Christian's rod,
And pastors trample down at will,
    The image of the living God.
While prayers go up in lofty strains,
    And pealing hymns ascend to heaven,
The captive, toiling in his chains,
    With tortured limbs and bosom riven,
Raises his fettered hand on high,
    And in the accents of despair,
To him who rules both earth and sky,
    Puts up a sad, a fervent prayer,
To free him from the awful blast
    Of slavery's bitter galling shame—
Although his portion should be cast
    With demons in eternal flame!
Almighty God! 'tis this they call
    The land of liberty and law;

Part of its sons in baser thrall
   Than Babylon or Egypt saw—
Worse scenes of rapine, lust and shame,
   Than Babylonian ever knew,
Are perpetrated in the name
   Of God, the holy, just, and true;
And darker doom than Egypt felt,
May yet repay this nation's guilt.
Almighty God! thy aid impart,
And fire anew each faltering heart,
And strengthen every patriot's hand,
Who aims to save our native land.
We do not come before thy throne,
   With carnal weapons drenched in gore,
Although our blood has freely flown,
   In adding to the tyrant's store.
Father! before thy throne we come,
   Not in the panoply of war,
With pealing trump, and rolling drum,
   And cannon booming loud and far;
Striving in blood to wash out blood,
   Through wrong to seek redress for wrong;
For while thou'rt holy, just and good,
   The battle is not to the strong;
But in the sacred name of peace,
   Of justice, virtue, love and truth,
We pray, and never mean to cease,
   Till weak old age and fiery youth
In freedom's cause their voices raise,
And burst the bonds of every slave;
Till, north and south, and east and west,
The wrongs we bear shall be redressed.

HOW LONG?

How long, O gracious God! how long,
 Shall power lord it over right?
The feeble, trampled by the strong,
 Remain in slavery's gloomy night?
In every region of the earth,
 Oppression rules with iron power;
And every man of sterling worth,
 Whose soul disdains to cringe or cower
Beneath a haughty tyrant's nod,
And, supplicating, kiss the rod
That, wielded by oppression's might,
Smites to the earth his dearest right,—
The right to speak, and think, and feel,
 And spread his uttered thoughts abroad,
To labor for the common weal,
 Responsible to none but God,—
Is threatened with the dungeon's gloom,
The felon's cell, the traitor's doom,
And treacherous politicians league
 With hireling priests, to crush and ban
All who expose their vile intrigue,
 And vindicate the rights of man.
How long shall Afric' raise to thee
 Her fettered hand, O Lord! in vain,
And plead in fearful agony
 For vengeance for her children slain?
I see the Gambia's swelling flood,
 And Niger's darkly rolling wave,
Bear on their bosoms, stained with blood,
 The bound and lacerated slave;
While numerous tribes spread near and far,

Fierce, devastating, barbarous war,
Earth's fairest scenes in ruin laid,
To furnish victims for that trade,
Which breeds on earth such deeds of shame,
As fiends might blush to hear or name.
I see where Danube's waters roll, .
    And where the Magyar vainly strove,
With valiant arm and faithful soul,
    In battle for the land he loved,—
A perjured tyrant's legions tread
The ground where Freedom's heroes bled,
And still the voice of those who feel
Their country's wrongs, with Austrian steel.
I see the "Rugged Russian Bear"
Lead forth his slavish hordes, to war
Upon the right of every State
Its own affairs to regulate;
To help each despot bind the chain
Upon the people's rights again,
And crush beneath his ponderous paw
All constitutions, rights, and law.
I see in France,—O burning shame!—
The shadow of a mighty name,
Wielding the power her patriot bands
Had boldly wrenched from kingly hands,
With more despotic pride of sway
Than ever monarch dared display.
The Fisher, too, whose world-wide nets
    Are spread to snare the souls of men,
By foreign tyrants' bayonets
    Established on his throne again,
Blesses the swords still reeking red
    With the best blood his country bore,

And prays for blessings on the head
 Of him who wades through Roman gore.
The same unholy sacrifice
Where'er I turn bursts on mine eyes,
Of princely pomp, and priestly pride,
 The people trampled in the dust,
Their dearest, holiest rights denied,
 Their hopes destroyed, their spirit crushed;
But when I turn the land to view,
 Which claims, par excellence, to be
The refuge of the brave and true,
 The strongest bulwark of the free,
The grand asylum for the poor
 And trodden down of every land,
Where they may rest in peace, secure,
 Nor fear the oppressor's iron hand,—
Worse scenes of rapine, lust, and shame,
Than e'er disgraced the Russian name,
Worse than the Austrian ever saw,
Are sanctioned here as righteous law.
Here might the Austrian butcher* make
 Progress in shameful cruelty,
Where women-whippers proudly take
 The meed and praise of chivalry.
Here might the cunning Jesuit learn,
 Though skilled in subtle sophistry,
And trained to persevere in stern
 Unsympathizing cruelty,
And call that good, which, right or wrong,
Will tend to make his order strong:

*Haynau.

He here might learn from those who stand
    High in the gospel ministry,
The very magnates of the land
    In evangelic piety,
That conscience must not only bend
    To everything the church decrees,
But it must also condescend,
    When drunken politicians please
To place their own inhuman acts
    Above the "higher law" of God,
And on the hunted victim's tracks
    Cheer the malignant fiends of blood,
To help the man-thief bind the chain
    Upon his Christian brother's limb,
And bear to slavery's hell again
    The bound and suffering child of Him
Who died upon the cross, to save
Alike, the master and the slave.
While all the oppressed from every land
Are welcomed here with open hand,
And fulsome praises rend the heaven
For those who have the fetters riven
Of European tyranny,
And bravely struck for liberty;
And while from thirty thousand fanes
    Mock prayers go up, and hymns are sung,
Three million drag their clanking chains,
    "Unwept, unhonored, and unsung:"
Doomed to a state of slavery,
    Compared with which the darkest night
Of European tyranny,
    Seems brilliant as the noonday light.

While politicians void of shame,
   Cry this is law and liberty,
The clergy lend the awful name
   And sanction of the Deity,
To help sustain the monstrous wrong,
And crush the weak beneath the strong.
Lord, thou hast said the tyrant's ear
   Shall not be always closed to thee,
But that thou wilt in wrath appear,
   And set the trembling captive free.
And even now dark omens rise
   To those who either see or hear,
And gather o'er the darkening skies
   The threatening signs of fate and fear;
Not like the plagues which Egypt saw,
   When rising in an evil hour,
A rebel 'gainst the "higher law,"
   And glorying in her mighty power,—
Saw blasting fire, and blighting hail,
Sweep o'er her rich and fertile vale,
And heard on every rising gale
Ascend the bitter mourning wail;
And blighted herd, and blasted plain,
Through all the land the first-born slain,
Her priests and magi made to cower
In witness of a higher power,
And darkness like a sable pall
   Shrouding the land in deepest gloom,
Sent sadly through the minds of all,
   Forebodings of approaching doom.
What though no real shower of fire
   Spreads o'er this land its withering blight,

Denouncing wide Jehovah's ire,
  Like that which palsied Egypt's might;
And though no literal darkness spreads
  Upon the land its sable gloom,
And seems to fling around our heads
  The awful terrors of the tomb?
Yet to the eye of him who reads
  The fate of nations past and gone,
And marks with care the wrongful deeds
  By which their power was overthrown,—
Worse plagues than Egypt ever felt
  Are seen wide-spreading through the land,
Announcing that the heinous guilt
  On which the nation proudly stands,
Has risen to Jehovah's throne,
  And kindled his Almighty ire,
And broadcast through the land has sown
  The seeds of a devouring fire;
Blasting with foul pestiferous breath
  The fountain springs of mortal life,
And planting deep the seeds of death,
  And future germs of deadly strife;
And moral darkness spreads its gloom
  Over the land in every part,
And buries in a living tomb
  Each generous prompting of the heart.
Vice in its darkest, deadliest stains,
  Here walks with brazen front abroad,
And foul corruption proudly reigns
  Triumphant in the church of God,
And sinks so low the Christian name
In foul degrading vice and shame,
That Moslem, Heathen, Atheist, Jew,

And men of every faith and creed,
To their professions far more true,
　　More liberal both in word and deed,
May well reject with loathing scorn
　　The doctrines taught by those who sell
Their brethren in the Saviour born,
　　Down into slavery's hateful hell;
And with the price of Christian blood
Build temples to the Christian's God,
And offer up as sacrifice,
　　And incense to the God of heaven,
The mourning wail, and bitter cries,
　　Of mothers from their children riven;
Of virgin purity profaned
　　To sate some brutal ruffian's lust,
Millions of godlike minds ordained
　　To grovel ever in the dust,
Shut out by Christian power and might
From every ray of Christian light.
How long, O Lord! shall such vile deeds
　　Be acted in thy holy name,
And senseless bigots o'er their creeds
　　Fill the whole world with war and flame?
How long shall ruthless tyrants claim
　　Thy sanction to their bloody laws,
And throw the mantle of thy name
　　Around their foul, unhallowed cause?
How long shall all the people bow
　　As vassals of the favored few,
And shame the pride of manhood's brow,—
　　Give what to God alone is due,
Homage to wealth and rank and power,
Vain shadows of a passing hour?

Oh, for a pen of living fire,
    A tongue of flame, an arm of steel!
To rouse the people's slumbering ire,
    And teach the tyrants' hearts to feel.
O Lord! in vengeance now appear,
    And guide the battles for the right,
The spirits of the fainting cheer,
    And nerve the patriot's arm with might;
Till slavery's banished from the world,
And tyrants from their power hurled;
And all mankind, from bondage free,
Exult in glorious liberty.

THE NORTH STAR

Star of the North! whose steadfast ray
    Pierces the sable pall of night,
Forever pointing out the way
    That leads to freedom's hallowed light:
The fugitive lifts up his eye
To where thy rays illume the sky.

That steady, calm, unchanging light,
    Through dreary wilds and trackless dells,
Directs his weary steps aright
    To the bright land where freedom dwells;
And spreads, with sympathizing breast,
Her aegis over the oppressed;

Written for *The North Star*, a newspaper edited by Frederick Douglass.

Though other stars may round thee burn,
   With larger disk and brighter ray,
And fiery comets round thee turn,
   While millions mark their blazing way;
And the pale moon and planets bright
Reflect on us their silvery light.

Not like that moon, now dark, now bright,
   In phase and place forever changing;
Or planets with reflected light,
   Or comets through the heavens ranging;
They all seem varying in our view,
While thou art ever fixed and true.

So may that other bright North Star,
   Beaming with truth and freedom's light,
Pierce with its cheering ray afar,
   The shades of slavery's gloomy night;
And may it never cease to be
The guard of truth and liberty.

Frederick Douglass

(1817?–1895)

Frederick Augustus Washington Bailey (Douglass) was the most famous African American in the antislavery movement and one of the most famous in the post–Civil War struggle for black equality and civil rights. Born (of an unknown white father) to a slave on the Eastern Shore of Maryland, he learned early the oppressive cruelty of slavery. During one brief period, however, a kind mistress encouraged the boy to learn to read and write. When he was twenty-one Frederick Bailey used his knowledge to forge papers which enabled him to escape. New York City attracted him, but he lingered just long enough to be joined by Anna Murray, a free black woman from Baltimore, who became his wife.

Frederick Bailey's work as an antislavery crusader began in New Bedford, Massachusetts. Taking the name Douglass, he soon became a leader of the black community in New England. At an antislavery convention in Nantucket in 1841, William Lloyd Garrison heard Douglass speak and, impressed by the ex-slave's intelligence and bearing, persuaded Douglass to become an agent for the Massachusetts Anti-Slavery Society. For the next four years Douglass lectured extensively and with such impact that many doubted the truth of his assertions that he was a self-taught ex-slave. To quiet such doubts, he wrote the *Narrative of the Life of Frederick Douglass, an American Slave* (1845). The book was so explicitly factual and became so popular that it exposed him to the hazard of seizure and reenslavement. Douglass fled to England, where he began to envision freedom as not only physical liberty but social equality and opportunity as well. With money raised by English friends, Douglass bought his freedom.

Returning to the States, Douglass broke with Garrison. The old abolitionist was advocating a policy of New England's seceding from the Union, but this act would leave slavery to flourish in the South, and Douglass would not support it. To avoid open factionalism and the disruption of the antislavery crusade, he moved to Rochester, New York. Here he established his paper, *The North Star* (in 1850 called *Frederick Douglass' Paper*), and vigorously plunged back into the abolition movement. The struggle was difficult, and sometimes Douglass was overcome by despair. During one of his most pessimistic lectures, Sojourner Truth rose in the audience and asked, "Frederick, is God dead?"

But in spite of bitter disappointment, especially after enactment of the Fugitive Slave Law in 1850, Douglass fought on. He lectured everywhere. His Rochester home was a station on the Underground Railroad. He engaged in politics, first as a member of the Liberty party and later as a Lincoln Republican. He was an intimate of the "extreme abolitionists"—although he did try to dissuade John Brown from his heroic, mad, and ill-fated attempt at insurrection.

When war broke out, Douglass joined Sojourner Truth in urging Lincoln to enlist blacks in the Union army, and when Lincoln yielded in 1862, Douglass helped to recruit two Massachusetts black regiments and enlisted his own sons. The end of the war found him organizing blacks to work against discrimination and segregation. Douglass's political prominence was such that he was appointed United States marshal for the District of Columbia under President Grant, recorder of deeds under President Hayes, and minister to Haiti under President Arthur.

As Benjamin Quarles states in *Dictionary of American Negro Biography,* "Frederick Douglass cast a long shadow because of his sense of humanity and his willingness to battle for his convictions. He is remembered too for his remarkable social insights. No one, for example, pointed out more insistently than he that the status of the Negro was the touchstone of American democracy, its inevitable and ultimate test."

In addition to the landmark 1845 *Narrative of the Life of Frederick Douglass, an American Slave* (reprinted 1982 with an introduction by Houston A. Baker, Jr.), Douglass published the following autobiographies: *My Bondage and My Freedom* (1855) and *The Life and Times of Frederick Douglass* (1881, updated 1892). For the fullest and most authoritative works on Douglass, see Benjamin Quarles, *Frederick Douglass* (1948); Phillip S. Foner, *Frederick Douglass* (1964); and Nathan Irvin Huggins, *Slave and Citizen: The Life of Frederick Douglass* (1980). In 1979 the Yale University Press published the first volume of a planned fourteen-volume edition of *The Frederick Douglass Papers,* edited by John W. Blassingame. For an interesting discussion of the literary merits of Douglass's autobiographical writings, see Marion Wilson

Starling's comments in *The Slave Narrative: Its Place in American History* (1988). See also Henry Louis Gates, Jr.'s discussion of Douglass's autobiographies in *Figures in Black: Words, Signs, and the "Racial" Self* (1987).

The first selection comes from *The Life and Times of Frederick Douglass,* now ranked as an American classic. The second is "The Fourth of July" speech given in Rochester, New York, on July 5, 1852, and comes from *Rhetoric of Black Revolution* by Arthur L. Smith.

FROM **THE LIFE AND TIMES OF FREDERICK DOUGLASS**

In the summer of 1841 a grand anti-slavery convention was held in Nantucket, under the auspices of Mr. Garrison and his friends. I had taken no holiday since establishing myself in New Bedford, and feeling the need of a little rest, I determined on attending the meeting, though I had no thought of taking part in any of its proceedings. Indeed, I was not aware that any one connected with the convention so much as knew my name. Mr. William C. Coffin, a prominent Abolitionist in those days of trial, had heard me speaking to my colored friends in the little school-house on Second street, where we worshipped. He sought me out in the crowd and invited me to say a few words to the convention. Thus sought out, and thus invited, I was induced to express the feelings inspired by the occasion, and the fresh recollection of the scenes through which I had passed as a slave.

It was with the utmost difficulty that I could stand erect, or that I could command and articulate two words without hesitation and stammering. I trembled in every limb. I am not sure that my embarrassment was not the most effective part of my speech, if speech it could be called. At any rate, this is about the only part of my performance that I now distinctly remember. The audience sympathized with me at once, and from having been remarkably quiet, became much excited.

Mr. Garrison followed me, taking me as his text, and now, whether *I* had made an eloquent plea in behalf of freedom, or not, his was one, never to be forgotten. Those who had heard him oftenest and had known him longest, were astonished at his masterly effort. For the time he possessed that almost fabulous inspiration often referred to, but seldom attained, in which a public meeting is transformed, as it were, into a single individuality, the orator swaying a thousand heads and hearts at once and, by the simple majesty of his all-controlling thought, converting his hearers into the express image of his own soul. That night there were at least a thousand Garrisonians in Nantucket!

At the close of this great meeting I was duly waited on by Mr. John A. Collins, then the general agent of the Massachusetts Anti-Slavery Society, and urgently solicited by him to become an agent of that society and publicly advocate its principles. I was reluctant to take the proffered position. I had not been quite three years from slavery and was honestly distrustful of my ability, and I wished to be excused. Besides, publicity might discover me to my master, and many other objections presented themselves. But Mr. Collins was not to be refused, and I finally consented to go out for three months, supposing I should in that length of time come to the end of my story and my consequent usefulness.

Here opened for me a new life—a life for which I had had no preparation. Mr. Collins used to say when introducing me to an audience, I was a "graduate from the peculiar institution, with my diploma *written on my back.*" The three years of my freedom had been spent in the hard school of adversity. My hands seemed to be furnished with something like a leather coating, and I had marked out for myself a life of rough labor, suited to the hardness of my hands, as a means of supporting my family and rearing my children.

Young, ardent and hopeful, I entered upon this new life in the full gush of unsuspecting enthusiasm. The cause was good, the men engaged in it were good, the means to attain its triumph, good. Heaven's blessings must attend all, and freedom must soon be given to the millions pining under a ruthless bondage. My whole heart went with the holy cause, and my most fervent prayer to the Almighty Disposer of the hearts of men was continually offered for its early triumph. In this enthusiastic spirit I dropped into the ranks of freedom's friends and went forth to the battle. For a time I was made to forget that my skin was dark and my hair crisped. For a time I regretted that I could not have shared the hardships and dangers endured by the earlier workers for the slave's release. I found, however, full soon that my enthusiasm had been extravagant, that hardships and dangers were not all over, and that the life now before me had its shadows also, as well as its sunbeams.

Among the first duties assigned me on entering the ranks was to travel in company with Mr. George Foster to secure subscribers to the *Anti-Slavery Standard* and the *Liberator.* With him I traveled and lectured through the eastern counties of Massachusetts. Much interest was awakened—large meetings assembled. Many came, no doubt from curiosity to hear what a Negro could say in his own cause. I was generally introduced as a "chattel"—a "thing"—a piece of Southern property—the chairman assuring the audience that it could speak. *Fugitive slaves* were rare then, and as a fugitive slave lecturer, I had the advantage of being a "bran new fact"—the first one out.

Up to that time, a colored man was deemed a fool who confessed himself a runaway slave, not only because of the danger to which he exposed himself of being retaken, but because it was a confession of a very low origin. Some of my colored friends in New Bedford thought very badly of my wisdom in thus exposing and degrading myself. The only precaution I took at the beginning, to prevent Master Thomas from knowing where I was and what I was about, was the withholding my former name, my master's name, and the name of the State and county from which I came.

During the first three or four months my speeches were almost exclusively made up of narrations of my own personal experience as a slave. "Let us have the facts," said the people. So also said Friend George Foster, who always wished to pin me down to a simple narrative. "Give us the facts," said Collins, "we will take care of the philosophy." Just here arose some embarrassment. It was impossible for me to repeat the same old story month after month and keep up my interest in it. It was new to the people, it is true, but it was an old story to me; and to go through with it night after night was a task altogether too mechanical for my nature.

"Tell your story, Frederick," would whisper my revered friend, Mr. Garrison, as I stepped upon the platform.

I could not always follow the injunction, for I was now reading and thinking. New views of the subject were being presented to my mind. It did not entirely satisfy me to *narrate* wrongs; I felt like *denouncing* them. I could not always curb my moral indignation for the perpetrators of slaveholding villainy long enough for a circumstantial statement of the facts which I felt almost sure everybody must know. Besides, I was growing and needed room.

"People won't believe you ever were a slave, Frederick, if you keep on this way," said friend Foster. "Be yourself," said Collins, "and tell your story." "Better have a little of the plantation speech than not," was said to me; "it is not best that you seem too learned." These excellent friends were actuated by the best of motives and were not altogether wrong in their advice; and still I must speak just the word that seemed to *me* the word to be spoken *by* me.

At last the apprehended trouble came. People doubted if I had ever been a slave. They said I did not talk like a slave, look like a slave, or act like a slave, and that they believed I had never been south of Mason and Dixon's line. "He don't tell us where he came from, what his master's name was, or how he got away; besides, he is educated, and is in this a contradiction of all the facts we have concerning the ignorance of the slaves." Thus I was in a pretty fair way to be denounced as an impostor. The committee of the Massachusetts Anti-Slavery Society knew all the facts in my case and agreed with me thus far in the prudence of keeping them private; but going down the aisles of the churches in which my meetings were held, and hearing the outspoken Yankees repeatedly saying, "He's never been a slave, I'll warrant you," I resolved that at no distant day, and by such a revelation of facts as could not be made by any other than a genuine fugitive, I would dispel all doubt.

In a little less than four years, therefore, after becoming a public lecturer, I was induced to write out the leading facts connected with my experience in slavery, giving names of persons, places, and dates, thus putting it in the power of any who doubted, to ascertain the truth or falsehood of my story. This statement soon became known in Maryland, and I had reason to believe that an effort would be made to recapture me.

It is not probable that any open attempt to secure me as a slave could have succeeded further than the obtainment by my master of the money value of my bones and sinews. Fortunately for me, in the four years of my labors in the Abolition cause I had gained many friends who would have suffered themselves to be taxed to almost any extent to save me from slavery. It was felt that I had committed the double offense of running away and exposing the secrets and crimes of slavery and slaveholders. There was a double motive for seeking my re-enslavement—avarice and vengeance; and while, as I have said, there was little probability of successful recapture, if attempted openly, I was constantly in danger of being spirited away at a moment when my friends could render me no assistance.

In traveling about from place to place, often alone, I was much exposed to this sort of attack. Anyone cherishing the desire to betray me could easily do so by simply tracing my whereabouts through the Anti-Slavery journals, for my movements and meetings were made through these in advance. My friends Mr. Garrison and Mr. Phillips had no faith in the power of Massachusetts to protect me in my right to liberty. Public sentiment and the law, in their opinion, would hand me over to the tormentors. Mr. Phillips especially considered me in danger, and said, when I showed him the manuscript of my story, if in my place he would "throw it into the fire." Thus the reader will observe that the overcoming of one difficulty only opened the way for another, and that though I had reached a free State, and had attained a position of public usefulness, I was still under the liability of losing all I had gained.

THE FOURTH OF JULY

Mr. President, Friends and Fellow Citizens:

He who could address this audience without a quailing sensation, has stronger nerves than I have. I do not remember ever to have appeared as a speaker before any assembly more shrinkingly, nor with greater distrust of my ability, than I do this day. A feeling has crept over me quite unfavorable to the exercise of my limited powers of speech. The task before me is one which requires much previous thought and study for its proper performance. I know that apologies of this sort are generally considered flat and unmeaning. I trust, however, that mine will not be so considered. Should I seem at ease, my appearance would much misrepresent me. The little experience I have had in addressing public meetings, in country school houses, avails me nothing on the present occasion.

The papers and placards say that I am to deliver a Fourth of July Oration. This certainly sounds large, and out of the common way, for me. It is true that I have often had the privilege to speak in this beautiful Hall, and to address many who now honor me with their presence. But neither their familiar faces, nor the perfect gage I think I have of Corinthian Hall seems to free me from embarrassment.

The fact is, ladies and gentlemen, the distance between this platform and the slave plantation, from which I escaped, is considerable—and the difficulties to be overcome in getting from the latter to the former are by no means slight. That I am here to-day is, to me, a matter of astonishment as well as of gratitude. You will not, therefore, be surprised, if in what I have to say I evince no elaborate preparation, nor grace my speech with any high sounding exordium. With little experience and with less learning, I have been able to throw my thoughts hastily and imperfectly together; and trusting to your patient and generous indulgence, I will proceed to lay them before you.

This, for the purpose of this celebration, is the Fourth of July. It is the birthday of your National Independence, and of your political freedom. This, to you, is what the Passover was to the emancipated people of God. It carries your minds back to the day, and to the act of your great deliverance; and to the signs, and to the wonders, associated with that act, and that day. This celebration also marks the beginning of another year of your national life; and reminds you that the Republic of America is now 76 years old. I am glad, fellow-citizens, that your nation is so young. Seventy-six years, though a good old age for a man, is but a mere speck in the life of a nation. Three score years and ten is the allotted time for individual men; but nations number their years by thousands. According to this fact, you are, even now, only in the beginning of your national career, still lingering in the period of childhood. I repeat, I am glad this is so. There is hope in the thought, and hope is much needed, under the dark clouds which lower above the horizon. The eye of the reformer is met with angry flashes, portending disastrous times; but his heart may well beat lighter at the thought that America is young, and that she is still in the impressible stage of her existence. May he not hope that high lessons of wisdom, of justice and of truth, will yet give direction to her destiny? Were the nation older, the patriot's heart might be sadder, and the reformer's brow heavier. Its future might be shrouded in gloom, and the hope of its prophets go out in sorrow. There is consolation in the thought that America is young. Great streams are not easily turned from channels, worn deep in the course of ages. They may sometimes rise in quiet and stately majesty, and inundate the land, refreshing and fertilizing the earth with their mysterious properties. They may also rise in wrath and fury, and bear away, on their angry waves, the accumulated wealth of years of toil and hardship. They, however, gradually flow back to the same old channel, and flow on as serenely as ever. But, while the river may not be turned aside, it may dry up, and leave nothing behind but the withered branch, and the unsightly rock, to howl in the abyss-sweeping wind, the sad tale of departed glory. As with rivers so with nations. . . .

Fellow-citizens, pardon me, allow me to ask, why am I called upon to speak here to-day? What have I, or those I represent, to do with your national independence? Are the great principles of political freedom and of natural justice, embodied in that Declaration of Independence, extended to us? and am I, therefore, called upon to bring our humble offering to the national altar, and to confess the benefits and express devout gratitude for the blessings resulting from your independence to us?

Would to God, both for your sakes and ours, that an affirmative answer could be truthfully returned to these questions! Then would my task be light, and my burden easy and delightful. For who is there so cold, that a nation's sympathy could not warm him? Who so obdurate and dead to the claims of gratitude, that would not thankfully acknowledge such priceless benefits? Who so stolid and selfish, that would not give his voice to swell the hallelujahs of a nation's jubilee, when the chains of servitude had been torn from his limbs? I am not that man. In a case like that, the dumb might eloquently speak, and the "lame man leap as an hart."

But such is not the state of the case. I say it with a sad sense of the disparity between us. I am not included within the pale of this glorious anniversary! Your high independence only reveals the immeasurable distance between us. The blessings in which you, this day, rejoice, are not enjoyed in common. The rich inheritance of justice, liberty, prosperity and independence, bequeathed by your fathers, is shared by you, not by me. The sunlight that brought light and healing to you, has brought stripes and death to me. This Fourth of July is yours, not mine. You may rejoice, I must mourn. To drag a man in fetters into the grand illuminated temple of liberty, and call upon him to join you in joyous an-

thems, were inhuman mockery and sacrilegious irony.
Do you mean, citizens, to mock me, by asking me to
speak today? If so, there is a parallel to your conduct.
And let me warn you that it is dangerous to copy the
example of a nation whose crimes, towering up to
heaven, were thrown down by the breath of the Almighty, burying that nation in irrevocable ruin! I can to-
day take up the plaintive lament of a peeled and
woe-smitten people!

By the rivers of Babylon, there we sat down. Yea!
we wept when we remembered Zion. We hanged
our harps upon the willows in the midst thereof. For
there, they that carried us away captive, required of
us a song; and they who wasted us required of us
mirth, saying, Sing us one of the songs of Zion.
How can we sing the Lord's song in a strange land?
If I forget thee, O Jerusalem, let my right hand forget her cunning. If I do not remember thee, let my
tongue cleave to the roof of my mouth.

Fellow-citizens, above your national, tumultuous joy,
I hear the mournful wail of millions; whose chains,
heavy and grievous yesterday, are, to-day, rendered
more intolerable by the jubilee shouts that reach them.
If I do forget, if I do not faithfully remember those
bleeding children of sorrow this day, "may my right
hand forget her cunning, and may my tongue cleave to
the roof of my mouth!" To forget them, to pass lightly
over their wrongs, and to chime in with the popular
theme, would be treason most scandalous and shocking,
and would make me a reproach before God and the
world. My subject, then, fellow-citizens, is AMERICAN

SLAVERY. I shall see this day and its popular characteristics from the slave's point of view. Standing there identified with the American bondman, making his wrongs mine, I do not hesitate to declare, with all my soul, that the character and conduct of this nation never looked blacker to me than on this 4th of July! Whether we turn to the declarations of the past, or to the professions of the present, the conduct of the nation seems equally hideous and revolting. America is false to the past, false to the present, and solemnly binds herself to be false to the future. Standing with God and the crushed and bleeding slave on this occasion, I will, in the name of humanity which is outraged, in the name of liberty which is fettered, in the name of the constitution and the Bible which are disregarded and trampled upon, dare to call in question and to denounce, with all the emphasis I can command, everything that serves to perpetuate slavery—the great sin and shame of America!

"I will not equivocate; I will not excuse"; I will use the severest language I can command; and yet not one word shall escape me that any man, whose judgment is not blinded by prejudice, or who is not at heart a slave-holder, shall not confess to be right and just.

But I fancy I hear some one of my audience say, "It is just in this circumstance that you and your brother abolitionists fail to make a favorable impression on the public mind. Would you argue more, and denounce less; would you persuade more, and rebuke less; your cause would be much more likely to succeed." But, I submit, where all is plain there is nothing to be argued. What point in the anti-slavery creed would you have me argue? On what branch of the subject do the people of this country need light? Must I undertake to prove that the slave is a man? That point is conceded already. Nobody doubts it. The slaveholders themselves acknowledge it in the enactment of laws for their government. They acknowledge it when they punish disobedience on the part of the slave. There are seventy-two crimes in the State of Virginia which, if committed by a black man (no matter how ignorant he be), subject him to the punishment of death; while only two of the same crimes will subject a white man to the like punishment. What is this but the acknowledgment that the slave is a moral, intellectual, and responsible being? The manhood of the slave is conceded. It is admitted in the fact that Southern statute books are covered with enactments forbidding, under severe fines and penalties, the teaching of the slave to read or to write. When you can point to any such laws in reference to the beasts of the field, then I may consent to argue the manhood of the slave. When the dogs in your streets, when the fowls of the air, when the cattle on your hills, when the fish of the sea, and the reptiles that crawl, shall be unable to distinguish the slave from a brute, then will I argue with you that the slave is a man!

For the present, it is enough to affirm the equal manhood of the Negro race. Is it not astonishing that, while we are ploughing, planting, and reaping, using all kinds of mechanical tools, erecting houses, constructing bridges, building ships, working in metals of brass, iron, copper, silver and gold; that, while we are reading, writing and ciphering, acting as clerks, merchants and secretaries, having among us lawyers, doctors, ministers, poets, authors, editors, orators and teachers; that, while we are engaged in all manner of enterprises common to other men, digging gold in California, capturing the whale in the Pacific, feeding sheep and cattle on the hill-side, living, moving, acting, thinking, planning, living in families as husbands, wives and children, and, above all, confessing and worshipping the Christian's God, and looking hopefully for life and immortality beyond the grave, we are called upon to prove that we are men!

Would you have me argue that man is entitled to liberty? that he is the rightful owner of his own body? You have already declared it. Must I argue the wrongfulness of slavery? Is that a question for Republicans? Is it to be settled by the rules of logic and argumentation, as matter beset with great difficulty, involving a doubtful application of the principle of justice, hard to be understood? How should I look to-day, in the presence of Americans, dividing, and subdividing a discourse, to show that men have a natural right to freedom? speaking of it relatively and positively, negatively and affirmatively. To do so, would be to make myself ridiculous, and to offer an insult to your understanding. There is not a man beneath the canopy of heaven that does not know that slavery is wrong for him.

What, am I to argue that it is wrong to make men brutes, to rob them of their liberty, to work them without wages, to keep them ignorant of their relations to their fellow men, to beat them with sticks, to flay their flesh with the lash, to load their limbs with irons, to hunt them with dogs, to sell them at auction, to sunder their families, to knock out their teeth, to burn their flesh, to starve them into obedience and submission to their masters? Must I argue that a system thus marked with blood, and stained with pollution, is wrong? No! I will not. I have better employment for my time and strength than such arguments would imply.

What, then, remains to be argued? Is it that slavery is not divine; that God did not establish it; that our doctors of divinity are mistaken? There is blasphemy in the thought. That which is inhuman, cannot be divine! Who can reason on such a proposition? They that can, may; I cannot. The time for such argument is passed.

At a time like this, scorching irony, not convincing argument, is needed. O! had I the ability, and could I reach the nation's ear, I would, to-day, pour out a fiery stream of biting ridicule, blasting reproach, withering sarcasm, and stern rebuke. For it is not light that is needed, but fire; it is not the gentle shower, but thunder. We need the storm, the whirlwind, and the earthquake. The feeling of the nation must be quickened; the conscience of the nation must be roused; the propriety of the nation must be startled; the hypocrisy of the nation must be exposed; and its crimes against God and man must be proclaimed and denounced.

What, to the American slave, is your 4th of July? I answer; a day that reveals to him, more than all other days in the year, the gross injustice and cruelty to which he is the constant victim. To him, your celebration is a sham; your boasted liberty, an unholy license; your national greatness, swelling vanity; your sounds of rejoicing are empty and heartless; your denunciation of tyrants, brass fronted impudence; your shouts of liberty and equality, hollow mockery; your prayers and hymns, your sermons and thanksgivings, with all your religious parade and solemnity, are to Him, mere bombast, fraud, deception, impiety, and hypocrisy—a thin veil to cover up crimes which would disgrace a nation of savages.

There is not a nation on the earth guilty of practices more shocking and bloody than are the people of the United States, at this very hour.

Go where you may, search where you will, roam through all the monarchies and despotisms of the Old World, travel through South America, search out every abuse, and when you have found the last, lay your facts by the side of the everyday practices of this nation, and you will say with me, that, for revolting barbarity and shameless hypocrisy, America reigns without a rival.

Take the American slave-trade, which we are told by the papers, is especially prosperous just now. Ex-Senator Benton tells us that the price of men was never higher than now. He mentions the fact to show that slavery is in no danger. This trade is one of the peculiarities of American institutions. It is carried on in all the large towns and cities in one-half of this confederacy; and millions are pocketed every year by dealers in this horrid traffic. In several states this trade is a chief source of wealth. It is called (in contradistinction to the foreign slave-trade) "the internal slave-trade." It is, probably, called so, too, in order to divert from it the horror with which the foreign slave-trade is contemplated. That trade has long since been denounced by this government as piracy. It has been denounced with burning words from the high places of the nation as an execrable traffic. To arrest it, to put an end to it, this nation keeps a squadron, at immense cost, on the coast of Africa. Everywhere, in this country, it is safe to speak of this foreign slave-trade as a most inhuman traffic, opposed alike to the laws of God and of man. The duty to extirpate and destroy it, is admitted even by our DOCTORS OF DIVINITY. In order to put an end to it, some of these last have consented that their colored brethren (nominally free) should leave this country, and establish themselves on the western coast of Africa! It is, however, a notable fact that, while so much execration is poured out by Americans upon all those engaged in the foreign slave-trade, the men engaged in the slave-trade between the states pass without condemnation, and their business is deemed honorable.

Behold the practical operation of this internal slave-trade, the American slave-trade, sustained by American politics and American religion. Here you will see men and women reared like swine for the market. You know what is a swine-drover? I will show you a man-drover. They inhabit all our Southern States. They perambulate the country, and crowd the highways of the nation, with droves of human stock. You will see one of these human flesh jobbers, armed with pistol, whip, and bowie-knife, driving a company of a hundred men, women, and children, from the Potomac to the slave market at New Orleans. These wretched people are to be sold singly, or in lots, to suit purchasers. They are food for the cottonfield and the deadly sugar-mill. Mark the sad procession, as it moves wearily along, and the inhuman wretch who drives them. Hear his savage yells and his blood-curdling oaths, as he hurries on his affrighted captives! There, see the old man with locks thinned and gray. Cast one glance, if you please, upon that young mother, whose shoulders are bare to the scorching sun, her briny tears falling on the brow of the babe in her arms. See, too, that girl of thirteen, weeping, yes! weeping, as she thinks of the mother from whom she has been torn! The drove moves tardily. Heat and sorrow have nearly consumed their strength; suddenly you hear a quick snap, like the discharge of a rifle; the fetters clank, and the chain rattles simultaneously; your ears are saluted with a scream, that seems to have torn its way to the centre of your soul! The crack you heard was the sound of the slave-whip; the scream you heard was from the woman you saw with the babe. Her speed had faltered under the weight of her child and her chains! that gash on her shoulder tells her to move on. Follow this drove to New Orleans. Attend the auction; see men examined like horses; see the forms of women rudely and brutally exposed to the shocking gaze of American slave-buyers. See this drove sold and separated forever; and never forget the deep, sad sobs that arose from that scattered multitude. Tell me, citizens, WHERE, under the sun, you can witness a spectacle more fiendish and shocking. Yet this is but a glance at the American slave-trade, as it exists, at this moment, in the ruling part of the United States.

I was born amid such sights and scenes. To me the American slave-trade is a terrible reality. When a child, my soul was often pierced with a sense of its horrors. I lived on Philpot Street, Fell's Point, Baltimore, and have watched from the wharves the slave ships in the Basin, anchored from the shore, with their cargoes of human flesh, waiting for favorable winds to waft them down the Chesapeake. There was, at that time, a grand slave mart kept at the head of Pratt Street, by Austin Woldfolk. His agents were sent into every town and county in Maryland, announcing their arrival, through the papers, and on flaming "hand-bills," headed CASH FOR NEGROES. These men were generally well dressed men, and very captivating in their manners; ever ready to drink, to treat, and to gamble. The fate of many a slave had depended upon the turn of a single card; and many a child has been snatched from the arms of its mother by bargains arranged in a state of brutal drunkenness.

The flesh-mongers gather up their victims by dozens, and drive them, chained, to the general depot at Baltimore. When a sufficient number has been collected here, a ship is chartered for the purpose of conveying the forlorn crew to Mobile, or to New Orleans. From the slave prison to the ship, they are usually driven in the darkness of night; for since the anti-slavery agitation, a certain caution is observed.

In the deep, still darkness of midnight, I have been aroused by the dead, heavy footsteps, and the piteous cries of the chained gangs that passed our door. The anguish of my boyish heart was intense; and I was often consoled, when speaking to my mistress in the morning, to hear her say that the custom was very wicked; that she hated to hear the rattle of the chains and the heart-rending cries. I was glad to find one who sympathized with me in my horror.

Fellow-citizens, this murderous traffic is, to-day, in active operation in this boasted republic. In the solitude of my spirit I see clouds of dust raised on the highways of the South; I see the bleeding footsteps; I hear the doleful wail of fettered humanity on the way to the slave-markets, where the victims are to be sold like horses, sheep, and swine, knocked off to the highest bidder. There I see the tenderest ties ruthlessly broken, to gratify the lust, caprice and rapacity of the buyers and sellers of men. My soul sickens at the sight.

> Is this the land your Fathers loved,
>   The freedom which they toiled to win?

> Is this the earth whereon they moved?
> Are these the graves they slumber in?

But a still more inhuman, disgraceful, and scandalous state of things remains to be presented. By an act of the American Congress, not yet two years old, slavery has been nationalized in its most horrible and revolting form. By that act, Mason and Dixon's line has been obliterated; New York has become as Virginia; and the power to hold, hunt, and sell men, women and children, as slaves, remains no longer a mere state institution, but is now an institution of the whole United States. The power is co-extensive with the star-spangled banner, and American Christianity. Where these go, may also go the merciless slave-hunter. Where these are, man is not sacred. He is a bird for the sportsman's gun. By that most foul and fiendish of all human decrees, the liberty and person of every man are put in peril. Your broad republican domain is hunting ground for men. Not for thieves and robbers, enemies of society, merely, but for men guilty of no crime. Your lawmakers have commanded all good citizens to engage in this hellish sport. Your President, your Secretary of State, your lords, nobles, and ecclesiastics enforce, as a duty you owe to your free and glorious country, and to your God, that you do this accursed thing. Not fewer than forty Americans have, within the past two years, been hunted down and, without a moment's warning, hurried away in chains, and consigned to slavery and excruciating torture. Some of these have had wives and children, dependent on them for bread; but of this, no account was made. The right of the hunter to his prey stands superior to the right of marriage, and to all rights in this republic, the rights of God included! For black men there is neither law nor justice, humanity nor religion. The Fugitive Slave Law makes MERCY TO THEM A CRIME; and bribes the judge who tries them. An American JUDGE GETS TEN DOLLARS FOR EVERY VICTIM HE CONSIGNS to slavery, and five, when he fails to do so. The oath of any two villains is sufficient, under this hell-black enactment, to send the most pious and exemplary black man into the remorseless jaws of slavery! His own testimony is nothing. He can bring no witnesses for himself. The minister of American justice is bound by the law to hear but one side; and that side is the side of the oppressor. Let this damning fact be perpetually told. Let it be thundered around the world that in tyrant-killing, king-hating, people-loving, democratic, Christian America the seats of justice are filled with judges who hold their offices under an open and palpable bribe, and are bound, in deciding the case of a man's liberty, to hear only his accusers!

In glaring violation of justice, in shameless disregard of the forms of administering law, in cunning arrangement to entrap the defenseless, and in diabolical intent this Fugitive Slave Law stands alone in the annals of tyrannical legislation. I doubt if there be another nation on the globe having the brass and the baseness to put such a law on the statute-book. If any man in this assembly thinks differently from me in this matter, and feels able to disprove my statements, I will gladly confront him at any suitable time and place he may select.

I take this law to be one of the grossest infringements of Christian Liberty, and, if the churches and

ministers of our country were not stupidly blind, or
most wickedly indifferent, they, too, would so regard it.

At the very moment that they are thanking God for
the enjoyment of civil and religious liberty, and for the
right to worship God according to the dictates of their
own consciences, they are utterly silent in respect to a
law which robs religion of its chief significance and
makes it utterly worthless to a world lying in wickedness. Did this law concern the "mint, anise, and cummin"—abridge the right to sing psalms, to partake of
the sacrament, or to engage in any of the ceremonies of
religion, it would be smitten by the thunder of a thousand pulpits. A general shout would go up from the
church demanding repeal, repeal, instant repeal!—And it
would go hard with that politician who presumed to solicit the votes of the people without inscribing this
motto on his banner. Further, if this demand were not
complied with, another Scotland would be added to the
history of religious liberty, and the stern old convenant-
ers would be thrown into the shade. A John Knox
would be seen at every church door and heard from
every pulpit, and Fillmore would have no more quarter
than was shown by Knox to the beautiful, but treacherous, Queen Mary of Scotland. The fact that the church
of our country (with fractional exceptions) does not esteem "the Fugitive Slave Law" as a declaration of war
against religious liberty, implies that that church regards
religion simply as a form of worship, an empty ceremony, and not a vital principle, requiring active benevolence, justice, love, and good will towards man. It
esteems sacrifice above mercy; psalm-singing above
right doing; solemn meetings above practical righteous-
ness. A worship that can be conducted by persons who

refuse to give shelter to the houseless, to give bread to the hungry, clothing to the naked, and who enjoin obedience to a law forbidding these acts of mercy is a curse, not a blessing to mankind. The Bible addresses all such persons as "scribes, pharisees, hypocrites, who pay tithe of mint, anise, and cummin, and have omitted the weightier matters of the law, judgment, mercy, and faith."

But the church of this country is not only indifferent to the wrongs of the slave, it actually takes sides with the oppressors. It has made itself the bulwark of American slavery, and the shield of American slave-hunters. Many of its most eloquent Divines, who stand as the very lights of the church, have shamelessly given the sanction of religion and the Bible to the whole slave system. They have taught that man may, properly, be a slave; that the relation of master and slave is ordained of God; that to send back an escaped bondman to his master is clearly the duty of all the followers of the Lord Jesus Christ; and this horrible blasphemy is palmed off upon the world for Christianity.

For my part, I would say, welcome infidelity! welcome atheism! welcome anything! in preference to the gospel, as preached by those Divines! They convert the very name of religion into an engine of tyranny and barbarous cruelty, and serve to confirm more infidels, in this age, than all the infidel writings of Thomas Paine, Voltaire, and Bolingbroke put together have done! These ministers make religion a cold and flinty-hearted thing, having neither principles of right action nor bowels of compassion. They strip the love of God of its beauty and leave the throne of religion a huge, horrible, repulsive form. It is a religion for oppressors, tyrants, man-stealers, and thugs. It is not that "pure and unde-filed religion" which is from above, and which is "first pure, then peaceable, easy to be entreated, full of mercy and good fruits, without partiality, and without hypoc-risy." But a religion which favors the rich against the poor; which exalts the proud above the humble; which divides mankind into two classes, tyrants and slaves; which says to the man in chains, stay there; and to the oppressor, oppress on; it is a religion which may be professed and enjoyed by all the robbers and enslavers of mankind; it makes God a respecter of persons, denies his fatherhood of the race, and tramples in the dust the great truth of the brotherhood of man. All this we affirm to be true of the popular church, and the popular wor-ship of our land and nation—a religion, a church, and a worship which, on the authority of inspired wisdom, we pronounce to be an abomination in the sight of God. In the language of Isaiah, the American church might be well addressed,

Bring no more vain oblations; incense is an abom-ination unto me: the new moons and Sabbaths, the calling of assemblies, I cannot away with; it is in-iquity, even the solemn meeting. Your new moons, and your appointed feasts my soul hateth. They are a trouble to me; I am weary to bear them; and when ye spread forth your hands I will hide mine eyes from you. Yea! when ye make many prayers, I will not hear. YOUR HANDS ARE FULL OF BLOOD; cease to do evil, learn to do well; seek judgment; relieve the oppressed; judge for the fatherless; plead for the widow.

The American church is guilty, when viewed in connection with what it is doing to uphold slavery; but it is superlatively guilty when viewed in its connection with its ability to abolish slavery.

The sin of which it is guilty is one of omission as well as of commission. Albert Barnes but uttered what the common sense of every man at all observant of the actual state of the case will receive as truth, when he declared that "There is no power out of the church that could sustain slavery an hour, if it were not sustained in it."

Let the religious press, the pulpit, the Sunday School, the conference meeting, the great ecclesiastical, missionary, Bible and tract associations of the land array their immense powers against slavery, and slave-holding; and the whole system of crime and blood would be scattered to the winds, and that they do not do this involves them in the most awful responsibility of which the mind can conceive.

In prosecuting the anti-slavery enterprise, we have been asked to spare the church, to spare the ministry; but how, we ask, could such a thing be done? We are met on the threshold of our efforts for the redemption of the slave, by the church and ministry of the country, in battle arrayed against us; and we are compelled to fight or flee. From what quarter, I beg to know, has proceeded a fire so deadly upon our ranks, during the last two years, as from the Northern pulpit? As the champions of oppressors, the chosen men of American theology have appeared—men honored for their so-called piety, and their real learning. The LORDS of Buffalo, the SPRINGS of New York, the LATHROPS of Auburn, the COXES and SPENCERS of Brooklyn, the

GANNETS and SHARPS of Boston, the DEWEYS of Washington, and other great religious lights of the land have, in utter denial of the authority of HIM by whom they professed to be called to the ministry, deliberately taught us, against the example of the Hebrews, and against the remonstrance of the Apostles, that we ought to obey man's law before the law of God.

My spirit wearies of such blasphemy; and how such men can be supported, as the "standing types and representatives of Jesus Christ," is a mystery which I leave others to penetrate. In speaking of the American church, however, let it be distinctly understood that I mean the great mass of the religious organizations of our land. There are exceptions, and I thank God that there are. Noble men may be found, scattered all over these Northern States, of whom Henry Ward Beecher, of Brooklyn; Samuel J. May, of Syracuse; and my esteemed friend (Rev. R. R. Raymond) on the platform, are shining examples; and let me say further, that, upon these men lies the duty to inspire our ranks with high religious faith and zeal, and to cheer us on in the great mission of the slave's redemption from his chains.

One is struck with the difference between the attitude of the American church towards the anti-slavery movement, and that occupied by the churches in England towards a similar movement in that country. There, the church, true to its mission of ameliorating, elevating and improving the condition of mankind, came forward promptly, bound up the wounds of the West Indian slave, and restored him to his liberty. There, the question of emancipation was a high religious question. It was demanded in the name of humanity, and according to the law of the living God. The Sharps, the Clarksons, the Wilberforces, the Buxtons, and the Burchells, and the Knibbs were alike famous for their piety and for their philanthropy. The anti-slavery movement there was not an anti-church movement, for the reason that the church took its full share in prosecuting that movement: and the anti-slavery movement in this country will cease to be an anti-church movement, when the church of this country shall assume a favorable instead of a hostile position towards that movement.

Americans! your republican politics, not less than your republican union, are flagrantly inconsistent. You boast of your love of liberty, your superior civilization, and your pure Christianity, which the whole political power of the nation (as embodied in the two great political parties) is solemnly pledged to support and perpetuate the enslavement of three millions of your countrymen. You hurl your anathemas at the crowned headed tyrants of Russia and Austria and pride yourselves on your Democratic institutions, while you yourselves consent to be the mere tools and body-guards of the tyrants of Virginia and Carolina. You invite to your shores fugitives of oppression from abroad, honor them with banquets, greet them with ovations, cheer them, toast them, salute them, protect them, and pour out your money to them like water; but the fugitives from your own land you advertise, hunt, arrest, shoot, and kill. You glory in your refinement and your universal education; yet you maintain a system as barbarous and dreadful as ever stained the character of a nation—a system begun in avarice, supported in pride, and perpetuated in cruelty. You shed tears over fallen Hungary, and make the sad story of her wrongs the theme of your poets, statesmen, and orators, till your gallant sons are ready to fly to arms to vindicate her cause against the oppressor; but, in regard to the ten thousand wrongs of the American slave, you would enforce the strictest silence, and would hail him as an enemy of the nation who dares to make those wrongs the subject of public discourse! You are all on fire at the mention of liberty for France or for Ireland; but are as cold as an iceberg at the thought of liberty for the enslaved of America. You discourse eloquently on the dignity of labor; yet, you sustain a system which, in its very essence, casts a stigma upon labor. You can bare your bosom to the storm of British artillery to throw off a three-penny tax on tea; and yet wring the last hard earned farthing from the grasp of the black laborers of your country. You profess to believe "that, of one blood, God made all nations of men to dwell on the face of all the earth," and hath commanded all men, everywhere, to love one another; yet you notoriously hate (and glory in your hatred) all men whose skins are not colored like your own. You declare before the world, and are understood by the world to declare that you "hold these truths to be self-evident, that all men are created equal; and are endowed by their Creator with certain inalienable rights; and that among these are, life, liberty, and the pursuit of happiness;" and yet, you hold securely, in a bondage which, according to your own Thomas Jefferson, "is worse than ages of that which your fathers rose in rebellion to oppose," a seventh part of the inhabitants of your country.

Fellow-citizens, I will not enlarge further on your national inconsistencies. The existence of slavery in this country brands your republicanism as a sham, your humanity as a base pretense, and your Christianity as a lie. It destroys your moral power abroad: it corrupts your politicians at home. It saps the foundation of religion; it makes your name a hissing and a bye-word to a mocking earth. It is the antagonistic force in your government, the only thing that seriously disturbs and endangers your Union. It fetters your progress; it is the enemy of improvement; the deadly foe of education; it fosters pride, it breeds insolence; it promotes vice; it shelters crime; it is a curse to the earth that supports it; and yet you cling to it as if it were the sheet anchor of all your hopes. Oh! be warned! a horrible reptile is coiled up in your nation's bosom; the venomous creature is nursing at the tender breast of your youthful republic; for the love of God, tear away, and fling from you the hideous monster, and let the weight of twenty millions crush and destroy it forever! . . .

Allow me to say, in conclusion, notwithstanding the dark picture I have this day presented, of the state of the nation, I do not despair of this country. There are forces in operation which must inevitably work the downfall of slavery. "The arm of the Lord is not shortened," and the doom of slavery is certain. I, therefore, leave off where I began, with hope. While drawing encouragement from "the Declaration of Independence," the great principles it contains, and the genius of American Institutions, my spirit is also cheered by the obvious tendencies of the age. Nations do not now stand in the same relation to each other that they did ages ago. No nation can now shut itself up from the surrounding world and trot round in the same old path of its fathers without interference. The time was when such could be done. Long established customs of hurtful character could formerly fence themselves in, and do their evil work with social impunity. Knowledge was then con-

fined and enjoyed by the privileged few, and the multitude walked on in mental darkness. But a change has
now come over the affairs of mankind. Walled cities
and empires have become unfashionable. The arm of
commerce has borne away the gates of the strong city.
Intelligence is penetrating the darkest corners of the
globe. It makes its pathway over and under the sea, as
well as on the earth. Wind, steam, and lightning are its
chartered agents. Oceans no longer divide, but link
nations together. From Boston to London is now a holiday excursion. Space is comparatively annihilated.—
Thoughts expressed on one side of the Atlantic are distinctly heard on the other.

The far off and almost fabulous Pacific rolls in grandeur at our feet. The Celestial Empire, the mystery of
ages, is being solved. The fiat of the Almighty, ''Let
there be Light,'' has not yet spent its force. No abuse,
no outrage whether in taste, sport or avarice, can now
hide itself from the all-pervading light. The iron shoe,
and crippled foot of China must be seen in contrast with
nature. Africa must rise and put on her yet unwoven
garment. ''Ethiopia shall stretch out her hand unto
God.''

PART 3

■■■━━━■■━━━■■━━━■■━━━■■

ACCOMMODATION AND PROTEST: 1865–1910

The North's military victory in the Civil War did not bring about change in the ways change was expected. Malice remained, not exorcised by President Lincoln's splendid words; charity, which he prayed for, did not appear. Between the agrarian-gentleman, whose ingrained attitudes and habits of mind dominated southern thought, and the industrialist-banker, whose money power determined northern polity, bitterness was not relieved. In fact, it was intensified, and the tide of enmity was freshened by the Reconstruction Act of 1867, for which northerners were held largely responsible. North and South, blacks were caught in that tide. Their situation was not new, nor was their reaction.

In the South, American blacks were still subject to the whims of the white world. A few blacks benefited from the activities of the Freedmen's Bureau, which helped to ease the transition from slavery to freedom; and a few were privileged to attend Yankee missionary schools, which were built somewhat less quickly than they were burned down by southern whites who opposed education for former slaves. It is true that between 1869 and 1874 southern blacks did vote in sufficient strength to have influence in some state legislatures and to send sixteen fellow blacks to the national Congress. But the terrorist activities of the Ku Klux Klan and other groups brought an effective end to black voting even before federal troops, charged with protecting the right to vote, were withdrawn.

Blacks in the North fared scarcely better. Few could afford schooling, even where free schools were provided—and they were not provided everywhere until the end of the century. Jobs were difficult to get and keep, for there was increasing competition with whites, who often mobbed black workers. Although the right to vote was generally acknowledged, few blacks were sophisticated enough to see the value of exercising that right.

The great majority of blacks in both the North and South accepted segregation and discrimination, believing, as Booker T. Washington persuaded them to believe, that as they approached the white world's standards, they would win the white world's tolerance, and "things" would be better. A handful of blacks protested. As their eloquent spokesman W. E. B. Du Bois wrote, "We demand every single right that belongs to a free born American, political, civil, and social; and until we get these rights we will never cease to protest and assail the ears of America."

An infinitesimal number of blacks reacted to the conditions of African American life by trying to escape them. While the imaginative writing of the period sets forth these varying attitudes and reactions symbolically, polemical writing states them straightforwardly. Between 1865 and 1910, an appreciable number of black writers, using both approaches, published significant works. Among the novelists are Charles W. Chesnutt, Paul Laurence Dunbar, Sutton Griggs, and a small number of lesser-known writers, including the recently discovered Harriet E. Wilson. The poets include Dunbar, William Stanley Braithwaite, and a number of dialect poets. The principal writers of autobiography/biography were Booker T. Washington, John M. Langston, and Frederick Douglass. The best-known historians of the period were George Washington Williams and William C. Nell.

Charles W. Chesnutt, the first black novelist of imposing stature, published three novels and two volumes of short stories. With the exception of his earliest stories, which began appearing in the *Atlantic Monthly* in 1887 and were later collected under the title *The Conjure Woman,* all of his work is in the protest tradition. Chesnutt's special theme was the African American of mixed blood, the ''tragic mulatto''; he was the first black author to deal in depth with the problem of the ''color line'' within the race, and the first to make imaginative capital of racism's consequences to the white man. In *The Marrow of Tradition* and *The Colonel's Dream,* which were both constructed around incidents from real life, Chesnutt's artistic control occasionally slips, and he makes didactic digressions that interrupt the story and add nothing to the theme. His short stories are free of this fault, and so is *The House behind the Cedars,* his first novel, and his best.

None of the fiction of Paul Laurence Dunbar matches the best of Charles Chesnutt. Three of Dunbar's four novels neither deal with racial themes nor present blacks as major characters. Dunbar's best novel, *The Sport of the Gods,* begins as a realistic depiction of black life in New

York but finally becomes a commitment to the southern white apologist's point of view. Indeed, it might have been written by Thomas Nelson Page or Maurice Thompson, both of whom were widely read southern apologists.

While Dunbar's prose fiction was popular in his own time, it is his dialect poetry for which he is best known today. His poetry, of course, did no violence to the acceptable notions of black life and character or mind and spirit. The widely held opinion of Dunbar the poet was best expressed by William Dean Howells, who was probably the most highly regarded of contemporary critics: "In nothing is [Dunbar's] essentially refined and delicate art so well shown as in those pieces, which . . . describe the range between appetite and emotion . . . which is the range of the race. He reveals in these a finely ironic perception of the Negro's limitations." Dunbar must have had this judgment in mind when, just prior to his death at the age of thirty-four, he wrote the lines that might very well have served as his epitaph:

> He sang of love when life was young,
> And Love itself was in his ways,
> But Ah, the world, it turned to praise
> A jingle in a broken tongue.

Sutton Griggs was a prolific and historically important novelist. Although he had less talent than Dunbar, he nevertheless vacillated between accommodation and militant protest, and his work reveals the ambivalence of many black intellectuals during that troubled period. *Imperium in Imperio,* for instance, advocates militant black nationalism, while *Unfettered* and *Pointing the Way* recommend an alliance between "upper class" blacks and Bourbon whites. Griggs, like Chesnutt, had contempt for poor whites. Because this was the one attitude from which he did not waver, his novels, whatever their story lines and themes, are bitter attacks upon the white poor—those "misguided souls [who] said and did all things, which [they] deemed necessary to leave behind . . . the greatest heritage of hatred the world has ever known."

There was little propaganda in the poetry of the time, and hard-line protest was out. Some poets have been designated as mockingbirds. Albery Whitman was one of these: he was by turns a "black Longfellow," a "black Byron," a "black Spenser." Lacking originality, Whitman's work was not truly significant, and he is remembered only for his versatility and for having composed the longest poem ever written by a Negro, "Not a Man and Yet a Man."

A small host of other poets were imitators, too, but they imitated the dialect poetry of Paul Dunbar. James Edwin Campbell and Daniel Webster Davis were fairly good as imitators, and Davis's only collection, *Wey Down Souf,* bears comparison with Dunbar's *Candle-Ligh'ing Time.* J. Mord Allen's *Rhymes, Tales, and Rhymed Tales* are noteworthy only in that they prove him more industrious than most of his contemporaries. Not much can be said for John Wesley Holloway's *From the Desert;* or for either of Ray Garfield Dandridge's two slim volumes, *Zalka Petruzza and Other Poems* and *The Poet and Other Poems.* George Marion McClellan refused to write dialect poetry. James D. Corrothers was probably the first American black poet to pursue African themes.

The best non-dialect poet of the period was William Stanley Braithwaite. Proud of his yearly anthologies of magazine verse, and of his position as a staff writer on the *Boston Transcript,* Braithwaite rejected the fact of his black heritage. In his autobiography, *The House of Falling Leaves,* he wrote, ''I am descended from a long line of English gentlemen.'' And this was true enough, if one considered only his father's line of descent; his mother was a West Indian black. As a poet, Braithwaite was a Pre-Raphaelite, and his work was haunting, mystical, romantic.

Certain autobiographical works and other prose pieces bridge the emotional gap between the pre–Civil War slave narratives and the racial apostasy of Braithwaite. An example of this type of literature is Elizabeth Keckley's *Behind the Scenes; or Thirty Years a Slave and Four Years in the White House.* John Mercer Langston, who was briefly dean of the law school at the predominantly black Howard University and even more briefly a member of Congress, wrote *From a Virginia Plantation to the National Capital* as a declaration of pride in his race. Then there is *Up from Slavery.* If certain of its episodes are suspect, its spirit and thrust are not. If Booker Washington lied and accommodated, he did so for a cause, and the cause was black advancement. This was also Frederick Douglass's cause, and his *Life and Times,* which was published in its final version in 1892, states it eloquently.

Two black historians deserve mention. Associated with Garrison on *The Liberator* and with Douglass on *The North Star,* William C. Nell was encouraged by John Greenleaf Whittier to do historical research. *The Colored Patriots of the American Revolution* is a work of careful scholarship and the first historical study by an African American to deserve the respect of the academic community. But *The Colored Patriots* was twice surpassed by George Washington Williams's books, *History of the Ne-*

gro Race in America from 1619 to 1880 and *A History of the Negro Troops in the War of the Rebellion,* which are still used as source books by reputable academic historians.

The customary view of black Reconstruction politicians is that they were both ignorant and venal, and that Congress reached its lowest level while these blacks were in office. This, of course, is a biased view, a view based upon racial antagonism rather than facts. By and large black members of Congress during Reconstruction were neither venal nor ignorant. As in all sessions of Congress then and now there were a few members not quite honest and not well educated, but they were the exception, not the general rule. Black congressmen did speak out bluntly for black rights and governmental reform. *This* was their crime; this lead to the general condemnation of all black members of Congress and officeholders. A look at the record will show that several of the blacks were better educated than their white colleagues. The two senators, Hiram R. Revels and B. K. Bruce, both from Mississippi, were educated men. Robert Brown Elliott of South Carolina was a graduate of Eton. John Mercer Langston of Virginia, who had studied at Oberlin, was a distinguished lawyer long before he went to Congress, and there were others equally well qualified. The last of these Reconstruction (and post-Reconstruction) congressmen was George H. White of North Carolina, a graduate of Howard University. His farewell speech to Congress, delivered on January 29, 1901, was often quoted during the first decades of this century.

Booker T. Washington

(1856–1915)

During his public career Booker Taliaferro Washington was the most popular and most influential Negro leader in the United States. Northern philanthropists like Andrew Carnegie subsidized him; Republican politicians like William Howard Taft and Theodore Roosevelt admired him, used him, and in turn were used by Washington; most southerners accepted him because of his accommodationist philosophy; and the black-man-in-the-street revered Booker T. and felt that his conservative you-must-crawl-before-you-can-walk message was the "way out" for African Americans. Black intellectuals like William Monroe Trotter, fiery editor of the *Boston Guardian,* and W. E. B. Du Bois fought Washington vigorously, even though Du Bois tried at first to work with him. Washington's black opponents objected not only to his "Uncle Tom" philosophy but also to the "Tuskegee Machine," which they felt had too much influence and power in bolstering Booker T. and in directing the course of black life in America. On the surface, Washington seemed to be a simple man with commonsense ideas expressed in down-to-earth terms. Booker T. Washington, however, as his opponents soon found out, was a complex character, a master of behind-the-scenes manipulation, and a superb salesman of his own philosophy.

Born on the Burrough's Plantation near Hale's Ford, Virginia, Booker T. Washington was the son of a slave woman and a white father. In 1865 the Washingtons moved to Malden, West Virginia, and Booker worked at odd jobs there until he heard of Hampton Normal and Industrial Institute (now Hampton University). With $1.50 in his pocket, he set out for the famous school.

After graduation from Hampton in 1875, Washington taught in Malden, then left for Washington, D.C., for a year's study at Wayland Seminary (now a part of Virginia Union University). In 1879 he returned to Hampton, where he took charge of a group of Native American students and organized Hampton's first night school. In 1881 he was sent to Tuskegee, Alabama, to start a new school of the Hampton type. Within a very short time, Washington built in the backwoods of Alabama one of America's best-known educational centers.

Although it is alleged that Booker T. Washington was "assisted" by others in many if not all of his works, he was a prolific author-editor. He published three autobiographies; one of them, *Up from Slavery* (1901), became an American classic often compared with Benjamin Franklin's autobiography. It was also for many years one of the most popular and most frequently reprinted books by an American black writer. One of his works, *The Negro in the South* (1907), was co-authored with Du Bois.

Though not an orator in the old-fashioned, thundering sense of that term, Booker T. Washington was one of the most popular and effective speakers of his generation. Relying heavily on concrete images, parable-like anecdotes ("cast down your buckets where you are"), and folk humor, usually at the expense of blacks, his speeches became an American institution. Among the best are the two that immediately follow and another he delivered in Boston in 1897 at the unveiling of the Robert Gould Shaw monument. In 1896, Harvard, the first New England college to give an honorary degree to a black, conferred upon Washington a Master of Arts degree. Booker T. Washington died in 1915 and was buried at Tuskegee. More than seven thousand people attended his funeral.

For a full and searching analysis of the great educator's life and for an equally helpful bibliography, see Emma Low Thornbrough's article in *Dictionary of American Negro Biography*. The Booker T. Washington Papers in the Library of Congress are also a most valuable source for scholars interested in Washington's life. For his speeches, see E. Davidson Washington, ed., *Selected Speeches of Booker T. Washington* (1932). See also Hugh Hawkins, ed., *Booker T. Washington and His Critics* (1962), and August Meier's *Negro Thought in America, 1880–1915: Racial Ideologies in the Age of Booker T. Washington* (1963).

Louis R. Harlan is editor of *The Booker T. Washington Papers* (1972–   ), which appears in thirteen volumes. See also Harlan's two-volume biography, *Booker T. Washington: The Making of a Black Leader, 1856–1901* (1972), and his *Booker T. Washington: The Wizard of Tuskegee, 1901–1915* (1983).

Among the most recent evaluations of Washington's writings are "The Lost Life of the Negro, 1859–1919: Black Literary and Intellectual Life before the Renaissance" by Wilson J. Moses, in *Black American Literature*

Forum 21, no. 1–2 (Spring–Summer 1987), and Houston A. Baker, Jr.'s *Modernism and the Harlem Renaissance* (1987).

The first selection is taken from *Up from Slavery;* the two speeches come from Carter G. Woodson's *Negro Orators and Their Orations* (1925).

THE STRUGGLE FOR AN EDUCATION

One day, while at work in the coal-mine, I happened to overhear two miners talking about a great school for coloured people somewhere in Virginia. This was the first time that I had ever heard anything about any kind of school or college that was more pretentious than the little coloured school in our town.

In the darkness of the mine I noiselessly crept as close as I could to the two men who were talking. I heard one tell the other that not only was the school established for the members of my race, but that opportunities were provided by which poor but worthy students could work out all or a part of the cost of board, and at the same time be taught some trade or industry.

As they went on describing the school, it seemed to me that it must be the greatest place on earth, and not even Heaven presented more attractions for me at that time than did the Hampton Normal and Agricultural Institute in Virginia, about which these men were talking. I resolved at once to go to that school, although I had no idea where it was, or how many miles away, or how I was going to reach it; I remembered only that I was on fire constantly with one ambition, and that was to go to Hampton. This thought was with me day and night.

After hearing of the Hampton Institute, I continued to work for a few months longer in the coal-mine. While at work there, I heard of a vacant position in the household of General Lewis Ruffner, the owner of the salt-furnace and coal-mine. Mrs. Viola Ruffner, the wife of General Ruffner, was a "Yankee" woman from Vermont. Mrs. Ruffner had a reputation all through the vicinity for being very strict with her servants, and especially with the boys who tried to serve her. Few of them had remained with her more than two or three weeks. They all left with the same excuse: she was too strict. I decided, however, that I would rather try Mrs. Ruffner's house than remain in the coal-mine, and so my mother applied to her for the vacant position. I was hired at a salary of $5 per month.

I had heard so much about Mrs. Ruffner's severity that I was almost afraid to see her, and trembled when I went into her presence. I had not lived with her many weeks, however, before I began to understand her. I soon began to learn that, first of all, she wanted everything kept clean about her, that she wanted things done promptly and systematically, and that at the bottom of everything she wanted absolute honesty and frankness. Nothing must be sloven or slipshod; every door, every fence, must be kept in repair.

I cannot now recall how long I lived with Mrs. Ruffner before going to Hampton, but I think it must have been a year and a half. At any rate, I here repeat what I have said more than once before, that the lessons that I learned in the home of Mrs. Ruffner were as valuable to me as any education I have ever gotten anywhere since. Even to this day I never see bits of paper scattered around a house or in the street that I do not want to

pick them up at once. I never see a filthy yard that I do
not want to clean it, a paling off of a fence that I do not
want to put it on, an unpainted or unwhitewashed house
that I do not want to paint or whitewash it, or a button
off one's clothes, or a grease-spot on them or on a
floor, that I do not want to call attention to it.

From fearing Mrs. Ruffner I soon learned to look
upon her as one of my best friends. When she found
that she could trust me she did so implicitly. During the
one or two winters that I was with her she gave me an
opportunity to go to school for an hour in the day during a portion of the winter months, but most of my
studying was done at night, sometimes alone, sometimes
under some one whom I could hire to teach me. Mrs.
Ruffner always encouraged and sympathized with me in
all my efforts to get an education. It was while living
with her that I began to get together my first library. I
secured a dry-goods box, knocked out one side of it, put
some shelves in it, and began putting into it every kind
of book that I could get my hands upon, and called it
my "library."

Notwithstanding my success at Mrs. Ruffner's I did
not give up the idea of going to the Hampton Institute.
In the fall of 1872 I determined to make an effort to get
there, although, as I have stated, I had no definite idea
of the direction in which Hampton was, or of what it
would cost to go there. I do not think that any one thoroughly sympathized with me in my ambition to go to
Hampton unless it was my mother, and she was troubled with a grave fear that I was starting out on a
"wild-goose chase." At any rate, I got only a
half-hearted consent from her that I might start. The
small amount of money that I had earned had been con-

sumed by my stepfather and the remainder of the family, with the exception of a very few dollars, and so I had very little with which to buy clothes and pay my travelling expenses. My brother John helped me all that he could, but of course that was not a great deal, for his work was in the coal mine, where he did not earn much, and most of what he did earn went in the direction of paying the household expenses.

Perhaps the thing that touched and pleased me most in connection with my starting for Hampton was the interest that many of the older coloured people took in the matter. They had spent the best days of their lives in slavery, and hardly expected to live to see the time when they would see a member of their race leave home to attend a boarding school. Some of these older people would give me a nickel, others a quarter, or a handkerchief.

Finally the great day came, and I started for Hampton. I had only a small, cheap satchel that contained what few articles of clothing I could get. My mother at the time was rather weak and broken in health. I hardly expected to see her again, and thus our parting was all the more sad. She, however, was very brave through it all. At that time there were no through trains connecting that part of West Virginia with eastern Virginia. Trains ran only a portion of the way, and the remainder of the distance was travelled by stage-coaches.

The distance from Malden to Hampton is about five hundred miles. I had not been away from home many hours before it began to grow painfully evident that I did not have enough money to pay my fare to Hampton. One experience I shall long remember. I had been travelling over the mountains most of the afternoon in an old-fashioned stage-coach, when, late in the evening, the coach stopped for the night at a common, unpainted house called a hotel. All the other passengers except myself were whites. In my ignorance I supposed that the little hotel existed for the purpose of accommodating the passengers who travelled on the stage-coach. The difference that the colour of one's skin would make I had not thought anything about. After all the other passengers had been shown rooms and were getting ready for supper, I shyly presented myself before the man at the desk. It is true I had practically no money in my pocket with which to pay for bed or food, but I had hoped in some way to beg my way into the good graces of the landlord, for at that season in the mountains of Virginia the weather was cold, and I wanted to get indoors for the night. Without asking as to whether I had any money, the man at the desk firmly refused to even consider the matter of providing me with food or lodging. This was my first experience in finding out what the colour of my skin meant. In some way I managed to keep warm by walking about, and so got through the night. My whole soul was so bent upon reaching Hampton that I did not have time to cherish any bitterness toward the hotel-keeper.

By walking, begging rides both in wagons and in the cars, in some way, after a number of days, I reached the city of Richmond, Virginia, about eighty-two miles from Hampton. When I reached there, tired, hungry, and dirty, it was late in the night. I had never been in a large city, and this rather added to my misery. When I reached Richmond, I was completely out of money. I had not a single acquaintance in the place, and, being unused to city ways, I did not know where to go. I applied at several places for lodging, but they all wanted money, and that was what I did not have. Knowing nothing else better to do, I walked the streets. In doing this I passed by many food-stands where fried chicken and half-moon apple pies were piled high and made to present a most tempting appearance. At that time it seemed to me that I would have promised all that I expected to possess in the future to have gotten hold of one of those chicken legs or one of those pies. But I could not get either of these, nor anything else to eat.

I must have walked the streets till after midnight. At last I became so exhausted that I could walk no longer. I was tired, I was hungry, I was everything but discouraged. Just about the time when I reached extreme physical exhaustion, I came upon a portion of a street where the board sidewalk was considerably elevated. I waited for a few minutes, till I was sure that no passers-by could see me, and then crept under the sidewalk and lay for the night upon the ground, with my satchel of clothing for a pillow. Nearly all night I could hear the tramp of feet over my head. The next morning I found myself somewhat refreshed, but I was extremely hungry, because it had been a long time since I had had sufficient food. As soon as it became light enough for me to see my surroundings I noticed that I was near a large ship, and that this ship seemed to be unloading a cargo of pig iron. I went at once to the vessel and asked the captain to permit me to help unload the vessel in order to get money for food. The captain, a white man, who seemed to be kindhearted, consented. I worked long enough to earn money for my breakfast, and it seems to me, as I remember it now, to have been about the best breakfast that I have ever eaten.

My work pleased the captain so well that he told me if I desired I could continue working for a small amount per day. This I was very glad to do. I continued working on this vessel for a number of days. After buying food with the small wages I received there was not much left to add to the amount I must get to pay my way to Hampton. In order to economize in every way possible, so as to be sure to reach Hampton in a reasonable time, I continued to sleep under the same sidewalk that gave me shelter the first night I was in Richmond. Many years after that the coloured citizens of Richmond very kindly tendered me a reception at which there must have been two thousand people present. This reception was held not far from the spot where I slept the first night I spent in that city, and I must confess that my mind was more upon the sidewalk that first gave me shelter than upon the reception, agreeable and cordial as it was.

When I had saved what I considered enough money with which to reach Hampton, I thanked the captain of the vessel for his kindness, and started again. Without any unusual occurrence I reached Hampton, with a surplus of exactly fifty cents with which to begin my education. To me it had been a long, eventful journey; but the first sight of the large, three-story, brick school building seemed to have rewarded me for all that I had undergone in order to reach the place. If the people who gave the money to provide that building could appreciate the influence the sight of it had upon me, as well as upon thousands of other youths, they would feel all the more encouraged to make such gifts. It seemed to me to be the largest and most beautiful building I had ever seen. The sight of it seemed to give me new life. I felt that a new kind of existence had now begun—that life would now have a new meaning. I felt that I had reached the promised land, and I resolved to let no obstacle prevent me from putting forth the highest effort to fit myself to accomplish the most good in the world.

As soon as possible after reaching the grounds of the Hampton Institute, I presented myself before the head teacher for assignment to a class. Having been so long without proper food, a bath, and change of clothing, I did not, of course, make a very favourable impression upon her, and I could see at once that there were doubts in her mind about the wisdom of admitting me as a student. I felt that I could hardly blame her if she got the idea that I was a worthless loafer or tramp. For some time she did not refuse to admit me, neither did she decide in my favour, and I continued to linger about her, and to impress her in all the ways I could with my worthiness. In the meantime I saw her admitting other students, and that added greatly to my discomfort, for I felt, deep down in my heart, that I could do as well as they, if I could only get a chance to show what was in me.

After some hours had passed, the head teacher said to me: "The adjoining recitation-room needs sweeping. Take the broom and sweep it."

It occurred to me at once that here was my chance. Never did I receive an order with more delight. I knew that I could sweep, for Mrs. Ruffner had thoroughly taught me how to do that when I lived with her.

I swept the recitation-room three times. Then I got a dusting-cloth and I dusted it four times. All the woodwork around the walls, every bench, table, and desk, I went over four times with my dusting-cloth. Besides, every piece of furniture had been moved and every closet and corner in the room had been thoroughly cleaned. I had the feeling that in a large measure my future depended upon the impression I made upon the teacher in the cleaning of that room. When I was through, I reported to the head teacher. She was a "Yankee" woman who knew just where to look for dirt. She went into the room and inspected the floor and closets; then she took her handkerchief and rubbed it on the woodwork about the walls, and over the table and benches. When she was unable to find one bit of dirt on the floor, or a particle of dust on any of the furniture, she quietly remarked, "I guess you will do to enter this institution."

I was one of the happiest souls on earth. The sweeping of that room was my college examination, and never did any youth pass an examination for entrance into Harvard or Yale that gave him more genuine satisfaction. I have passed several examinations since then, but I have always felt that this was the best one I ever passed. . . .

AN ADDRESS DELIVERED AT THE OPENING OF THE COTTON STATES' EXPOSITION IN ATLANTA, GEORGIA, SEPTEMBER, 1895

Mr. President and Gentlemen of the Board of Directors and Citizens: One-third of the population of the South is of the Negro race. No enterprise seeking the material, civil, or moral welfare of this section can disregard this element of our population and reach the highest success.

I but convey to you, Mr. President and Directors, the sentiment of the masses of my race when I say that in no way have the value and manhood of the American Negro been more fittingly and generously recognized than by the managers of this magnificent Exposition at every stage of its progress. It is a recognition that will do more to cement the friendship of the two races than any occurrence since the dawn of freedom.

Not only this, but the opportunity here afforded will awaken among us a new era of industrial progress. Ignorant and inexperienced, it is not strange that in the first years of our new life we began at the top instead of at the bottom; that a seat in Congress or the State Legislature was more sought than real estate or industrial skill; that the political convention or stump speaking had more attractions than starting a dairy farm or truck garden.

A ship lost at sea for many days suddenly sighted a friendly vessel. From the mast of the unfortunate vessel was seen a signal, "Water, water; we die of thirst!" The answer from the friendly vessel at once came back: "Cast down your bucket where you are." A second time the signal, "Water, water; send us water!" ran up from the distressed vessel, and was answered: "Cast down your bucket where you are." The captain of the distressed vessel, at last heeding the injunction, cast down his bucket, and it came up full of fresh, sparkling water from the mouth of the Amazon River. To those of

Negro Orators and Their Orations. Copyright © 1925 by The Associated Publishers, Inc., published by The Association for the Study of Afro-American Life and History. Reprinted by permission.

my race who depend upon bettering their condition in a foreign land, or who underestimate the importance of cultivating friendly relations with the Southern white man, who is his next door neighbor, I would say: "Cast down your bucket where you are"—cast it down in making friends in every manly way of the people of all races by whom we are surrounded.

Cast it down in agriculture, mechanics, in commerce, in domestic service, and in the professions. And in this connection it is well to bear in mind that whatever other sins the South may be called to bear, when it comes to business, pure and simple, it is in the South that the Negro is given a man's chance in the commercial world, and in nothing is this Exposition more eloquent than in emphasizing this chance. Our greatest danger is, that in the great leap from slavery to freedom we may overlook the fact that the masses of us are to live by the productions of our hands, and fail to keep in mind that we shall prosper in proportion as we learn to dignify and glorify common labor, and put brains and skill into the common occupations of life; shall prosper in proportion as we learn to draw the line between the superficial and the substantial, the ornamental gewgaws of life and the useful. No race can prosper till it learns that there is as much dignity in tilling a field as in writing a poem. It is at the bottom of life we must begin, and not at the top. Nor should we permit our grievances to overshadow our opportunities.

To those of the white race who look to the incoming of those of foreign birth and strange tongue and habits for the prosperity of the South, were I permitted I would repeat what I say to my own race, "Cast down your bucket where you are." Cast it down among the

8,000,000 Negroes whose habits you know, whose fidelity and love you have tested in days when to have proved treacherous meant the ruin of your firesides. Cast down your bucket among these people who have, without strikes and labor wars, tilled your fields, cleared your forests, built your railroads and cities, and brought forth treasures from the bowels of the earth, and helped make possible this magnificent representation of the progress of the South. Casting down your bucket among my people, helping and encouraging them as you are doing on these grounds, and, with education of head, hand and heart, you will find that they will buy your surplus land, make blossom the waste places in your fields, and run your factories. While doing this, you can be sure in the future, as in the past, that you and your families will be surrounded by the most patient, faithful, law-abiding, and unresentful people that the world has seen. As we have proved our loyalty to you in the past, in nursing your children, watching by the sick bed of your mothers and fathers, and often following them with tear-dimmed eyes to their graves, so in the future, in our humble way, we shall stand by you with a devotion that no foreigner can approach, ready to lay down our lives, if need be, in defense of yours, interlacing our industrial, commercial, civil, and religious life with yours in a way that shall make the interests of both races one. In all things that are purely social we can be as separate as the fingers, yet one as the hand in all things essential to mutual progress.

There is no defense or security for any of us except in the highest intelligence and development of all. If anywhere there are efforts tending to curtail the fullest growth of the Negro, let these efforts be turned into stimulating, encouraging, and making him the most useful and intelligent citizen. Effort or means so invested will pay a thousand per cent interest. These efforts will be twice blessed—blessing him that gives and him that takes.

There is no escape through law of man or God from the inevitable:

> The laws of changeless justice bind
> Oppressor with oppressed;
> And close as sin and suffering joined
> We march to fate abreast.

Nearly sixteen millions of hands will aid you in pulling the load upwards or they will pull against you the load downwards. We shall constitute one-third and more of the ignorance and crime of the South, or one-third its intelligence and progress; we shall contribute one-third to the business and industrial prosperity of the South, or we shall prove a veritable body of death, stagnating, depressing, retarding every effort to advance the body politic.

Gentlemen of the Exposition, as we present to you our humble effort at an exhibition of our progress, you must not expect overmuch. Starting thirty years ago with ownership here and there in a few quilts and pumpkins and chickens (gathered from miscellaneous sources), remember the path that has led from these to the invention and production of agricultural implements, buggies, steam engines, newspapers, books, statuary, carving, paintings, the management of drug stores and banks has not been trodden without contact with thorns and thistles. While we take pride in what we exhibit as a result of our independent efforts, we do not for a moment forget that our part in this exhibition would fall far short of your expectations but for the constant help that has come to our educational life, not only from the Southern States, but especially from Northern philanthropists, who have made their gifts a constant stream of blessing and encouragement.

The wisest among my race understand that the agitation of questions of social equality is the extremest folly, and that progress in the enjoyment of all the privileges that will come to us must be the result of severe and constant struggle rather than of artificial forcing. No race that has anything to contribute to the markets of the world is long in any degree ostracized. It is important and right that all privileges of the law be ours, but it is vastly more important that we be prepared for the exercise of those privileges. The opportunity to earn a dollar in a factory just now is worth infinitely more than the opportunity to spend a dollar in an opera house.

In conclusion, may I repeat that nothing in thirty years has given us more hope and encouragement, and drawn us so near to you of the white race, as this opportunity offered by the Exposition; and here bending, as it were, over the altar that represents the results of the struggles of your race and mine, both starting practically empty-handed three decades ago, I pledge that, in your effort to work out the great and intricate problem which God has laid at the doors of the South, you shall have at all times the patient, sympathetic help of my race; only let this be constantly in mind that, while from representations in these buildings of the products of field, of forest, of mine, of factory, letters, and art, much good will come, yet far above and beyond mate-

rial benefits will be the higher good, that let us pray
God will come, in a blotting out of sectional differences
and racial animosities and suspicions, in a determination
to administer absolute justice, in a willing obedience
among all classes to the mandates of law. This, coupled
with our material prosperity, will bring into our beloved
South a new heaven and a new earth.

ADDRESS DELIVERED AT THE
HARVARD ALUMNI DINNER IN 1896

Mr. President and Gentlemen: It would in some measure
relieve my embarrassment if I could, even in a slight
degree, feel myself worthy of the great honor which you
do me today. Why you have called me from the Black
Belt of the South, from among my humble people, to
share in the honors of this occasion, is not for me to ex-
plain; and yet it may not be inappropriate for me to
suggest that it seems to me that one of the most vital
questions that touch our American life is how to bring
the strong, wealthy and learned into helpful touch with
the poorest, most ignorant and humblest, and at the
same time make the one appreciate the vitalizing,
strengthening influence of the other. How shall we make
the mansions on yon Beacon Street feel and see the
need of the spirits in the lowliest cabin in Alabama cotton fields or Louisiana sugar bottoms? This problem
Harvard University is solving, not by bringing itself
down, but by bringing the masses up.

If through me, an humble representative, seven millions of my people in the South might be permitted to
send a message to Harvard—Harvard that offered up on

death's altar young Shaw, and Russell, and Lowell, and scores of others, that we might have a free and united country—that message would be, "Tell them that the sacrifice was not in vain. Tell them that by habits of thrift and economy, by way of the industrial school and college, we are coming. We are crawling up, working up, yea, bursting up. Often through oppression, unjust discrimination and prejudice, but through them all we are coming up, and with proper habits, intelligence and property, there is no power on earth that can permanently stay our progress."

If my life in the past has meant anything in the lifting up of my people and the bringing about of better relations between your race and mine, I assure you from this day it will mean doubly more. In the economy of God there is but one standard by which an individual can succeed—there is but one for a race. This country demands that every race shall measure itself by the American standard. By it a race must rise or fall, succeed or fail, and in the last analysis mere sentiment counts for little. During the next half century and more, my race must continue passing through the severe American crucible. We are to be tested in our patience, our forbearance, our perseverance, our power to endure wrong, to withstand temptations, to economize, to acquire and use skill; in our ability to compete, to succeed in commerce, to disregard the superficial for the real, the appearance for the substance, to be great and yet small, learned and yet simple, high and yet the servant of all. This, this is the passport to all that is best in the life of our Republic, and the Negro must possess it, or be debarred.

While we are thus being tested, I beg of you to remember that wherever our life touches yours, we help or hinder. Wherever your life touches ours, you make us stronger or weaker. No member of your race in any part of our country can harm the meanest member of mine without the proudest and bluest blood in Massachusetts being degraded. When Mississippi commits crime, New England commits crime, and in so much, lowers the standard of your civilization. There is no escape—man drags man down, or man lifts man up.

In working out our destiny, while the main center of activity must be with us, we shall need, in a large measure in the years that are to come as we have in the past, the help, the encouragement, the guidance that the strong can give the weak. Thus helped, we of both races in the South soon shall throw off the shackles of racial and sectional prejudice and rise, as Harvard University has risen and as we all should rise, above the clouds of ignorance, narrowness and selfishness, into that atmosphere, that pure sunshine, where it will be our highest ambition to serve man, our brother, regardless of race or previous condition.

Frances Ellen Watkins Harper

(1825–1911)

Born of free parents in Baltimore, Maryland, Frances Ellen Watkins was educated first at home, and after the loss of her parents, at a school for free Negroes run by her uncle, the Reverend William Watkins. In 1845, according to William Still, with whom she later worked on the Underground Railroad, Watkins published an early collection of prose and poetry, *Forest Leaves.* No copy of this early work has yet been found. From 1850 to 1852, Watkins taught sewing at the A.M.E. Union Seminary, which was near Columbus, Ohio, but she soon left for a better teaching position in York, Pennsylvania. In 1854, reacting to a new and harsh anti-black law in Maryland, she pledged herself to the antislavery cause. Because of her success as a speaker (in her talks she often included portions of her own poems), she was employed by the Maine Antislavery Movement and lectured extensively.

In 1860 Watkins married Fenton Harper and moved to a farm near Columbus, Ohio. The Harpers had one child, who died at an early age. Mr. Harper died soon after, and Frances Harper returned to the antislavery lecture program and in addition toured the South speaking for the Women's Christian Temperance Union (WCTU). A pioneer feminist in essence, Harper advocated higher and fairer standards of domestic morality and better education for women. She worked with the American Women Suffrage Association for a while, but by 1869 was doing more for black suffrage than for women's. During her last years, however, she returned to the WCTU.

Harper was a very popular poet and fiction writer. *Poems on Miscellaneous Subjects* (1854; enlarged 1857) was reprinted many times; finally, with an introduction by William Lloyd Garrison, it went to its twentieth edition. *Moses: A Story of the Nile* (1869; enlarged 1889) became the major part of her *Idylls of the Bible* (1901). *Poems*, at first a small volume in 1871, had grown to ninety pages in 1895. *Sketches of Southern Life* (1872) was enlarged in 1896. These statistics come from William Still, mentioned earlier.

Harper's verse was conventional and, measured by the standards of her era, competent. Its subject matter varied with the periods through which she lived and the particular group with which she was currently connected. She wrote about the evils of drink, women's rights, and the double standard of morality. She put into verse biblical stories, classical myths, and oriental legends, but returned again and again to the black cause. Her novel, *Iola Leroy; or, Shadows Uplifted* (1892), is a "race" novel.

For biographical and critical comment on Frances Ellen Watkins Harper, see the articles by Daniel Walden in *Dictionary of American Negro Biography* and by Maryemma Graham in *Dictionary of Literary Biography, Volume 50;* see also Vernon Loggins's *The Negro Author* (1931), Benjamin Brawley, *Early Negro American Writ-*

ers (1935), Louis Filler, *Notable American Women* (1971), and most important, William Still, *The Underground Rail Road* (1872).

For more recent evaluations see the following: *Black Feminist Criticism: Perspectives on Black Women Writers* (1985) by Barbara Christian; Paula Gidding's *When and Where I Enter: The Impact of Black Women on Race and Sex in America* (1984); and *Invisible Poets* by Joan R. Sherman (1974). See also *Reconstructing Womanhood: The Emergence of the Afro-American Woman Novelist* by Hazel V. Carby (1987) and *Invented Lives: Narratives of Black Women, 1860–1960* by Mary Helen Washington (1987).

The selections that follow come from Harper's most popular poetic volumes: *Poems on Miscellaneous Subjects; Poems;* and *Sketches of Southern Life.*

THE SLAVE AUCTION

The sale began—young girls were there,
   Defenceless in their wretchedness,
Whose stifled sobs of deep despair
   Revealed their anguish and distress.

And mothers stood with streaming eyes,
   And saw their dearest children sold;
Unheeded rose their bitter cries,
   While tyrants bartered them for gold.

And woman, with her love and truth—
   For these in sable forms may dwell—
Gaz' on the husband of her youth,
   With anguish none may paint or tell.

And men, whose sole crime was their hue,
   The impress of their Maker's hand,
And frail and shrinking children, too,
   Were gathered in that mournful band.

Ye who have laid your love to rest,
   And wept above their lifeless clay,
Know not the anguish of that breast,
   Whose lov'd are rudely torn away.

Ye may not know how desolate
   Are bosoms rudely forced to part,
And how a dull and heavy weight
   Will press the life-drops from the heart.

THE DYING BONDMAN

Life was trembling, faintly trembling
On the bondman's latest breath,
And he felt the chilling pressure
Of the cold, hard hand of Death.

He had been an Afric chieftain,
Worn his manhood as a crown;
But upon the field of battle
Had been fiercely stricken down.

He had longed to gain his freedom,
Waited, watched and hoped in vain,
Till his life was slowly ebbing—
Almost broken was his chain.

By his bedside stood the master,
Gazing on the dying one,

Knowing by the dull grey shadows
That life's sands were almost run.

"Master," said the dying bondman,
"Home and friends I soon shall see;
But before I reach my country,
Master write that I am free;

"For the spirits of my fathers
Would shrink back from me in pride,
If I told them at our greeting
I a slave had lived and died;—

"Give to me the precious token,
That my kindred dead may see—
Master! write it, write it quickly!
Master! write that I am free!"

At his earnest plea the master
Wrote for him the glad release,
O'er his wan and wasted features
Flitted one sweet smile of peace.

Eagerly he grasped the writing;
"I am free!" at last he said.
Backward fell upon the pillow,
He was free among the dead.

BURY ME IN A FREE LAND

Make me a grave where'er you will,
In a lowly plain, or a lofty hill;
Make it among earth's humblest graves,
But not in a land where men are slaves.

I could not rest if around my grave
I heard the steps of a trembling slave;
His shadow above my silent tomb
Would make it a place of fearful gloom.

I could not rest if I heard the tread
Of a coffle gang to the shambles led,
And the mother's shriek of wild despair
Rise like a curse on the trembling air.

I could not sleep if I saw the lash
Drinking her blood at each fearful gash,
And I saw her babes torn from her breast,
Like trembling doves from their parent nest.

I'd shudder and start if I heard the bay
Of bloodhounds seizing their human prey,
And I heard the captive plead in vain
As they bound afresh his galling chain.

If I saw young girls from their mothers' arms
Bartered and sold for their youthful charms,
My eye would flash with a mournful flame,
My death-paled cheek grow red with shame.

I would sleep, dear friends, where bloated might
Can rob no man of his dearest right;
My rest shall be calm in any grave
Where none can call his brother a slave.

I ask no monument, proud and high,
To arrest the gaze of the passers-by;
All that my yearning spirit craves,
Is bury me not in a land of slaves.

A DOUBLE STANDARD

Do you blame me that I loved him?
  If when standing all alone
I cried for bread a careless world
  Pressed to my lips a stone.

Do you blame me that I loved him,
  That my heart beat glad and free,
When he told me in the sweetest tones
  He loved but only me?

Can you blame me that I did not see
  Beneath his burning kiss
The serpent's wiles, nor even hear
  The deadly adder hiss?

Can you blame me that my heart grew cold
  The tempted, tempter turned;
When he was feted and caressed
  And I was coldly spurned?

Would you blame him, when you draw from me
  Your dainty robes aside,
If he with gilded baits should claim
  Your fairest as his bride?

Would you blame the world if it should press
  On him a civic crown;
And see me struggling in the depth
  Then harshly press me down?

Crime has no sex and yet to-day
  I wear the brand of shame;
Whilst he amid the gay and proud
  Still bears an honored name.

Can you blame me if I've learned to think
  Your hate of vice a sham,
When you so coldly crushed me down
  And then excused the man?

Would you blame me if to-morrow
  The coroner should say,
A wretched girl, outcast, forlorn,
  Has thrown her life away?

Yes, blame me for my downward course,
  But oh! remember well,
Within your homes you press the hand
  That led me down to hell.

I'm glad God's ways are not our ways,
  He does not see as man;
Within His love I know there's room
  For those whom others ban.

I think before His great white throne,
  His throne of spotless light,
That whited sepulchres shall wear
  The hue of endless night.

That I who fell, and he who sinned,
  Shall reap as we have sown;
That each the burden of his loss
  Must bear and bear alone.

No golden weights can turn the scale
  Of justice in His sight;
And what is wrong in woman's life
  In man's cannot be right.

LEARNING TO READ

Very soon the Yankee teachers
   Came down and set up school;
But, oh! how the Rebs did hate it,—
   It was agin' their rule.

Our masters always tried to hide
   Book learning from our eyes;
Knowledge didn't agree with slavery—
   'Twould make us all too wise.

But some of us would try to steal
   A little from the book,
And put the words together,
   And learn by hook or crook.

I remember Uncle Caldwell,
   Who took pot liquor fat
And greased the pages of his book,
   And hid it in his hat,

And had his master ever seen
   The leaves upon his head,
He'd have thought them greasy papers,
   But nothing to be read.

And there was Mr. Turner's Ben,
   Who heard the children spell,
And picked the words right up by heart,
   And learned to read 'em well.

Well, the Northern folks kept sending
   The Yankee teachers down;
And they stood right up and helped us,
   Though Rebs did sneer and frown.

And, I longed to read my Bible,
    For precious words it said;
But when I begun to learn it,
    Folks just shook their heads,

And said there is no use trying,
    Oh! Chloe, you're too late;
But as I was rising sixty,
    I had no time to wait.

So I got a pair of glasses,
    And straight to work I went,
And never stopped till I could read
    The hymns and Testament.

Then I got a little cabin
    A place to call my own—
And I felt as independent
    As the queen upon her throne.

Pauline E. Hopkins

(1856–1930)

A versatile and talented person, Pauline Elizabeth Hopkins deserves to be better known than she is today. She was, among other things, an editor of an important Negro magazine, a publisher, a journalist, a novelist and writer of short stories, and a producer of a musical drama in which she sang one of the stellar parts. These were pursuits followed by very few women, white or black, of her generation.

Born in Portland, Maine, Pauline Hopkins was the daughter of Northrup and Sarah (Allen) Hopkins. Her mother, who was born in Exeter, New Hampshire, belonged to a well-known New England African American family, one that included the outstanding clergyman and abolitionist Nathaniel Paul. She was also the grandniece of the poet James Whitfield.

During her early years Pauline Hopkins lived in Boston and attended the public schools of that city. At the age of fifteen she won a prize for her essay ''The Evils of Intemperance and Their Remedies'' in a contest sponsored by William Wells Brown. The prize inspired her to seek a writing career after graduation from high school. In 1880 Hopkins created and produced a musical presentation called "Hopkins' Coloured Troubadors in the Great Musical Drama, Escape from Slavery." The cast consisted of such well-known performers as Sam Lucas and the Hyers Sisters, a sixty-member chorus, members of her family, and the author-producer herself, billed as "Boston's Colored Soprano." This musical drama ran to five performances.

In 1892 Hopkins won widespread praise for her illustrated lecture on Toussaint L'Ouverture, presented in the famous Tremont Temple for the Robert A. Bell Boston Post of the Grand Army of the Republic. In 1900 she published her first novel, *Contending Forces: A Romance Illustrative of Negro Life North and South.* The work dealt with middle-class Negro life of her generation. She promoted the book by reading portions of it to women's clubs throughout the nation.

Because of the success of this novel, Hopkins was asked to serve as editor of and contributor to the *Colored American,* one of the best-known periodicals of its day. Coming into existence in 1900, it was the first Negro magazine of the twentieth century devoted to the "development of Afro-American art and literature." Pauline Hopkins wrote for the magazine's first issue a short story entitled "The Mystery within Us." For subsequent issues, she wrote three long serials: "Hagar's Daughters: A Story of Southern Caste Prejudice" (March 1901 to March 1902); "Winona: A Tale of Negro Life in the South and Southwest" (May 1902 to October 1902); and "Of One Blood; or, The Hidden Self" (November 1902 to November 1903). These novels and some of her short stories dealt largely with interracial relationships. In addition to these works of fiction, Hopkins also wrote biographical sketches of "Famous Men of the Negro Race" and "Famous Women of the Negro Race."

According to Dorothy Porter, "the illustrated *Colored American Magazine* [under Hopkins's editorship] is a major source for the literature, science, music, arts, religions, facts, and traditions of the Negro race during four years." On the grounds of poor health, Hopkins left the *Colored American* in 1904. The real reason was probably the purchase of the magazine by accommodationist Fred R. Moore, with money furnished by Booker T. Washington, who was then trying to gain control over newspapers owned by blacks.

After leaving the *Colored American,* Hopkins engaged in several activities: she wrote briefly for the *Voice of the Negro,* founded her own publishing firm, contributed articles to and edited the *New Era,* and wrote several biographies of distinguished black and white abolitionists like Henry Highland Garnet and William Lloyd Garrison. After living in obscurity for more than a decade, Pauline Elizabeth Hopkins died in 1930.

For excellent articles on Pauline Hopkins, see Dorothy Porter's entry in *Dictionary of American Negro Biography* and Jane Campbell's entry in *Dictionary of Literary Biography, Volume 50.* See also Hugh M. Gloster, *Negro Voices in American Fiction* (1948); Ann Allen Shockley, "Pauline Elizabeth Hopkins: A Biographical Excursion into Obscurity," *Phylon* 33 (Spring 1972); Abby A. Johnson and Ronald M. Johnson, "Away from Accommodation: Radical Editors and Protest Journalism, 1900–1910," *Journal of Negro History* (October 1977); and Claudia Tate, "Pauline Hopkins: Our Literary Foremother," in *Conjuring: Black Women, Fiction, and Lit-*

erary Tradition, ed. Marjorie Pryse and Hortense J. Spillers (1985). For the most recent commentary see Mary Helen Washington, *Invented Lives* (1987) and Hazel V. Carby, *Reconstructing Womanhood* (1987).

The following selection comes from *Contending Forces,* originally published in 1900, reprinted in 1975 by AMS Press.

BRO'R ABR'M JIMSON'S WEDDING
A Christmas Story

It was a Sunday in early spring the first time that Caramel Johnson dawned on the congregation of _____ Church in a populous New England City.

The Afro-Americans of that city are well-to-do, being of a frugal nature, and considering it a lasting disgrace for any man among them, desirous of social standing in the community, not to make himself comfortable in this world's goods against the coming time, when old age creeps on apace and renders him unfit for active business.

Therefore the members of the said church had not waited to be exhorted by reformers to own their unpretentious homes and small farms outside the city limits, but they vied with each other in efforts to accumulate a small competency urged thereto by a realization of what pressing needs the future might bring, or that might have been because of the constant example of white neighbors, and a due respect for the dignity which *their* foresight had brought to the superior race.

Of course, these small Vanderbilts and Astors of a darker hue must have a place of worship in accord with

their worldly prosperity, and so it fell out that _____
church was the richest plum in the ecclesiastical pud-
ding, and greatly sought by scholarly divines as a rest-
ing place for four years,—the extent of the time-limit
allowed by conference to the men who must be provided with suitable charges according to the demands of
their energy and scholarship.

The attendance was unusually large for morning service, and a restless movement was noticeable all
through the sermon. How strange a thing is nature; the
change of the seasons announces itself in all humanity
as well as in the trees and flowers, the grass, and in the
atmosphere. Something within us responds instantly to
the touch of kinship that dwells in all life.

The air, soft and balmy, laden with rich promise for
the future, came through the massive, half-open windows, stealing in refreshing waves upon the congregation. The sunlight fell through the colored glass of the
windows in prismatic hues, and dancing all over the
lofty star-gemmed ceiling, painted the hue of the broad
vault of heaven, creeping down in crinkling shadows to
touch the deep garnet cushions of the sacred desk, and
the rich wood of the altar with a hint of gold.

The offertory was ended. The silvery cadences of a
rich soprano voice still lingered on the air, "O, Worship
the Lord in the beauty of holiness." There was a suppressed feeling of expectation, but not the faintest rustle
as the minister rose in the pulpit, and after a solemn
pause, gave the usual invitation:

"If there is anyone in this congregation desiring to
unite with this church, either by letter or on probation,
please come forward to the altar."

The words had not died upon his lips when a woman

started from her seat near the door and passed up the main aisle. There was a sudden commotion on all sides. Many heads were turned—it takes so little to interest a church audience. The girls in the choir-box leaned over the rail, nudged each other and giggled, while the men said to one another, "She's a stunner, and no mistake."

The candidate for membership, meanwhile, had reached the altar railing and stood before the man of God, to whom she had handed her letter from a former Sabbath home, with head decorously bowed as became the time and the holy place. There was no denying the fact that she was a pretty girl; brown of skin, small of feature, with an ever-lurking gleam of laughter in eyes coal black. Her figure was slender and beautifully moulded, with a seductive grace in the undulating walk and erect carriage. But the chief charm of the sparkling dark face lay in its intelligence, and the responsive play of facial expression which was enhanced by two mischievous dimples pressed into the rounded cheeks by the caressing fingers of the god of Love.

The minister whispered to the candidate, coughed, blew his nose on his snowy clerical handkerchief, and, finally, turned to the expectant congregation:

"Sister Chocolate Caramel Johnson—"

He was interrupted by a snicker and a suppressed laugh, again from the choir-box, and an audible whisper which sounded distinctly throughout the quiet church,—

"I'd get the Legislature to change that if it was mine, 'deed I would!" then silence profound caused by the reverend's stern glance of reproval bent on the offenders in the choir-box.

"Such levity will not be allowed among the members of the choir. If it occurs again, I shall ask the

choir master for the names of the offenders and have
their places taken by those more worthy to be gospel
singers.''

Thereupon Mrs. Tilly Anderson whispered to Mrs.
Nancy Tobias that, ''them choir gals is the mos' deceiv-
ines' hussies in the church, an' for my part, I'm glad
the pastor called 'em down. That sister's too good
lookin' for 'em, an' they'll be after her like er pack o'
houn's, min' me, Sis' Tobias.''

Sister Tobias ducked her head in her lap and shook
her fat sides in laughing appreciation of the sister's
foresight.

Order being restored the minister proceeded:

''Sister Chocolate Caramel Johnson brings a letter to
us from our sister church in Nashville, Tennessee. She
has been a member in good standing for ten years, having been received into fellowship at ten years of age.
She leaves them now, much to her regret, to pursue the
study of music at one of the large conservatories in this
city, and they recommend her to our love and care. You
know the contents of the letter. All in favor of giving
Sister Johnson the right hand of fellowship, please manifest the same by a rising vote.'' The whole congregation rose.

''Contrary minded? None. The ayes have it. Be
seated, friends. Sister Johnson, it gives me great pleasure to receive you into this church. I welcome you to
its joys and sorrows. May God bless you. Brother Jimson?'' (Brother Jimson stepped from his seat to the pastor's side.) ''I assign this sister to your class. Sister
Johnson, this is Brother Jimson, your future spiritual
teacher.''

Brother Jimson shook the hand of his new member,

warmly, and she returned to her seat. The minister pronounced the benediction over the waiting congregation; the organ burst into richest melody. Slowly the crowd of worshippers dispersed.

Abraham Jimson had made his money as a janitor for the wealthy people of the city. He was a bachelor, and when reproved by some good Christian brother for still dwelling in single blessedness always offered as an excuse that he had been too busy to think of a wife, but that now he was "well fixed," pecuniarily, he would begin to "look over" his lady friends for a suitable companion.

He owned a house in the suburbs and a fine brick dwelling-house in the city proper. He was a trustee of prominence in the church, in fact, its "solid man," and his opinion was sought and his advice acted upon by his associates on the Board. It was felt that any lady in the congregation would be proud to know herself his choice.

When Caramel Johnson received the right hand of fellowship, her aunt, the widow Maria Nash, was ahead in the race for the wealthy class-leader. It had been neck-and-neck for a while between her and Sister Viney Peters, but, finally it had settled down to Sister Maria with a hundred to one, among the sporting members of the Board, that she carried off the prize, for Sister Maria owned a house adjoining Brother Jimson's in the suburbs, and property counts these days.

Sister Nash had "no idea" when she sent for her niece to come to B. that the latter would prove a rival; her son Andy was as good as engaged to Caramel. But it is always the unexpected that happens. Caramel came, and Brother Jimson had no eyes for the charms of other women after he had gazed into her coal black orbs, and watched her dimples come and go.

Caramel decided to accept a position as housemaid in order to help defray the expenses of her tuition at the conservatory, and Brother Jimson interested himself so warmly in her behalf that she soon had a situation in the home of his richest patron where it was handy for him to chat with her about the business of the church, and the welfare of her soul, in general. Things progressed very smoothly until the fall, when one day Sister Maria had occasion to call, unexpectedly, on her niece and found Brother Jimson basking in her smiles while he enjoyed a sumptuous dinner of roast chicken and fixings.

To say that Sister Maria was "set way back" would not accurately describe her feelings; but from that time Abraham Jimson knew that he had a secret foe in the Widow Nash.

Before many weeks had passed it was publicly known that Brother Jimson would lead Caramel Johnson to the altar "come Christmas." There was much sly speculation as to the "widder's gittin' left," and how she took it from those who had cast hopeless glances toward the chief man of the church. Great preparations were set on foot for the wedding festivities. The bride's trousseau was a present from the groom and included a white satin wedding gown and a costly gold watch. The town house was refurnished and a trip to New York was in contemplation.

"Hump!" grunted Sister Nash when told the rumors, "there's no fool like an ol' fool. Car'mel's a han'ful he'll fin', ef he gits her."

"I reckon he'll git her all right, Sis' Nash," laughed the neighbor, who had run in to talk over the news.

"I've said my word an' I ain't goin' change it, Sis'r. Min' me, I says, *ef he gits her,* an, I mean it."

Andy Nash was also a member of Brother Jimson's class; he possessed, too, a strong sweet baritone voice which made him a great value to the choir. He was an immense success in the social life of the city, and had created sad havoc with the hearts of the colored girls; he could have his pick of the best of them because of his graceful figure and fine easy manners. Until Caramel had been dazzled by the wealth of her elderly lover, she had considered herself fortunate as the lady of his choice.

It was Sunday, three weeks before the wedding that Andy resolved to have it out with Caramel.

"She's been hot an' she's been col', an' now she's luke warm, an' today ends it before this gent-man sleeps," he told himself as he stood before the glass and tied his pale blue silk tie in a stunning knot, and settled his glossy tile at a becoming angle.

Brother Jimson's class was a popular one and had a large membership; the hour spent there was much enjoyed, even by visitors. Andy went into the vestry early resolved to meet Caramel if possible. She was there, at the back of the room sitting alone on a settee. Andy immediately seated himself in the vacant place by her side. There were whispers and much head-shaking among the few early worshippers, all of whom knew the story of the young fellow's romance and his disappointment.

As he dropped into the seat beside her, Caramel turned her large eyes on him intently, speculatively, with a doubtful sort of curiosity suggested in her expression, as to how he took her flagrant desertion.

"Howdy, Car'mel?" was his greeting without a shade of resentment.

"I'm well; no need to ask how you are," was the quick response. There was a mixture of cordiality and coquetry in her manner. Her eyes narrowed and glittered under lowered lids, as she gave him a long side-glance. How could she help showing her admiration for the supple young giant beside her? "Surely," she told herself, "I'll have long time enough to git sick of old rheumatics," her pet name for her elderly lover.

"I ain't sick much," was Andy's surly reply.

He leaned his elbow on the back of the settee and gave his recreant sweetheart a flaming glance of mingled love and hate, oblivious to the presence of the assembled class-members.

"You ain't over friendly these days, Car'mel, but I gits news of your capers 'roun' 'bout some of the members."

"My—Yes?" she answered as she flashed her great eyes at him in pretended surprise. He laughed a laugh not good to hear.

"Yes," he drawled. Then he added with sudden energy, "Are you goin' to tie up to old Rheumatism sure 'nuff, come Chris'mas?"

"Come Chris'mas, Andy, I be. I hate to tell you but I have to do it."

He recoiled as from a blow. As for the girl, she found a keen relish in the situation: it flattered her vanity.

"How comes it you've changed your mind, Car'mel,

'bout you an' me? You've tol' me often that I was your first choice.''

"We—ll," she drawled, glancing uneasily about her and avoiding her aunt's gaze, which she knew was bent upon her every movement, "I did reckon once I would. But a man with money suits me best, an' you ain't got a cent."

"No more have you. You ain't no better than other women to work an' help a man along, is you?"

The color flamed an instant in her face turning the dusky skin to a deep, dull red.

"Andy Nash, you always was a fool, an' as ignerunt as a wil' Injun. I mean to have a sure nuff brick house an' plenty of money. That makes people respec' you. Why don' you quit bein' so shifless and save your money. You ain't worth your salt."

"Your head's turned with pianorer-playin' an' livin' up North. Ef you'll turn *him* off an' come back home, I'll turn over a new leaf, Car'mel," his voice was soft and persuasive enough now.

She had risen to her feet; her eyes flashed, her face was full of pride.

"I won't. I've quit likin' you, Andy Nash."

"Are you in earnest?" he asked, also rising from his seat.

"Dead earnes'."

"Then there's no more to be said."

He spoke calmly, not raising his voice above a whisper. She stared at him in surprise. Then he added as he swung on his heel preparatory to leaving her:

"You ain't got him yet, my gal. But remember, I'm waitin' for you when you need me."

While this whispered conference was taking place in

the back of the vestry, Brother Jimson had entered, and many an anxious glance he cast in the direction of the couple. Andy made his way slowly to his mother's side as Brother Jimson rose in his place to open the meeting. There was a commotion on all sides as the members rustled down on their knees for prayer. Widow Nash whispered to her son as they knelt side by side:

"How did you make out, Andy?"

"Didn't make out at all, mammy; she's as obstinate as a mule."

"Well, then, there's only one thing mo' to do."

Andy was unpleasant company for the remainder of the day. He sought, but found nothing to palliate Caramel's treachery. He had only surly, bitter words for his companions who ventured to address him, as the outward expression of inward tumult. The more he brooded over his wrongs the worse he felt. When he went to work on Monday morning he was feeling vicious. He had made up his mind to do something desperate. The wedding should not come off. He would be avenged.

Andy went about his work at the hotel in gloomy silence unlike his usual gay hilarity. It happened that all the female help at the great hostelry was white, and on that particular Monday morning was the duty of Bridget McCarthy's watch to clean the floors. Bridget was also not in the best of humors, for Pat McClosky, her special company, had gone to the priest's with her rival, Kate Connerton, on Sunday afternoon, and Bridget had not yet got over the effects of a strong rum punch taken to quiet her nerves after hearing the news.

Bridget had scrubbed a wide swath of the marble floor when Andy came through with a rush order carried in scientific style high above his head, balanced on one hand. Intent upon satisfying the guest who was princely in his "tips," Andy's unwary feet became entangled in the maelstrom of brooms, scrubbing-brushes and pails. In an instant the "order" was sliding over the floor in a general mix-up.

To say Bridget was mad wouldn't do her state justice. She forgot herself and her surroundings and relieved her feelings in elegant Irish, ending a tirade of abuse by calling Andy a "wall-eyed, bandy-legged nagur."

Andy couldn't stand that from "common, po' white trash," so calling all his science into play he struck out straight from the shoulder with his right, and brought her a swinging blow on the mouth, which seated her neatly in the five-gallon bowl of freshly made lobster salad which happened to be standing on the floor behind her.

There was a wail from the kitchen force that reached to every department. It being the busiest hour of the day when they served dinner, the dish-washers and scrubbers went on a strike against the "nagur who struck Bridget McCarthy, the baste,"* mingled with cries of "lynch him!" Instantly the great basement floor was a battle ground. Every colored man seized whatever was handiest and ranged himself by Andy's side, and stood ready to receive the onslaught of the Irish brigade. For the sake of peace, and sorely against his inclinations, the proprietor surrendered Andy to the police on a charge of assault and battery.

On Wednesday morning of the eventful week,

---

*"Baste" is "beast" as Hopkins tries to imitate an Irish brogue.

Brother Jimson wended his way to his house in the suburbs to collect the rent. Unseen by the eye of man, he
was wrestling with a problem that had shadowed his life
for many years. No one on earth suspected him unless it
might be the widow. Brother Jimson boasted of his consistent Christian life—rolled his piety like a sweet mor-
sel beneath his tongue, and had deluded himself into
thinking that *he* could do no sin. There were scoffers in
the church who doubted the genuineness of his preten-
tions, and he believed that there was a movement on
foot against his power led by Widow Nash.

Brother Jimson groaned in bitterness of spirit. His
only fear was that he might be parted from Caramel. If
he lost her he felt that all happiness in life was over for
him, anxiety gave him a sickening feeling of unrest. He
was tormented, too, by jealousy; and when he was
called upon by Andy's anxious mother to rescue her son
from the clutches of the law, he had promised her fair
enough, but in reality resolved to do nothing but—tell
the judge that Andy was a dangerous character whom it
was best to quell by severity. The pastor and all the
other influential members of the church were at court on
Tuesday, but Brother Jimson was conspicuous by his
absence.

Today Brother Jimson resolved to call on Sister
Nash, and as he had heard nothing of the outcome of
the trial, make cautious inquiries concerning that, and
also sound her on the subject nearest his heart.

He opened the gate and walked down the side path
to the back door. From within came the rhythmic sound
of a rubbing board. The brother knocked, and then
cleared his throat with a preliminary cough.

"Come," called a voice within. As the door swung

open it revealed the spare form of the widow, who with sleeves rolled above her elbows stood at the tub cutting her way through piles of foaming suds.

"Mornin', Sis' Nash! How's all?"

"That you, Bro'r Jimson? How's yourself? Take a cheer an' make yourself to home."

"Cert'nly, Sis' Nash, don' care ef I do," and the good brother scanned the sister with an eagle eye. "Yas'm I'm purty tol'rable these days, thank God. Bleeg'd to you, Sister, I jes' will stop an res' myself befo' I repair myself back to the city." He seated himself in the most comfortable chair in the room, tilted it on the two back legs against the wall, lit his pipe and with a grunt of satisfaction settled back to watch the white rings of smoke curl about his head.

"These are mighty ticklish times, Sister. How's you continue on the journey? Is you strong in the faith?"

"I've got the faith, my brother, but I ain't on no mountain top this week. I'm way down in the valley; I'm jes' coaxin' the Lord to keep me sweet," and Sister Nash wiped the ends from her hands and prodded the clothes in the boiler with the clothes-stick, added fresh pieces and went on with her work.

"This is a worl' strewed with wrecks an' floatin' with tears. It's the valley of tribulation. May your faith continue. I hear Jim Jinkins has bought a farm up Taunton way."

"Wan'ter know!"

"Doctor tells me Bro'r Waters is comin' after Chrismus. They do say as how he's stirrin' up things turrible; he's easin' his min' on this lynchin' business, an' it's high time—high time."

"Sho! Don' say so! What you reck'n he's goin tell us now, Brother Jimson?"

"Suthin' 'stonishin', Sister; it'll stir the country from end to end. Yes'm the Council is powerful strong as an organization."

"Sho! sho!" and the "thrub, thrub" of the board could be heard a mile away.

The conversation flagged. Evidently Widow Nash was not in a talkative mood that morning. The brother was disappointed.

"Well, it's mighty comfort'ble here, but I mus' be goin'."

"What's your hurry, Brother Jimson?"

"Business, Sister, business," and the brother brought his chair forward preparatory to rising. "Where's Andy? How'd he come out of that little difficulty?"

"Locked up."

"You don' mean to say he's in jail?"

"Yes, he's in jail 'tell I git's his bail."

"What might the sentence be, Sister?"

"Twenty dollars fine or six months at the Islan'." There was silence for a moment, broken only by the "thrub, thrub" of the washboard, while the smoke curled upward from Brother Jimson's pipe as he enjoyed a few last puffs.

"These are mighty ticklish times, Sister. Po' Andy, the way of the transgressor is hard."

Sister Nash took her hands out of the tub and stood with arms akimbo, a statue of Justice carved in ebony. Her voice was like the trump of doom.

"Yes; an' men like you is the cause of it. You leadin' men with money an' chances don' do your duty. I arst you, I arst you fair, to go down to the jedge an'

bail that po' chile out. Did you go? No; you hard-faced
old devil, you lef him be there, an' I had to git the
money from my white folks. Yes, an I'm breakin' my
back now, over that pile of clo's to pay that twenty dollars. Um! all the trouble comes to us women.''

"That's so, Sister; that's the livin' truth,'' murmured
Brother Jimson furtively watching the rising storm and
wondering where the lightning of her speech would
strike next.

"I tell you that it is our receiptfulness to each other
is the reason we don' prosper an' God's a-punishin' us
with fire an' with sward 'cause we's so jealous an'
snaky to each other.''

"That's so, Sister; that's the livin' truth.''

"Yes, sir; a nigger's boun' to be a nigger 'tell the
trump of doom. You kin skin him, but he's a nigger
still. Broad-cloth, biled shirts an' money won' make
him more or less, no, sir.''

"That's so, Sister; that's jes' so.''

"A nigger can't holp himself. White folks can run
agin the law all the time an' they never gits caught, but
a nigger! Every time he opens his mouth he puts his
foot in it—got to hit that po' white trash gal in the
mouth an' git jailed an' leave his po'r ol' mother to
work her fingers to the secon' jint to get him out. Um!''

"These are mighty ticklish times, Sister. Man's
boun' to sin; it's his nat'ral state. I hope this will teach
Andy humility of the sperit.''

"A little humility'd be good for yourself, Abra'm
Jimson.'' Sister Nash ceased her sobs and set her teeth
hard.

"Lord, Sister Nash, what compar'son is there 'twixt
me an' a worthless nigger like Andy? My business is

with the salt of the earth, an' so I have dwelt ever since I was consecrated.''

"Salt of the earth! But ef the salt have los' its saver how you goin' salt it ergin? No, sir, you cain't do it; it mus' be cas' out an' trodded under foot of men. That's who's goin' happen you Abe Jimson, hyar me? An' I'd like to trod on you with my foot, an' every ol' good fer nuthin' bag o' salt like you,'' shouted Sister Nash. "You're a snake in the grass; you done stole the boy's gal an' then try to git him sent to the Islan'. You cain't deny it, fer the jedge done tol' me all you said, you ol' rhinoceros-hided hypercrite. Salt of the earth! You!''

Brother Jimson regretted that Widow Nash had found him out. Slowly he turned, settling his hat on the back of his head.

"Good mornin', Sister Nash. I ain't no hard feelin's agains' you. I too near to the kingdom to let trifles jar me. My bowels of compassion yearns over you, Sister, a pilgrim an' a stranger in this unfriendly worl'.''

No answer from Sister Nash. Brother Jimson lingered.

"Good mornin', Sister.'' Still no answer.

"I hope to see you at the weddin', Sister.''

"Keep on hopin', I'll be there. That gal's my own sister's chile. What in time she wants of a rheumatic ol' sap-head like you for, beats me. I wouldn't marry you for no money, myself; no, sir; it's my belief that you've done goophered her.''

"Yes, Sister; I've hearn tell of people refusin' befo' they was ask'd,'' he retorted, giving her a sly look.

For answer the widow grabbed the clothes-stick and flung it at him in speechless rage.

"My, what a temper it's got,'' remarked Brother

Jimson soothingly as he dodged the shovel, the broom, the coal-hod and the stove-covers. But he sighed with relief as he turned into the street and caught the faint sound of the washboard now resumed.

To a New Englander the season of snow and ice with its clear biting atmosphere, is the ideal time for the great festival. Christmas morning dawned in royal splendor; the sun kissed the snowy streets and turned the icicles into brilliant stalactites. The bells rang a joyous call from every steeple, and soon the churches were crowded with eager worshippers—eager to hear again the oft-repeated, the wonderful story on which the heart of the whole Christian world feeds its faith and hope. Words of tender faith, marvelous in their simplicity fell from the lips of a world-renowned preacher, and touched the hearts of the listening multitude:

"The winter sunshine is not more bright and clear than the atmosphere of living joy, which stretching back between our eyes and that picture of Bethlehem, shows us its beauty in unstained freshness. And as we open once again those chapters of the gospel in which the ever fresh and living picture stands, there seems from year to year always to come some newer, brighter meaning into the words that tell the tale.

"St. Matthew says that when Jesus was born in Bethlehem the wise men came from the East to Jerusalem. The East means man's search after God; Jerusalem means God's search after man. The East means the religion of the devout soul; Jerusalem means the religion of the merciful God. The East means Job's cry, 'Oh, that I knew where I might find him!' Jerusalem means 'Immanuel—God with us.' ''

Then the deep-toned organ joined the grand chorus of human voices in a fervent hymn of praise and thanksgiving:

> Lo! the Morning Star appeareth,
>   O'er the world His beams are cast;
> He the Alpha and Omega,
>   He, the Great, the First the Last!
> Hallelujah! hallelujah!
>   Let the heavenly portal ring!
> Christ is born, the Prince of glory!
>   Christ the Lord, Messiah, King!

Everyone of prominence in church circles had been bidden to the Jimson wedding. The presents were many and costly. Early after service on Christmas morning the vestry room was taken in hand by leading sisters to prepare the tables for the supper, for on account of the host of friends bidden to the feast, the reception was to be held in the vestry.

The tables groaned beneath their loads of turkey, salads, pies, puddings, cakes and fancy ices.

Yards and yards of evergreen wreaths encircled the granite pillars; the altar was banked with potted plants and cut flowers. It was a beautiful sight. The main aisle was roped off for the invited guests with white satin ribbons.

Brother Jimson's patrons were to be present in a body, and they had sent the bride a solid silver service, so magnificent that the sisters could only sigh with envy.

The ceremony was to take place at seven sharp. Long before that hour the ushers in full evening dress were ready to receive the guests. Sister Maria Nash was among the first to arrive, and even the Queen of Sheba was not arrayed like unto her. At fifteen minutes before the hour, the organist began an elaborate instrumental performance. There was an expectant hush and much head-turning when the music changed to the familiar strains of the "Wedding March." The minister took his place inside the railing ready to receive the party. The groom waited at the altar.

First came the ushers, then the maids of honor, then the flower girl—daughter of a prominent member—carrying a basket of flowers which she scattered before the bride, who was on the arm of the best man. In the bustle and confusion incident to the entrance of the wedding party no one noticed a group of strangers accompanied by Andy Nash enter and occupy seats near the door.

The service began. All was quiet. The pastor's words fell clearly upon the listening ears. He had reached the words:

"If any man can show just cause, etc.," when like a thunder-clap came a voice from the back part of the house—an angry excited voice, and a woman of ponderous avoirdupois advanced up the aisle.

"Hol' on that, pastor, hol' on! A man cain't have but one wife 'cause it's agin' the law. I'm Abe Jimson's lawful wife, an' hyars his six children—all boys—to pint out their daddy." In an instant the assembly was in confusion.

"My soul," exclaimed Viney Peters, "the ol' ser-

pent! An' to think how near I come to takin' up with
him. I'm glad I ain't Car'mel.''

Sis'r Maria said nothing, but a smile of triumph lit
up her countenance.

''Brother Jimson, is this true?'' demanded the minister, sternly. But Abraham Jimson was past answering.
His face was ashen, his teeth chattering, his hair standing on end. His shaking limbs refused to uphold his
weight; he sank upon his knees on the steps of the altar.

But now a hand was laid upon his shoulder and Mrs.
Jimson hauled him upon his feet with a jerk.

''Abe Jimson, you know me. You run'd 'way from
me up North fifteen year ago, an' you hid yourself like
a groun' hog in a hole, but I've got you. There'll be no
new wife in the Jimson family this week. I'm yer fus'
wife and I'll be yer las' one. Git up hyar now, you
mis'able sinner an' tell the pastor who I be.'' Brother
Jimson meekly obeyed the clarion voice. His sanctified
air had vanished; his pride humbled into the dust.

''Pastor,'' came in trembling tones from his quiver-
ing lips. ''These are mighty ticklish times.'' He paused.
A deep silence followed his words. ''I'm a weak-kneed,
mis'able sinner. I have fallen under temptation. This is
Ma' Jane, my wife, an' these hyar boys is my sons,
God forgive me.''

The bride, who had been forgotten now, broke in:

''Abraham Jimson, you ought to be hung. I'm going
to sue you for breach of promise.'' It was a fatal remark. Mrs. Jimson turned upon her.

''You will, will you? Sue him, will you? I'll make a
choc'late Car'mel of you befo' I'm done with you, you
'ceitful hussy, hoo-dooin' hones' men from thar wives.''

She sprang upon the girl, tearing, biting, rendering.

The satin gown and gossamer veil were reduced to rags. Caramel emitted a series of ear-splitting shrieks, but the biting and tearing went on. How it might have ended no one can tell if Andy had not sprang over the backs of the pews and grappled with the infuriated woman.

The excitement was intense. Men and women struggled to get out of the church. Some jumped from the windows and others crawled under the pews, where they were secure from violence. In the midst of the melee, Brother Jimson disappeared and was never seen again, and Mrs. Jimson came into the possession of his property by due process of law.

In the church Abraham Jimson's wedding and his fall from grace is still spoken of in eloquent whispers.

In the home of Mrs. Andy Nash a motto adorns the parlor walls worked in scarlet wool and handsomely framed in gilt. The text reads: "Ye are the salt of the earth; there is nothing hidden that shall not be revealed."

Charles W. Chesnutt

(1858–1932)

The best Negro fiction writer before Richard Wright, Charles Waddell Chesnutt wrote usually about some aspects of the American "color line," whether within the race or between the races. A "volunteer Negro" himself, that is, one who could easily "pass for white" and who was offered two promising opportunities to do so, Chesnutt remained with his people and devoted his life to the black's fight for equality. Unlike Dunbar, he was a "protest" writer, attacking in his fiction the portrayal of American blacks given by such nationally popular southern writers as Joel Chandler Harris, Thomas Dixon, Thomas Nelson Page, and others.

Born in Cleveland, Ohio, of free parents who had left their home in Fayetteville, North Carolina, because of pressures put on free blacks, Chesnutt was eight years old when his father in 1866 decided to take his family back to Fayetteville. There he attended the public rural school, his only formal education; there he finally became a teacher himself and was offered the principalship of a state normal school. Possessing a brilliant mind and an indomitable will, Chesnutt taught himself Latin, German, French, mathematics, and subsequently stenography and law. After his marriage in 1878, he became tired of the South and decided to leave for greener pastures. In 1883 he spent a year in New York City as a court stenographer and journalist. The following year he moved his family back to Cleveland. There he became a successful legal stenographer and lawyer, having passed in 1887 the Ohio bar at the top of his "class"; at this time his writing career began.

After several minor works of his were printed in minor publications, Chesnutt's "The Goophered Grapevine" was accepted by the *Atlantic Monthly* in 1887 and "Po Sandy" in 1888. These two short stories were the opening door to the nation's top publishing opportunities, but the door was not yet fully opened. Chesnutt by 1889 had finished his first novel, which was called initially *Rena Walden;* it was turned down because of its subject: interracial marriage. The publishers were saying in effect: short stories about folk material are all right for a black author, but the interracial marriage theme—No! After several rewrites, the book was eventually published in 1900 with the title *The House behind the Cedars.*

In 1899, with the help of Walter Hines Page, editor of the *Atlantic Monthly,* Chesnutt's *The Conjure Woman,* seven southern folklore stories, was published by Houghton Mifflin. In the same year *The Wife of His Youth and Other Stories of the Color Line,* a second volume of stories, was brought out. Two novels followed: *The Marrow of Tradition* (1901), based on the Wilmington Riot, and *The Colonel's Dream* (1905), one of Chesnutt's bitterest protest works. One of his best short stories, "Baxter's Procrustes," was published in the *Atlantic* (June 1904). It had nothing to do with race. Charles W. Chesnutt was given the Spingarn Medal in 1928 for his "pioneer work as a literary artist." He published his last work in 1931, an article for the *Colophon* called "Post Bellum–Pre-Harlem." Chesnutt died in 1932.

Charles W. Chesnutt is not as popular among readers and scholars as he should be. Post-1960s generation do not understand fully the conditions, particularly the color-line emphasis, about which he writes so consistently and dramatically. However, his works helped to make possible the freedom (however limited) which blacks now have in America. As a strong writer of protest fiction, as a pioneer in opening doors for blacks to the nation's major periodicals and publishing firms, as a skillful user of folk material, especially in his short stories, and as a fighter for civil rights in his private and public life, Chesnutt deserves much more recognition than he now has. Any scholar interested in the black's position in America from roughly 1890 to 1920 could benefit greatly from an in-depth reading of Chesnutt's works.

For comment on Charles W. Chesnutt's life and writings see the full-length critical biography by Frances R. Keller, *An American Crusade: The Life of Charles Waddell Chesnutt* (1977); see also the biography by his daughter, Helen M. Chesnutt, *Charles Waddell Chesnutt: Pioneer of the Color Line* (1952). This work contains *inter alia* many letters showing Chesnutt's intimacy with such people as George W. Cable, Walter Hines Page, Mark Twain, Booker T. Washington, and others. Sylvia Lyons Render's edition of *The Short Fiction of Charles W. Chesnutt* (1974, 1980) has an excellent introduction. The entry in *Dictionary of American Negro Biography* by John W. Wideman gives among other fine things "nec-

essarily short descriptions of Chesnutt's major works,"
which are quite useful. The most recent evaluation of
Chesnutt's literary achievement is *The Literary Career of
Charles W. Chesnutt* by William L. Andrews (1980).
Charles W. Chesnutt: A Reference Guide by Curtis W.
Ellison and E. W. Metcalf, Jr., was published in 1977.
Additional recent commentary can be found in Bernard
W. Bell's *The Afro-American Novel and Its Tradition*
(1987).

"The Goophered Grapevine" was originally published
in *The Conjure Woman* by Houghton Mifflin Company in
1899. "The Wife of His Youth" comes originally from
*The Wife of His Youth and Other Stories of the Color
Line,* also published in 1899 by Houghton Mifflin. Both
stories are found in Sylvia Lyons Render's *The Short Fiction of Charles W. Chesnutt* (1974).

THE GOOPHERED GRAPEVINE

Some years ago my wife was in poor health, and our
family doctor, in whose skill and honesty I had implicit
confidence, advised a change of climate. I shared, from
an unprofessional standpoint, his opinion that the raw
winds, the chill rains, and violent changes of tempera-
ture that characterized the winters in the region of the
Great Lakes tended to aggravate my wife's difficulty,
and would undoubtedly shorten her life if she remained
exposed to them. The doctor's advice was that we seek,
not a temporary place of sojourn, but a permanent residence, in a warmer and more equable climate. I was engaged at the time in grape-culture in northern Ohio, and,
as I liked the business and had given it much study, I

decided to look for some other locality suitable for carrying it on. I thought of sunny France, of sleepy Spain, of Southern California, but there were objections to them all. It occurred to me that I might find what I wanted in some one of our own Southern States. It was a sufficient time after the war for conditions in the South to have become somewhat settled; and I was enough of a pioneer to start a new industry, if I could not find a place where grape-culture had been tried. I wrote to a cousin who had gone into the turpentine business in central North Carolina. He assured me, in response to my inquiries, that no better place could be found in the South than the State and neighborhood where he lived; the climate was perfect for health, and, in conjunction with the soil, ideal for grape-culture; labor was cheap, and land could be bought for a mere song. He gave us a cordial invitation to come and visit him while we looked into the matter. We accepted the invitation, and after several days of leisurely travel, the last hundred miles of which were up a river on a side-wheel steamer, we reached our destination, a quaint old town, which I shall call Patesville, because, for one reason, that is not its name. There was a red brick market-house in the public square, with a tall tower, which held a four-faced clock that struck the hours, and from which there pealed out a curfew at nine o'clock. There were two or three hotels, a court-house, a jail, stores, offices, and all the appurtenances of a county seat and a commercial emporium; for while Patesville numbered only four or five thousand inhabitants, of all shades of complexion, it was one of the principal towns in North Carolina, and had a considerable trade in cotton and naval stores. This business activity was not immediately apparent to my unaccustomed eyes. Indeed, when I first saw the town, there brooded over it a calm that seemed almost sabbatic in its restfulness, though I learned later on that underneath its somnolent exterior the deeper currents of life—love and hatred, joy and despair, ambition and avarice, faith and friendship—flowed not less steadily than in livelier latitudes.

We found the weather delightful at that season, the end of summer, and were hospitably entertained. Our host was a man of means and evidently regarded our visit as a pleasure, and we were therefore correspondingly at our ease, and in a position to act with the coolness of judgment desirable in making so radical a change in our lives. My cousin placed a horse and buggy at our disposal, and himself acted as our guide until I became somewhat familiar with the country.

I found that grape-culture, while it had never been carried on to any great extent, was not entirely unknown in the neighborhood. Several planters thereabouts had attempted it on a commercial scale, in former years, with greater or less success; but like most Southern industries, it had felt the blight of war and had fallen into desuetude.

I went several times to look at a place that I thought might suit me. It was a plantation of considerable extent, that had formerly belonged to a wealthy man by the name of McAdoo. The estate had been for years involved in litigation between disputing heirs, during which period shiftless cultivation had well-nigh exhausted the soil. There had been a vineyard of some extent on the place, but it had not been attended to since the war, and had lapsed into utter neglect. The vines—here partly supported by decayed and broken-down trellises, there twining themselves among the branches of the slender saplings which had sprung up among them—grew in wild and unpruned luxuriance, and the few scattered grapes they bore were the undisputed prey of the first comer. The site was admirably adapted to grape-raising; the soil, with a little attention, could not have been better; and with the native grape, the luscious scuppernong, as my main reliance in the beginning, I felt sure that I could introduce and cultivate successfully a number of other varieties.

One day I went over with my wife to show her the place. We drove out of the town over a long wooden bridge that spanned a spreading mill-pond, passed the long whitewashed fence surrounding the county fair-ground, and struck into a road so sandy that the horse's feet sank to the fetlocks. Our route lay partly up hill and partly down, for we were in the sand-hill county; we drove past cultivated farms, and then by abandoned fields grown up in scrub-oak and short-leaved pine, and once or twice through the solemn aisles of the virgin forest, where the tall pines, well-nigh meeting over the narrow road, shut out the sun, and wrapped us in clois-tral solitude. Once, at a cross-roads, I was in doubt as to the turn to take, and we sat there waiting ten minutes— we had already caught some of the native infection of restfulness—for some human being to come along, who could direct us on our way. At length a little negro girl appeared, walking straight as an arrow, with a piggin full of water on her head. After a little patient investiga-tion, necessary to overcome the child's shyness, we learned what we wished to know, and at the end of about five miles from the town reached our destination.

We drove between a pair of decayed gateposts—the

gate itself had long since disappeared—and up a straight
sandy lane, between two lines of rotting rail fence,
partly concealed by jimson-weeds and briers, to the
open space where a dwelling-house had once stood, evidently a spacious mansion, if we might judge from the
ruined chimneys that were still standing, and the brick
pillars on which the sills rested. The house itself, we
had been informed, had fallen a victim to the fortunes
of war.

We alighted from the buggy, walked about the yard
for a while, and then wandered off into the adjoining
vineyard. Upon Annie's complaining of weariness I led
the way back to the yard, where a pine log, lying under
a spreading elm, afforded a shady though somewhat
hard seat. One end of the log was already occupied by a
venerable-looking colored man. He held on his knees a
hat full of grapes, over which he was smacking his lips
with great gusto, and a pile of grape-skins near him indicated that the performance was no new thing. We approached him at an angle from the rear, and were close
to him before he perceived us. He respectfully rose as
we drew near, and was moving away, when I begged
him to keep his seat.

"Don't let us disturb you," I said. "There is plenty
of room for us all."

He resumed his seat with somewhat of embarrassment. While he had been standing, I had observed that
he was a tall man, and, though slightly bowed by the
weight of years, apparently quite vigorous. He was not
entirely black, and this fact, together with the quality of
his hair, which was about six inches long and very
bushy, except on the top of his head, where he was
quite bald, suggested a slight strain of other than negro

blood. There was a shrewdness in his eyes, too, which was not altogether African, and which, as we afterwards learned from experience, was indicative of a corresponding shrewdness in his character. He went on eating the grapes, but did not seem to enjoy himself quite so well as he had apparently done before he became aware of our presence.

"Do you live around here?" I asked, anxious to put him at his ease.

"Yas, suh. I lives des ober yander, behine de nex' san'-hill, on de Lumberton plank-road."

"Do you know anything about the time when this vineyard was cultivated?"

"Lawd bless you, suh, I knows all about it. Dey ain' na'er a man in dis settlement w'at won' tell you ole Julius McAdoo 'uz bawn en raise' on dis yer same plantation. Is you de Norv'n gemman w'at's gwine ter buy de ole vimya'd?"

"I am looking at it," I replied; "but I don't know that I shall care to buy unless I can be reasonably sure of making something out of it."

"Well, suh, you is a stranger ter me, en I is a stranger ter you, en we is bofe strangers ter one anudder, but 'f I 'uz in yo' place, I would n' buy dis vimya'd."

"Why not?" I asked.

"Well, I dunno whe'r you b'lieves in cunj'in' er not,—some er de w'ite folks don't, er says dey don't,—but de truf er de matter is dat dis yer ole vimya'd is goophered."

"Is what?" I asked, not grasping the meaning of this unfamiliar word.

"Is goophered,—conju'd, bewitch'."

He imparted this information with such solemn earnestness, and with such an air of confidential mystery, that I felt somewhat interested, while Annie was evidently much impressed, and drew closer to me.

"How do you know it is bewitched?" I asked.

"I would n' spec' fer you ter b'lieve me 'less you know all 'bout de fac's. But ef you en young miss dere doan' mine' lis'nin' ter a ole nigger run on a minute er two w'ile you er restin', I kin 'splain to you how it all happen'."

We assured him that we would be glad to hear how it all happened, and he began to tell us. At first the current of his memory—or imagination—seemed somewhat sluggish; but as his embarrassment wore off, his language flowed more freely, and the story acquired perspective and coherence. As he became more and more absorbed in the narrative, his eyes assumed a dreamy expression, and he seemed to lose sight of his auditors, and to be living over again in monologue his life on the old plantation.

"Ole Mars Dugal' McAdoo," he began, "bought dis place long many years befo' de wah, en I 'member well w'en he sot out all dis yer part er de plantation in scuppernon's. De vimes growed monst'us fas', en Mars Dugal' made a thousan' gallon er scuppernon' wine eve'y year.

"Now, ef dey's an'thing a nigger lub, nex' ter 'possum, en chick'n, en watermillyums, it's scuppernon's. Dey ain' nuffin dat kin stan' up side'n de scuppernon' for sweetness; sugar ain't a suckumstance ter scuppernon'. W'en de season is nigh 'bout ober, en de grapes begin ter swivel up des a little wid de wrinkles er ole age,—w'en de skin git sof' en brown,—den de scupper-

non' make you smack yo' lip en roll yo' eye en wush
fer mo'; so I reckon it ain' very 'stonishin' dat niggers
lub scuppernon'.

"Dey wuz a sight er niggers in de naberhood er de
vimya'd. Dere wuz ole Mars Henry Brayboy's niggers,
en ole Mars Jeems McLean's niggers, en Mars Dugal's
own niggers; den dey wuz a settlement er free niggers
en po' buckrahs down by de Wim'l'ton Road, en Mars
Dugal' had de only vimya'd in de naberhood. I reckon
it ain' so much so nowadays, but befo' de wah, in
slab'ry times, a nigger did n' mine goin' fi' er ten mile
in a night, w'en dey wuz sump'n good ter eat at de
yuther een'.

"So atter a w'ile Mars Dugal' begin ter miss his
scuppernon's. Co'se he 'cuse' de niggers er it, but dey
all 'nied it ter de las'. Mars Dugal' sot spring guns en
steel traps, en he en de oberseah sot up nights once't er
twice't, tel one night Mars Dugal'—he 'uz a monst'us
keerless man—got his leg shot full er cow-peas. But
somehow er nudder dey could n' nebber ketch none er
de niggers. I dunner how it happen, but it happen des
like I tell you, en de grapes kep' on agoin' des de same.

"But bimeby ole Mars Dugal' fix' up a plan ter stop
it. Dey wuz a conjuh 'oman livin' down 'mongs' de
free niggers on de Wim'l'ton Road, en all de darkies
fum Rockfish ter Beaver Crick wuz feared er her. She
could wuk de mos' powerfulles' kin' er goopher,—
could make people hab fits, er rheumatiz, er make 'em
des dwinel away en die; en dey say she went out ridin'
de niggers at night, fer she wuz a witch 'sides bein' a
conjuh 'oman. Mars Dugal' hearn 'bout Aun' Peggy's
doin's, en begun ter 'flect whe'r er no he could n' git
her ter he'p him keep de niggers off'n de grapevimes.

One day in de spring er de year, ole miss pack' up a basket er chick'n en poun'-cake, en a bottle er scuppernon' wine, en Mars Dugal' tuk it in his buggy en driv ober ter Aun' Peggy's cabin. He tuk de basket in, en had a long talk wid Aun' Peggy.

"De nex' day Aun' Peggy come up ter de vimya'd. De niggers seed her slippin' 'roun', en dey soon foun' out what she 'uz doin' dere. Mars Dugal' had hi'ed her ter goopher de grapevimes. She sa'ntered 'roun' 'mongs' de vimes, en tuk a leaf fum dis one, en a grape-hull fum dat one, en a grape-seed fum anudder one; en den a little twig fum here, en a little pinch er dirt fum dere,—en put it all in a big black bottle, wid a snake's toof en a speckle' hen's gall en some ha'rs fum a black cat's tail, en den fill' de bottle wid scuppernon' wine. W'en she got de goopher all ready en fix', she tuk'n went out in de woods en buried it under de root uv a red oak tree, en den come back en tole one er de niggers she done goopher de grapevimes, en a'er a nigger w'at eat dem grapes 'ud be sho ter die inside'n twel' mont's.

"Atter dat de niggers let de scuppernon's 'lone, en Mars Dugal' did n' hab no 'casion ter fine no mo' fault; en de season wuz mos' gone, w'en a strange gemman stop at de plantation one night ter see Mars Dugal' on some business; en his coachman, seein' de scuppernon's growin' so nice en sweet, slip 'roun' behine de smoke-house, en et all de scuppernon's he could hole. Nobody did n' notice it at de time, but dat night, on de way home, de gemman's hoss runned away en kill' de coachman. W'en we hearn de noos, Aun' Lucy, de cook, she up 'n say she seed de strange nigger eat'n' er de scuppernon's behine de smoke-house; en den we

knowed de goopher had b'en er wukkin'. Den one er de
nigger chilluns runned away fum de quarters one day,
en got in de scuppernon's, en died de nex' week. W'ite
folks say he die' er de fevuh, but de niggers knowed it
wuz de goopher. So you k'n be sho de darkies did n'
hab much ter do wid dem scuppernon' vimes.

"W'en de scuppernon' season 'uz ober fer dat year,
Mars Dugal' foun' he had made fifteen hund'ed gallon
er wine; en one er de niggers hearn him laffin' wid de
oberseah fit ter kill, en sayin' dem fifteen hund'ed gallon er wine wuz monst'us good intrus' on de ten dollars
he laid out on de vimya'd. So I 'low ez he paid Aun'
Peggy ten dollars fer to goopher de grapevimes.

"De goopher did n' wuk no mo' tel de nex' summer,
we'n 'long to'ds de middle er de season one er de fiel'
han's died; en ez dat lef' Mars Dugal' sho't er han's, he
went off ter town fer ter buy anudder. He fotch de noo
nigger home wid 'im. He wuz er ole nigger, er de color
er a gingy-cake, en ball ez a hoss-apple on de top er his
head. He wuz a peart ole nigger, do', en could do a big
day's wuk.

"Now it happen dat one er de niggers on de nex'
plantation, one er ole Mars Henry Brayboy's niggers,
had runned away de day befo', en tuk ter de swamp, en
ole Mars Dugal' en some er de yuther nabor w'ite folks
had gone out wid dere guns en dere dogs fer ter he'p
'em hunt fer de nigger; en de han's on our own plantation wuz all so flusterated dat we fuhgot ter tell de noo
han' 'bout de goopher on de scuppernon' vimes. Co'se
he smell de grapes en see de vimes, an atter dahk de
fus' thing he done wuz ter slip off ter de grapevimes
'dout sayin' nuffin to nobody. Nex' mawnin' he tole

some er de niggers 'bout de fine bait er scuppernon' he
et de night befo'.

"W'en dey tole 'im 'bout de goopher on de grapevimes, he 'uz dat tarrified dat he turn pale, en look des
like he gwine ter die right in his tracks. De oberseah
come up en axed w'at 'uz de matter; en w'en dey tole
'im Henry be'n eatin' er de scuppernon's, en got de
goopher on 'im, he gin Henry a big drink er w'iskey, en
'low dat de nex' rainy day he take 'im ober ter Aun'
Peggy's, en see ef she would n' take de goopher off'n
him, seein' ez he did n' know nuffin erbout it tel he
done et de grapes.

"Sho nuff, it rain de nex' day, en de oberseah went
ober ter Aun' Peggy's wid Henry. En Aun' Peggy say
dat bein' ez Henry did n' know 'bout de goopher, en et
de grapes in ign'ance er de conseq'ences, she reckon
she mought be able fer ter take de goopher off'n him.
So she fotch out er bottle wid some conjuh medicine in
it, en po'd some out in a go'd fer Henry ter drink. He
manage ter git it down; he say it tas'e like whiskey wid
sump'n bitter in it. She 'lowed dat 'ud keep de goopher
off'n him tel de spring; but w'en de sap begin ter rise
in de grapevimes he ha'ter come en see her ag'in, en
she tell him w'at e's ter do.

"Nex' spring, w'en de sap commence' ter rise in de
scuppernon' vime, Henry tuk a ham one night. Whar 'd
he git de ham? *I* doan know; dey wa'n't no hams on de
plantation 'cep'n' w'at 'uz in de smoke-house, but *I*
never see Henry 'bout de smoke-house. But ez I wuz a-
sayin', he tuk de ham ober ter Aun' Peggy's; en Aun'
Peggy tole 'im dat w'en Mars Dugal' begin ter prune de
grapevimes, he mus' go en take 'n scrape off de sap
whar it ooze out'n de cut een's er de vimes, en 'n'int

his ball head wid it; en ef he do dat once't a year de goopher would n' wuk agin 'im long ez he done it. En bein' ez he fotch her de ham, she fix' it so he kin eat all de scuppernon' he want.

"So Henry 'n'int his head wid de sap out'n de big grapevime des ha'f way 'twix' de quarters en de big house, en de goopher nebber wuk agin him dat summer. But de beatenes' thing you eber see happen ter Henry. Up ter dat time he wuz ez ball ez a sweeten' 'tater, but des ez soon ez de young leaves begun ter come out on de grapevimes, de ha'r begun ter grow out on Henry's head, en by de middle er de summer he had de bigges' head er ha'r on de plantation. Befo' dat, Henry had tol'-able good ha'r 'round' de aidges, but soon ez de young grapes begun ter come, Henry's ha'r begun to quirl all up in little balls, des like dis yer reg'lar grapy ha'r, en by de time de grapes got ripe his head look des like a bunch er grapes. Combin' it did n' do no good; he wuk at it ha'f de night wid er Jim Crow,* en think he git it straighten' out, but in de mawnin' de grapes 'ud be dere des de same. So he gin it up, en tried ter keep de grapes down by havin' his ha'r cut sho't.

"But dat wa'n't de quares' thing 'bout de goopher. When Henry come ter de plantation, he wuz gittin' a lit-tle ole an stiff in de j'ints. But dat summer he got des ez spry en libely ez any young nigger on de plantation; fac', he got so biggity dat Mars Jackson, de oberseah, ha' ter th'eaten ter whip 'im, if he did n' stop cuttin' up his didos en behave hisse'f. But de mos' cur'ouses'

---

*A small card, resembling a currycomb in construction, and used by negroes [sic] in the rural districts instead of a comb.

thing happen' in de fall, when de sap begin ter go down in de grapevimes. Fus', when de grapes 'uz gethered, de knots begun ter straighten out'n Henry's ha'r; en w'en de leaves begin ter fall, Henry's ha'r 'mence' ter drap out; en when de vimes 'uz bar', Henry's head wuz baller 'n it wuz in de spring, en he begin ter git ole en stiff in de j'ints ag'in, en paid no mo' 'tention ter de gals dyoin' er de whole winter. En nex' spring, w'en he rub de sap on ag'in, he got young ag'in, en so soopl en libely dat none er de young niggers on de plantation could n' jump, ner dance, ner hoe ez much cotton ez Henry. But in de fall er de year his grapes 'mence' ter straighten out, en his j'ints ter git stiff, en his ha'r drap off, en de rheumatiz begin ter wrastle wid'im.

"Now, ef you'd 'a' knowed ole Mars Dugal' Mc-Adoo, you'd 'a' knowed dat it ha' ter be a mighty rainy day when he could n' fine sump'n fer his niggers ter do, en it ha' ter be a mighty little hole he could n' crawl thoo, en ha' ter be a monst'us cloudy night when a dollar git by him in de dahkness; en w'en he see how Henry git young in de spring en ole in de fall, he 'lowed ter hisse'f ez how he could make mo' money out'n Henry dan by wukkin' him in de cotton-fiel'. 'Long de nex' spring, atter de sap 'mence' ter rise, en Henry 'n'int 'is head en sta'ted fer ter git young en soopl, Mars Dugal' up 'n tuk Henry ter town, en sole 'im fer fifteen hunder' dollars. Co'se de man w'at bought Henry did n' know nuffin 'bout de goopher, en Mars Dugal' did n' see no 'casion fer ter tell 'im. Long to'ds de fall, w'en de sap went down, Henry begin ter git ole ag'in same ez yu-zhal, en his noo marster begin to git skeered les'n he gwine ter lose his fifteen-hunder'-dollar nigger. He sent fer a mighty fine doctor,

but de med'cine did n' 'pear ter do no good; de
goopher had a good holt. Henry tole de doctor 'bout de
goopher, but de doctor des laff at 'im.

"One day in de winter Mars Dugal' went ter town,
en wuz santerin' 'long de Main Street, when who
should he meet but Henry's noo marster. Dey said
'Hoddy,' en Mars Dugal' ax 'im ter hab a seegyar; en
atter dey run on awhile 'bout de craps en de weather,
Mars Dugal' ax 'im, sorter keerless, like ez ef he des
thought of it,—

" 'How you like de nigger I sole you las' spring?'

"Henry's master shuck his head en knock de ashes
off'n his seegyar.

" 'Spec' I made a bad bahgin when I bought dat nigger. Henry done good wuk all de summer, but sence de
fall set in he 'pears ter be sorter pinin' away. Dey ain'
nuffin pertickler de matter wid 'im—leastways de doctor
say so—'cep'n' a tech er de rheumatiz; but his ha'r is
all fell out, en ef he don't pick up his strenk mighty
soon, I spec' I'm gwine ter lose 'im.'

"Dey smoked on awhile, en bimeby ole mars say,
'Well, a bahgin's a bahgin, but you en me is good
fren's, en I doan wan 'ter see you lose all de money
you paid fer dat nigger; en ef wa't you say is so, en I
ain't 'sputin' it, he ain't wuf much now. I 'spec's you
wukked him too ha'd dis summer, er e'se de swamps
down here don't agree wid de san'-hill nigger. So you
des lemme know, en ef he gits any wusser I 'll be wil-
lin' ter gib yer five hund'ed dollars fer 'im, en take my
chances on his livin'.'

"Sho 'nuff, when Henry begun ter draw up wid de
rheumatiz en it look like he gwine ter die fer sho, his
noo marster sen' fer Mars Dugal', en Mars Dugal' gin

him what he promus, en brung Henry home ag'in. He tuk good keer uv 'im dyoin' er de winter,—give 'im w'iskey ter rub his rheumatiz, en terbacker ter smoke, en all he want ter eat,—'caze a nigger w'at he could make a thousan' dollars a year off'n did n' grow on eve'y huckleberry bush.

"Nex' spring, w'en de sap ris en Henry's ha'r commence' ter sprout, Mars Dugal' sole 'im ag'in, down in Robeson County dis time; en he kep' dat sellin' business up fer five year er mo'. Henry nebber say nuffin 'bout de goopher ter his noo marsters, 'caze he know he gwine ter be tuk good keer uv de nex' winter, w'en Mars Dugal' buy him back. En Mars Dugal' made 'nuff money off'n Henry ter buy anudder plantation ober on Beaver Crick.

"But 'long 'bout de een' er dat five year dey come a stranger ter stop at de plantation. De fus' day he 'uz dere he went out wid Mars Dugal' en spent all de mawnin' lookin' ober de vimya'd, en atter dinner dey spent all de evenin' playin' kya'ds. De niggers soon 'skiver' dat he wuz a Yankee, en dat he come down ter Norf C'lina fer ter l'arn de w'ite folks how to raise grapes en make wine. He promus Mars Dugal' he c'd make de grapevimes b'ar twice't ez many grapes, en dat de noo winepress he wuz a-sellin' would make mo' d'n twice't ez many gallons er wine. En ole Mars Dugal' des drunk it all in, des 'peared ter be bewitch' wid dat Yankee. W'en de darkies see dat Yankee runnin' 'roun' de vimya'd en diggin' under de grapevimes, dey shuk dere heads, en 'lowed dat dey feared Mars Dugal' losin' his min'. Mars Dugal' had all de dirt dug away fum under de roots er all de scuppernon' vimes, an' let 'em stan' dat away fer a week er mo'. Den dat Yankee made de niggers fix up a mixtry er lime en ashes en manyo, en po' it 'roun' de roots er de grapevimes. Den he 'vise Mars Dugal' fer ter trim de vimes close't, en Mars Dugal' tuck 'n done eve'ything de Yankee tole him ter do. Dyoin' all er dis time, mind yer, dis yer Yankee wuz libbin' off'n de fat er de lan', at de big house, en playin' kya'ds wid Mars Dugal' eve'y night; en dey say Mars Dugal' los' mo'n a thousan' dollars dyoin' er de week dat Yankee wuz a-ruinin' de grapevimes.

"W'en de sap ris nex' spring, ole Henry 'n'inted his head ez yuzhal, en his ha'r 'mence' ter grow des de same ez it done eve'y year. De scuppernon' vimes growed monst's fas', en de leaves wuz greener en thicker dan dey eber be'n dyoin' my remem'ance; en Henry's ha'r growed out thicker dan eber, en he 'peared ter git younger 'n younger, en soopler 'n soopler; en seein' ez he wuz sho't ter han's dat spring, havin' tuk in consid'able noo groun', Mars Dugal' 'cluded he would n' sell Henry 'tel he git de crap in en de cotton chop'. So he kep' Henry on de plantation.

"But 'long 'bout time fer de grapes ter come on de scuppernon' vimes, dey 'peared ter come a change ober 'em; de leaves withered en swivel' up, en de young grapes turn' yaller, en bimeby eve'ybody on de plantation could see dat de whole vimeya'd wuz dyin'. Mars Dugal' tuk 'n water de vimes en done all he could, but 't wa'n' no use; dat Yankee had done bus' de watermillyum. One time de vimes picked up a bit, en Mars Dugal' 'lowed dey wuz gwine ter come out ag'in; but dat Yankee done dug too close under de roots, en prune de branches too close ter de vime, en all dat lime en ashes

done burn' de life out'n de vimes, en dey des kep' a-
with'in' en a-swivelin'.

"All dis time de goopher wuz a-wukkin.' When de
vimes sta'ted ter wither, Henry 'mence' ter complain er
his rheumatiz; en when de leaves begin ter dry up, his
ha'r 'mence' ter drap out. When de vimes fresh' up a
bit, Henry 'd git peart ag'in, en when de vimes wither'
ag'in, Henry 'd git ole ag'in, en des kep' gittin' mo' en
mo' fitten fer nuffin; he des pined away, en pined away,
en fine'ly tuk ter his cabin; en when de big vime whar
he got de sap ter 'n'int his head withered en turned
yaller en died, Henry died too,—des went out sorter like
a cannel. Dey did n't 'pear ter be nuffin de matter wid
'im, 'cep'n' de rheumatiz, but his strenk des dwinel'
away 'tel he did n' hab ernuff lef' ter draw his bref. De
goopher had got de under holt, en th'owed Henry dat
time fer good en all.

"Mars Dugal' tuk on might'ly 'bout losin' his vimes
en his nigger in de same year; en he swo' dat ef he
could git holt er dat Yankee he'd wear 'im ter a frazzle,
en den chaw up de frazzle; en he'd done it, too, for
Mars Dugal' 'uz a monst'us brash man w'en he once git
started. He sot de vimya'd out ober ag'in, but it wuz
th'ee er fo' year befo' de vimes got ter b'arin' any
scuppernon's.

"W'en de wah broke out, Mars Dugal' raise' a
comp'ny, en went off ter fight de Yankees. He say he
wuz mighty glad dat wah come, en he des want ter kill
a Yankee fer eve'y dollar he los' 'long er dat grape-
raisin' Yankee. En I 'spec' he would 'a' done it, too, if
de Yankees had n' s'picioned sump'n, en killed him
fus'. Atter de s'render ole miss move' ter town, de nig-

gers all scattered 'way fum de plantation, en de vimya'd
ain' be'n cultervated sence.''

"Is that story true?'' asked Annie doubtfully, but seriously, as the old man concluded his narrative.

"It's des ez true ez I 'm a-settin' here, miss. Dey 's
a easy way ter prove it: I kin lead de way right ter Henry's grave ober yander in de plantation buryin'-groun'.
En I tell yer w'at, marster, I would n' 'vise you to buy
dis yer ole vimya'd, 'case de goopher 's on it yit, en
dey ain' no tellin' w'en it's gwine ter crap out.''

"But I thought you said all the old vines died.''

"Dey did 'pear ter die, but a few un 'em come out
ag'in, en is mixed in 'mongs' de yuthers. I ain' skeered
ter eat de grapes, 'caze I knows de old vimes fum de
noo ones; but wid strangers dey ain' no tellin' w'at
mought happen. I would n' 'vise yer ter buy dis vimya'd.''

I bought the vineyard, nevertheless, and it has been
for a long time in a thriving condition, and is often referred to by the local press as a striking illustration of
the opportunities open to Northern capital in the development of Southern industries. The luscious scuppernong holds first rank among our grapes, though we
cultivate a great many other varieties, and our income
from grapes packed and shipped to the Northern markets is quite considerable. I have not noticed any devel-
opments of the goopher in the vineyard, although I have
a mild suspicion that our colored assistants do not suffer
from want of grapes during the season.

I found, when I bought the vineyard, that Uncle Julius had occupied a cabin on the place for many years,
and derived a respectable revenue from the product of
the neglected grapevines. This, doubtless, accounted for

his advice to me not to buy the vineyard, though whether it inspired the goopher story I am unable to state. I believe, however, that the wages I paid him for his services as coachman, for I gave him employment in that capacity, were more than an equivalent for anything he lost by the sale of the vineyard.

THE WIFE OF HIS YOUTH

1

Mr. Ryder was going to give a ball. There were several reasons why this was an opportune time for such an event.

Mr. Ryder might aptly be called the dean of the Blue Veins. The original Blue Veins were a little society of colored persons organized in a certain Northern city shortly after the war. Its purpose was to establish and maintain correct social standards among a people whose social condition presented almost unlimited room for improvement. By accident, combined perhaps with some natural affinity, the society consisted of individuals who were, generally speaking, more white than black. Some envious outsider made the suggestion that no one was eligible for membership who was not white enough to show blue veins. The suggestion was readily adopted by those who were not of the favored few, and since that time the society, though possessing a longer and more pretentious name, had been known far and wide as the "Blue Vein Society," and its members as the "Blue Veins."

The Blue Veins did not allow that any such requirement existed for admission to their circle, but, on the contrary, declared that character and culture were the only things considered; and that if most of their members were light-colored, it was because such persons, as a rule, had better opportunities to qualify themselves for membership. Opinions differed, too, as to the usefulness of the society. There were those who had been known to assail it violently as a glaring example of the very prejudice from which the colored race had suffered most; and later, when such critics had succeeded in getting on the inside, they had been heard to maintain with zeal and earnestness that the society was a life-boat, an anchor, a bulwark and a shield,—a pillar of cloud by day and of fire by night, to guide their people through the social wilderness. Another alleged prerequisite for Blue Vein membership was that of free birth; and while there was really no such requirement, it is doubtless true that very few of the members would have been unable to meet it if there had been. If there were one or two of the older members who had come up from the South and from slavery, their history presented enough romantic circumstances to rob their servile origin of its grosser aspects.

While there were no such tests of eligibility, it is true that the Blue Veins had their notions on these subjects, and that not all of them were equally liberal in regard to the things they collectively disclaimed. Mr. Ryder was one of the most conservative. Though he had not been among the founders of the society, but had come in some years later, his genius for social leadership was such that he had speedily become its recognized adviser and head, the custodian of its standards, and the preserver of its traditions. He shaped its social policy, was active in providing for its entertainment, and when the interest fell off, as it sometimes did, he fanned the embers until they burst again into a cheerful flame.

There were still other reasons for his popularity. While he was not as white as some of the Blue Veins, his appearance was such as to confer distinction upon them. His features were of a refined type, his hair was almost straight; he was always neatly dressed; his manners were irreproachable, and his morals above suspicion. He had come to Groveland a young man, and obtaining employment in the office of a railroad company as messenger had in time worked himself up to the position of stationery clerk, having charge of the distribution of the office supplies for the whole company. Although the lack of early training had hindered the orderly development of a naturally fine mind, it had not prevented him from doing a great deal of reading or from forming decidedly literary tastes. Poetry was his passion. He could repeat whole pages of the great English poets; and if his pronunciation was sometimes faulty, his eye, his voice, his gestures, would respond to the changing sentiment with a precision that revealed a poetic soul and disarmed criticism. He was economical, and had saved money; he owned and occupied a very comfortable house on a respectable street. His residence was handsomely furnished, containing among other things a good library, especially rich in poetry, a piano, and some choice engravings. He generally shared his house with some young couple, who looked after his wants and were company for him; for Mr. Ryder was a single man. In the early days of his connection with the Blue Veins he had been regarded as quite a catch, and young ladies and their mothers had manœuvered with much ingenuity to capture him. Not, however, until Mrs. Molly Dixon visited Groveland had any woman ever made him wish to change his condition to that of a married man.

Mrs. Dixon had come to Groveland from Washington in the spring, and before the summer was over she had won Mr. Ryder's heart. She possessed many attractive qualities. She was much younger than he; in fact, he was old enough to have been her father, though no one knew exactly how old he was. She was whiter than he, and better educated. She had moved in the best colored society of the country, at Washington, and had taught in the schools of that city. Such a superior person had been eagerly welcomed to the Blue Vein Society, and had taken a leading part in its activities. Mr. Ryder had at first been attracted by her charms of person, for she was very good looking and not over twenty-five; then by her refined manners and the vivacity of her wit. Her husband had been a government clerk, and at his death had left a considerable life insurance. She was visiting friends in Groveland, and, finding the town and the people to her liking, had prolonged her stay indefinitely. She had not seemed displeased at Mr. Ryder's attentions, but on the contrary had given him every proper encouragement; indeed, a younger and less cautious man would long since have spoken. But he had made up his mind, and had only to determine the time when he would ask her to be his wife. He decided to give a ball in her honor, and at some time during the evening of the ball to offer her his heart and hand. He had no special fears about the outcome, but, with a little touch of romance, he wanted the surroundings to be in harmony with his own feelings when he should have received the answer he expected.

Mr. Ryder resolved that this ball should mark an epoch in the social history of Groveland. He knew, of course,—no one could know better,—the entertainments that had taken place in past years, and what must be done to surpass them. His ball must be worthy of the lady in whose honor it was to be given, and must, by the quality of its guests, set an example for the future. He had observed of late a growing liberality, almost a laxity, in social matters, even among members of his own set, and had several times been forced to meet in a social way persons whose complexions and callings in life were hardly up to the standard which he considered proper for the society to maintain. He had a theory of his own.

"I have no race prejudice," he would say, "but we people of mixed blood are ground between the upper and the nether millstone. Our fate lies between absorption by the white race and extinction in the black. The one doesn't want us, but may take us in time. The other would welcome us, but it would be for us a backward step. 'With malice towards none, with charity for all,' we must do the best we can for ourselves and those who are to follow us. Self-preservation is the first law of nature."

His ball would serve by its exclusiveness to counteract leveling tendencies, and his marriage with Mrs. Dixon would help to further the upward process of absorption he had been wishing and waiting for.

2

The ball was to take place on Friday night. The house
had been put in order, the carpets covered with canvas,
the halls and stairs decorated with palms and potted
plants; and in the afternoon Mr. Ryder sat on his front
porch, which the shade of a vine running up over a wire
netting made a cool and pleasant lounging place. He expected to respond to the toast "The Ladies" at the supper, and from a volume of Tennyson—his favorite
poet—was fortifying himself with apt quotations. The
volume was open at "A Dream of Fair Women." His
eyes fell on these lines, and he read them aloud to judge
better of their effect:—

> At length I saw a lady within call,
>   Stiller than chisell'd marble, standing there;
> A daughter of the gods, divinely tall,
>   And most divinely fair.

He marked the verse, and turning the page read the
stanza beginning,—

> O sweet pale Margaret,
>   O rare pale Margaret.

He weighed the passage a moment, and decided that it
would not do. Mrs. Dixon was the palest lady he expected at the ball, and she was of a rather ruddy complexion, and of lively disposition and buxom build. So
he ran over the leaves until his eye rested on the description of Queen Guinevere:—

She seem'd a part of joyous Spring:
A gown of grass-green silk she wore,
Buckled with golden clasps before;
A light-green tuft of plumes she bore
Closed in a golden ring.

She look'd so lovely, as she sway'd
The rein with dainty finger-tips,
A man had given all other bliss,
And all his worldly worth for this,
To waste his whole heart in one kiss
Upon her perfect lips.

As Mr. Ryder murmured these words audibly, with
an appreciative thrill, he heard the latch of his gate
click, and a light footfall sounding on the steps. He
turned his head, and saw a woman standing before his
door.

She was a little woman, not five feet tall, and propor-
tioned to her height. Although she stood erect, and
looked around her with very bright and restless eyes,
she seemed quite old; for her face was crossed and re-
crossed with a hundred wrinkles, and around the edges
of her bonnet could be seen protruding here and there a
tuft of short gray wool. She wore a blue calico gown of
ancient cut, a little red shawl fastened around her shoulders with an old-fashioned brass brooch, and a large
bonnet profusely ornamented with faded red and yellow
artificial flowers. And she was very black,—so black
that her toothless gums, revealed when she opened her
mouth to speak, were not red, but blue. She looked like
a bit of the old plantation life, summoned up from the
past by the wave of a magician's wand, as the poet's

fancy had called into being the gracious shapes of which Mr. Ryder had just been reading.

He rose from his chair and came over to where she stood.

"Good-afternoon, madam," he said.

"Good-evenin', suh," she answered, ducking suddenly with a quaint curtsy. Her voice was shrill and piping, but softened somewhat by age. "Is dis yere whar Mistuh Ryduh lib, suh?" she asked, looking around her doubtfully, and glancing into the open windows, through which some of the preparations for the evening were visible.

"Yes," he replied, with an air of kindly patronage, unconsciously flattered by her manner, "I am Mr. Ryder. Did you want to see me?"

"Yas, suh, ef I ain't 'sturbin' of you too much."

"Not at all. Have a seat over here behind the vine, where it is cool. What can I do for you?"

" 'Scuse me, suh," she continued, when she had sat down on the edge of a chair, " 'scuse me, suh, I 's lookin' for my husban'. I heered you wuz a big man an' had libbed heah a long time, an' I 'lowed you wouldn't min' ef I 'd come roun' an' ax you ef you'd ever heered of a merlatter man by de name er Sam Taylor 'quirin' roun' in de chu'ches ermongs' de people fer his wife 'Liza Jane?"

Mr. Ryder seemed to think for a moment.

"There used to be many such cases right after the war," he said, "but it has been so long that I have forgotten them. There are very few now. But tell me your story, and it may refresh my memory."

She sat back farther in her chair so as to be more comfortable, and folded her withered hands in her lap.

"My name is 'Liza," she began, " 'Liza Jane. W'en
I wuz young I us'ter b'long ter Marse Bob Smif, down
in ole Missoura. I wuz bawn down dere. W'en I wuz a
gal I wuz married ter a man named Jim. But Jim died,
an' after dat I married a merlatter man named Sam Taylor. Sam wuz freebawn, but his mammy and daddy
died, an' de w'ite folks 'prenticed him ter my marster
fer ter work fer 'im 'tel he wuz growed up. Sam
worked in de fiel', an' I wuz de cook. One day Ma'y
Ann, ole miss's maid, came rushin' out ter de kitchen,
an' says she, ' 'Liza Jane, ole marse gwine sell yo' Sam
down de ribber.'

" 'Go way f'm yere,' says I; 'my husban' 's free!'

" 'Don' make no diff'ence. I heerd ole marse tell ole
miss he wuz gwine take yo' Sam 'way wid 'im ter-
morrow, fer he needed money, an' he knowed whar he
could git a t'ousan' dollars fer Sam an' no questions
axed.'

"W'en Sam come home f'm de fiel' dat night, I tole
him 'bout ole marse gwine steal 'im, an' Sam run erway. His time wuz mos' up, an' he swo' dat w'en he
wuz twenty-one he would come back an' he'p me run
erway, er else save up de money ter buy my freedom.
An' I know he'd 'a' done it, fer he thought a heap er
me, Sam did. But w'en he come back he did n' fin' me,
fer I wuz n' dere. Ole marse had heerd dat I warned
Sam, so he had me whip' an' sol' down de ribber.

"Den de wah broke out, an' w'en it wuz ober de
cullud folks wuz scattered. I went back ter de ole home;
but Sam wuz n' dere, an' I could n' l'arn nuffin' 'bout
'im. But I knowed he 'd be'n dere to look fer me an'
had n' foun' me, an' had gone erway ter hunt fer me.

"I 's be'n lookin' fer 'im eber sence," she added

simply, as though twenty-five years were but a couple of weeks, "an' I knows he 's be'n lookin' fer me. Fer he sot a heap er sto' by me, Sam did, an' I know he's be'n huntin' fer me all dese years,—'less'n he 's be'n sick er sump'n, so he could n' work, er out'n his head, so he could n' 'member his promise. I went back down de ribber, fer I 'lowed he 'd gone down dere lookin' fer me. I 's be'n ter Noo Orleens, an' Atlanty, an' Charleston, an' Richmon'; an' w'en I 'd be'n all ober de Souf I come ter de Norf. Fer I knows I 'll fin' 'im some er dese days," she added softly, "er he 'll fin' me, an' den we 'll bofe be as happy in freedom as we wuz in de ole days befo' de wah." A smile stole over her withered countenance as she paused a moment, and her bright eyes softened into a far-away look.

This was the substance of the old woman's story. She had wandered a little here and there. Mr. Ryder was looking at her curiously when she finished.

"How have you lived all these years?" he asked.

"Cookin', suh. I 's a good cook. Does you know anybody w'at needs a good cook, suh? I 's stoppin' wid a cullud fam'ly roun' de corner yonder 'tel I kin git a place."

"Do you really expect to find your husband? He may be dead long ago."

She shook her head emphatically. "Oh no, he ain' dead. De signs an' de tokens tells me. I dremp three nights runnin' on'y dis las' week dat I foun' him."

"He may have married another woman. Your slave marriage would not have prevented him, for you never lived with him after the war, and without that your marriage doesn't count."

"Would n' make no diff'ence wid Sam. He would n'

marry no yuther 'ooman 'tel he foun' out 'bout me. I knows it,'' she added. ''Sump'n 's be'n tellin' me all dese years dat I 's gwine fin' Sam 'fo' I dies.''

''Perhaps he's outgrown you, and climbed up in the world where he wouldn't care to have you find him.''

''No, indeed, suh,'' she replied, ''Sam ain' dat kin' er man. He wuz good ter me, Sam wuz, but he wuz n' much good ter nobody e'se, fer he wuz one er de triflin'- 'es' han's on de plantation. I 'spec's ter haf ter suppo't 'im w'en I fin' im, fer he nebber would work 'less'n he had ter. But den he wuz free, an' he did n' git no pay fer his work, an' I don' blame 'im much. Mebbe he's done better sence he run erway, but I ain' 'spectin' much.''

''You may have passed him on the street a hundred times during the twenty-five years, and not have known him; time works great changes.''

She smiled incredulously. ''I 'd know 'im 'mongs' a hund'ed men. Fer dey wuz n' no yuther merlatter man like my man Sam, an' I could n' be mistook. I 's toted his picture roun' wid me twenty-five years.''

''May I see it?'' asked Mr. Ryder. ''It might help me to remember whether I have seen the original.''

As she drew a small parcel from her bosom he saw that it was fastened to a string that went around her neck. Removing several wrappers, she brought to light an old-fashioned daguerreotype in a black case. He looked long and intently at the portrait. It was faded with time, but the features were still distinct, and it was easy to see what manner of man it had represented.

He closed the case, and with a slow movement handed it back to her.

''I don't know of any man in town who goes by that

name," he said, "nor have I heard of any one making such inquiries. But if you will leave me your address, I will give the matter some attention, and if I find out anything I will let you know."

She gave him the number of a house in the neighborhood, and went away, after thanking him warmly.

He wrote the address on the fly-leaf of the volume of Tennyson, and, when she had gone, rose to his feet and stood looking after her curiously. As she walked down the street with mincing step, he saw several persons whom she passed turn and look back at her with a smile of kindly amusement. When she had turned the corner, he went upstairs to his bedroom, and stood for a long time before the mirror of his dressing-case, gazing thoughtfully at the reflection of his own face.

3

At eight o'clock the ballroom was a blaze of light and the guests had begun to assemble; for there was a literary programme and some routine business of the society to be gone through with before the dancing. A black servant in evening dress waited at the door and directed the guests to the dressing-rooms.

The occasion was long memorable among the colored people of the city; not alone for the dress and display, but for the high average of intelligence and culture that distinguished the gathering as a whole. There were a number of school-teachers, several young doctors, three or four lawyers, some professional singers, an editor, a lieutenant in the United States army spending his furlough in the city, and others in various polite callings; these were colored, though most of them would not

have attracted even a casual glance because of any
marked difference from white people. Most of the ladies
were in evening costume, and dress coats and dancing
pumps were the rule among the men. A band of string
music, stationed in an alcove behind a row of palms,
played popular airs while the guests were gathering.

The dancing began at half past nine. At eleven
o'clock supper was served. Mr. Ryder had left the ballroom some little time before the intermission, but reappeared at the supper-table. The spread was worthy of
the occasion, and the guests did full justice to it. When
the coffee had been served, the toast-master, Mr. Solo-
mon Sadler, rapped for order. He made a brief introduc-
tory speech, complimenting host and guests, and then
presented in their order the toasts of the evening. They
were responded to with a very fair display of after-
dinner wit.

"The last toast," said the toast-master, when he
reached the end of the list, "is one which must appeal
to us all. There is no one of us of the sterner sex who is
not at some time dependent upon woman,—in infancy
for protection, in manhood for companionship, in old
age for care and comforting. Our good host has been
trying to live alone, but the fair faces I see around me
to-night prove that he too is largely dependent upon the
gentler sex for most that makes life worth living,—the
society and love of friends,—and rumor is at fault if he
does not soon yield entire subjection to one of them.
Mr. Ryder will now respond to the toast,—The Ladies."

There was a pensive look in Mr. Ryder's eyes as he
took the floor and adjusted his eye-glasses. He began by
speaking of woman as the gift of Heaven to man, and

after some general observations on the relations of the sexes he said: "But perhaps the quality which most distinguishes woman is her fidelity and devotion to those she loves. History is full of examples, but has recorded none more striking than one which only to-day came under my notice."

He then related, simply but effectively, the story told by his visitor of the afternoon. He gave it in the same soft dialect, which came readily to his lips, while the company listened attentively and sympathetically. For the story had awakened a responsive thrill in many hearts. There were some present who had seen, and others who had heard their fathers and grandfathers tell, the wrongs and sufferings of this past generation, and all of them still felt, in their darker moments, the shadow hanging over them. Mr. Ryder went on:—

"Such devotion and confidence are rare even among women. There are many who would have searched a year, some who would have waited five years, a few who might have hoped ten years; but for twenty-five years this woman has retained her affection for and her faith in a man she has not seen or heard of in all that time.

"She came to me to-day in the hope that I might be able to help her find this long-lost husband. And when she was gone I gave my fancy rein, and imagined a case I will put to you.

"Suppose that this husband, soon after his escape, had learned that his wife had been sold away, and that such inquiries as he could make brought no information of her whereabouts. Suppose that he was young, and she much older than he; that he was light; and she was black; that their marriage was a slave marriage, and legally binding only if they chose to make it so after the war. Suppose, too, that he made his way to the North, as some of us have done, and there, where he had larger opportunities, had improved them, and had in the course of all these years grown to be as different from the ignorant boy who ran away from fear of slavery as the day is from the night. Suppose, even, that he had qualified himself, by industry, by thrift, and by study, to win the friendship and be considered worthy the society of such people as these I see around me to-night, gracing my board and filling my heart with gladness; for I am old enough to remember the day when such a gathering would not have been possible in this land. Suppose, too, that, as the years went by, this man's memory of the past grew more and more indistinct, until at last it was rarely, except in his dreams, that any image of this bygone period rose before his mind. And then suppose that accident should bring to his knowledge the fact that the wife of his youth, the wife he had left behind him,—not one who had walked by his side and kept pace with him in his upward struggle, but one upon whom advancing years and a laborious life had set their mark,—was alive and seeking him, but that he was absolutely safe from recognition or discovery, unless he chose to reveal himself. My friends, what would the man do? I will presume that he was one who loved honor, and tried to deal justly with all men. I will even carry the case further, and suppose that perhaps he had set his heart upon another, whom he had hoped to call his own. What would he do, or rather what ought he to do, in such a crisis of a lifetime?

"It seemed to me that he might hesitate, and I imagined that I was an old friend, a near friend, and that he

had come to me for advice; and I argued the case with
him. I tried to discuss it impartially. After we had
looked upon the matter from every point of view, I said
to him, in words that we all know:—

> This above all: to thine own self be true,
> And it must follow, as the night the day,
> Thou canst not then be false to any man.

Then, finally, I put the question to him, 'Shall you acknowledge her?'

"And now, ladies and gentlemen, friends and companions, I ask you, what should he have done?"

There was something in Mr. Ryder's voice that
stirred the hearts of those who sat around him. It suggested more than mere sympathy with an imaginary situation; it seemed rather in the nature of a personal
appeal. It was observed, too, that his look rested more
especially upon Mrs. Dixon, with a mingled expression
of renunciation and inquiry.

She had listened, with parted lips and streaming eyes.
She was the first to speak: "He should have acknowledged her."

"Yes," they all echoed, "he should have acknowledged her."

"My friends and companions," responded Mr. Ryder, "I thank you, one and all. It is the answer I expected, for I knew your hearts."

He turned and walked toward the closed door of an
adjoining room, while every eye followed him in wondering curiosity. He came back in a moment, leading by
the hand his visitor of the afternoon, who stood startled
and trembling at the sudden plunge into this scene of

brilliant gayety. She was neatly dressed in gray, and wore the white cap of an elderly woman.

"Ladies and gentlemen," he said, "this is the woman, and I am the man, whose story I have told you. Permit me to introduce to you the wife of my youth."

Paul Laurence Dunbar

(1872–1906)

Poet, short story writer, novelist, and writer of articles, dramatic sketches, plays, and song lyrics, Dunbar was the most popular black author of his generation. He was also the best writer of dialect verse, and his mastery in this genre accounted in large measure for this singular popularity.

The son of ex-slave parents, Dunbar was born in Dayton, Ohio. His father was an escaped slave who returned from Canada to fight in the Union army. His mother, who even in bondage had learned to read and write, was a strong influence on the poet's life and encouraged him in his literary efforts. Both parents furnished their son with firsthand information about slavery which Dunbar used brilliantly in his works.

Dunbar went to high school in Dayton and was elected editor of the school paper. Too poor to attend college, he became an elevator boy, wrote verses on the job, and peddled them to his riders. In 1893 he collected all of his poems and with a loan from a white friend published them under the title *Oak and Ivy*. Shortly after the publication of this work, another white friend, a judge, offered Dunbar a job as courthouse messenger with the opportunity to "read" law; but in the spring of 1893, when the Chicago World's Fair was opened, Dunbar, feeling that there would be more promising jobs there, elected to go to the Windy City. He was disappointed in his search for jobs, but he met Frederick Douglass, who was commissioner in charge of the Haitian exhibit. Douglass made the young poet his clerical assistant, paying him five dollars a week from his own funds.

In 1895 Dunbar, again with the help of other white friends, published his second collection of poems, *Majors and Minors*. It was this work which was reviewed by William Dean Howells for *Harper's Weekly* in 1896. Although 86 of the volume's 148 pages dealt with poems in standard English, Howells practically dismissed these poems and stressed the ones in dialect. In the same year, Dodd, Mead and Company published Dunbar's third volume, *Lyrics of Lowly Life,* and with it the famous introduction by Howells, which said: "[This] was the first instance of an American Negro who had evinced innate distinction in literature. . . . So far as I could remember, Paul Dunbar was the only man of pure African blood and of American civilization to feel the Negro life aesthetically and express it lyrically." It is easy to disagree strongly with the critic's statement, but its effect is hardly debatable. Howells's introduction made Dunbar the most popular black writer in America.

In 1897 the poet made a not-too-successful tour of England. On his return he was given, through the influence of Robert G. Ingersoll, a minor position in the Library of Congress, which he held for two years. In 1898 he married Alice Ruth Moore, a fairly well-known writer, but the marriage failed. A victim of overwork, of drink, and of tuberculosis, Paul Laurence Dunbar died in his birthplace in 1906, still in his thirties.

In addition to the poetical works mentioned previously, Dunbar published the following collections: *Lyrics of the Hearthside* (1899), *Lyrics of Love and Laughter* (1903), and *Lyrics of Sunshine and Shadow* (1905). He published four novels: *The Uncalled* (1898), *The Love of Landry* (1900), *The Fanatics* (1901), and *The Sport of the Gods* (1902), the only novel that had black major characters. It is also, most critics feel, Dunbar's best novel. He also published four collections of short stories: *Folks from Dixie* (1898), *The Strength of Gideon* (1900), *In Old Plantation Days* (1903), and *The Heart of Happy Hollow* (1904).

An accommodationist, Dunbar avoided almost entirely in his works any mention of racial injustice. Predominantly a pastoral poet, he wrote generally about the joys of plantation life both before and after the war, of contented slaves and untroubled freedom. Though he seldom mentioned the harshness of slavery and the viciousness of Reconstruction, he wrote a small number of poems which could be classified as protest poems, among them "We Wear the Mask" and "The Haunted Oak," an antilynching poem. These, however, are the exceptions. Although Dunbar felt it unfair to judge his standing as a poet by his "jingles in a broken tongue," his best poetry is written in dialect. Even though he paints only two aspects of black life—pathos and humor—his works show a deeper understanding and insight than the portrayal by any of his contemporaries, white or black. On the other hand, his poems in standard English are highly uneven, running the gamut from banal and sentimental verses to lyrics of undoubted excellence.

Like his dialect verse, Dunbar's short stories, with but few exceptions, present only the humorous or pathetic side of plantation life. He wrote for a white audience seemingly; he wrote the kind of stories found in the works of Thomas Nelson Page and other southern white apologists.

For biographical and critical comment on Dunbar's life and work, see the full-length study by Benjamin Brawley, *Paul Laurence Dunbar: Poet of His People* (1916). See also the following works: Victor Lawson's *Dunbar Critically Examined* (1941); Vernon Loggins's *The Negro Author* (1931); Sterling A. Brown's *Negro Poetry and Drama* (1937); Addison Gayle, Jr.'s *Oak and Ivy: A Biography of Paul Laurence Dunbar* (1971); and the entry in *Dictionary of American Negro Biography* by Arthur P. Davis. Bernard W. Bell's *The Afro-American Novel* (1987) should be consulted. Also useful for its exploration of the poet's psyche and its expression in Dunbar's poetry, see Jean Wagner's *Black Poets* (1973). The original source of much of the present-day knowledge of the poet's career is *The Life and Works of Paul Laurence Dunbar* (1907) by Lida Keck Wiggins.

The following poems are reprinted from *The Complete Poems of Paul Laurence Dunbar* (1913); the short story is from *The Best Stories of Paul Laurence Dunbar,* ed. Benjamin Brawley (1938).

AN ANTE-BELLUM SERMON

We is gathahed hyeah, my brothahs,
    In dis howlin' wildaness,

Fu' to speak some words of comfo't
  To each othah in distress.
An' we chooses fu' ouah subjic'
  Dis—we'll 'splain it by an' by;
"An' de Lawd said, 'Moses, Moses,'
  An' de man said, 'Hyeah am I.' "

Now ole Pher'oh, down in Egypt,
  Was de wuss man evah bo'n,
An' he had de Hebrew chillun
  Down dah wukin' in his co'n;
'T well de Lawd got tiahed o' his foolin',
  An' sez he: "I 'll let him know—
Look hyeah, Moses, go tell Pher'oh
  Fu' to let dem chillun go."

"An' ef he refuse to do it,
  I will make him rue de houah,
Fu' I 'll empty down on Egypt
  All de vials of my powah."
Yes, he did—an' Pher'oh's ahmy
  Was n't wuth a ha'f a dime;
Fu' de Lawd will he'p his chillun,
  You kin trust him evah time.

An' yo' enemies may 'sail you
  In de back an' in de front;
But de Lawd is all aroun' you,
  Fu' to ba' de battle's brunt.
Dey kin fo'ge yo' chains an' shackles
  F'om de mountains to de sea;
But de Lawd will sen' some Moses
  Fu' to set his chillun free.

An' de lan' shall hyeah his thundah,
   Lak a blas' f'om Gab'el's ho'n,
Fu' de Lawd of hosts is mighty
   When he girds his ahmor on.
But fu' feah some one mistakes me,
   I will pause right hyeah to say,
Dat I'm still a-preachin' ancient,
   I ain't talkin' 'bout to-day.

But I tell you, fellah christuns,
   Things 'll happen mighty strange;
Now, de Lawd done dis fu' Isrul,
   An' his ways don't nevah change,
An' de love he showed to Isrul
   Was n't all on Isrul spent;
Now don't run an' tell yo' mastahs
   Dat I 's preachin' discontent.

'Cause I is n't; I 'se a-judgin'
   Bible people by deir ac's;
I 'se a-givin' you de Scriptuah,
   I 'se a-handin' you de fac's.
Cose ole Pher'oh b'lieved in slav'ry,
   But de Lawd he let him see,
Dat de people he put bref in,—
   Evah mothah's son was free.

An' dahs othahs thinks lak Pher'oh,
   But dey calls de Scriptuah liar,
Fu' de Bible says "a servant
   Is a-worthy of his hire."
An' you cain't git roun' nor thoo dat,
   An' you cain't git ovah it,
Fu' whatevah place you git in,
   Dis hyeah Bible too 'll fit.

So you see de Lawd's intention,
    Evah sence de worl' began,
Was dat His almighty freedom
    Should belong to evah man,
But I think it would be bettah,
    Ef I 'd pause again to say,
Dat I'm talkin' 'bout ouah freedom
    In a Bibleistic way.

But de Moses is a-comin',
    An' he 's comin', suah and fas'
We kin hyeah his feet a-trompin',
    We kin hyeah his trumpit blas'.
But I want to wa'n you people,
    Don't you git too brigity;
An' don't you git to braggin'
    'Bout dese things, you wait an' see.

But when Moses wif his powah
    Comes an' sets us chillun free,
We will praise de gracious Mastah
    Dat has gin us liberty;
An' we 'll shout ouah halleluyahs,
    On dat mighty reck'nin' day,
When we 'se reco'nised ez citiz'—
    Huh uh! Chillun, let us pray!

ODE TO ETHIOPIA

O Mother Race! to thee I bring
This pledge of faith unwavering,
    This tribute to thy glory.
I know the pangs which thou didst feel,

When Slavery crushed thee with its heel,
  With thy dear blood all gory.

Sad days were those—ah, sad indeed!
But through the land the fruitful seed
  Of better times was growing.
The plant of freedom upward sprung,
And spread its leaves so fresh and young—
  Its blossoms now are blowing.

On every hand in this fair land,
Proud Ethiope's swarthy children stand
  Beside their fairer neighbor;
The forests flee before their stroke,
Their hammers ring, their forges smoke,—
  They stir in honest labour.

They tread the fields where honour calls;
Their voices sound through senate halls
  In majesty and power.
To right they cling; the hymns they sing
Up to the skies in beauty ring,
  And bolder grow each hour.

Be proud, my Race, in mind and soul;
Thy name is writ on Glory's scroll
  In characters of fire.
High 'mid the clouds of Fame's bright sky
Thy banner's blazoned folds now fly,
  And truth shall lift them higher.

Thou hast the right to noble pride,
Whose spotless robes were purified
  By blood's severe baptism.
Upon thy brow the cross was laid,

And labour's painful sweat-beads made
  A consecrating chrism.

No other race, or white or black,
When bound as thou wert, to the rack,
  So seldom stooped to grieving;
No other race, when free again,
Forgot the past and proved them men
  So noble in forgiving.

Go on and up! Our souls and eyes
Shall follow thy continuous rise;
  Our ears shall list thy story
From bards who from thy root shall spring,
And proudly tune their lyres to sing
  Of Ethiopia's glory.

WHEN DE CO'N PONE 'S HOT

Dey is times in life when Nature
  Seems to slip a cog an' go,
Jes' a-rattlin' down creation,
  Lak an ocean's overflow;
When de worl' jes' stahts a-spinnin'
  Lak a picaninny's top,
An' yo' cup o' joy is brimmin'
  'Twell it seems about to slop,
An' you feel jes' lak a racah,
  Dat is trainin' fu' to trot—
When yo' mammy says de blessin'
  An' de co'n pone 's hot.

When you set down at de table,
  Kin' o' weary lak an' sad,

An' you 'se jes' a little tiahed
   An' purhaps a little mad;
How yo' gloom tu'ns into gladness,
   How yo' joy drives out de doubt
When de oven do' is opened,
   An' de smell comes po'in' out;
Why, de 'lectric light o' Heaven
   Seems to settle on de spot,
When yo' mammy says de blessin'
   An' de co'n pone 's hot.

When de cabbage pot is steamin'
   An' de bacon good an' fat,
When de chittlins is a-sputter'n'
   So 's to show you whah dey 's at;
Tek away yo' sody biscuit,
   Tek away yo' cake an' pie,
Fu' de glory time is comin',
   An' it 's 'proachin' mighty nigh,
An' you want to jump an' hollah,
   Dough you know you'd bettah not,
When yo' mammy says de blessin'
   An' de co'n pone 's hot.

I have hyeahd o' lots o' sermons,
   An' I've hyeahd o' lots o' prayers,
An' I've listened to some singin'
   Dat has tuck me up de stairs
Of de Glory-Lan' an' set me
   Jes' below de Mastah's th'one,
An' have lef' my hea't a-singin'
   In a happy aftah tone;
But dem wu'ds so sweetly murmured
   Seem to tech de softes' spot,

When my mammy says de blessin',
  An' de co'n pone 's hot.

SIGNS OF THE TIMES

Air a-gittin' cool an' coolah,
  Frost a-comin' in de night,
Hicka' nuts an' wa'nuts fallin',
  Possum keepin' out o'sight.
Tu'key struttin' in de ba'nya'd,
  Nary step so proud ez his;
Keep on struttin', Mistah Tu'key,
  Yo' do' know what time it is.

Cidah press commence a-squeakin'
  Eatin' apples sto'ed away,
Chillun swa'min' 'roun' lak ho'nets,
  Huntin' aigs ermung de hay.
Mistah Tu'key keep on gobblin'
  At de geese a-flyin' souf,
Oomph! dat bird do' know whut 's comin';
  Ef he did he'd shet his mouf.

Pumpkin gittin' good an' yallah
  Mek me open up my eyes;
Seems lak it 's a-lookin' at me
  Jes' a-la'in' dah sayin' "Pies."
Tu'key gobbler gwine 'roun' blowin',
  Gwine 'roun' gibbin' sass an' slack;
Keep on talkin', Mistah Tu'key,
  You ain't seed no almanac.

Fa'mer walkin' th'oo de ba'nya'd
  Seein' how things is comin' on,

Sees ef all de fowls is fatt'nin'—
  Good times comin' sho 's you bo'n.
Hyeahs dat tu'key gobbler braggin',
  Den his face break in a smile—
Nebbah min', you sassy rascal,
  He's gwine nab you atter while.

Choppin' suet in de kitchen,
  Stonin' raisins in de hall,
Beef a-cookin' fu' de mince meat,
  Spices groun'—I smell 'em all.
Look hyeah, Tu'key, stop dat gobblin',
  You ain' luned de sense ob feah,
You ol' fool, yo' naik 's in dangah,
  Do' you know Thanksgibbin 's hyeah!

WE WEAR THE MASK

We wear the mask that grins and lies,
It hides our cheeks and shades our eyes,—
This debt we pay to human guile;
With torn and bleeding hearts we smile,
And mouth with myriad subtleties.

Why should the world be overwise,
In counting all our tears and sighs?
Nay, let them only see us, while
  We wear the mask.

We smile, but, O great Christ, our cries
To thee from tortured souls arise.
We sing, but oh the clay is vile
Beneath our feet, and long the mile;

But let the world dream otherwise,
  We wear the mask!

CHRISMUS ON THE PLANTATION

It was Chrismus Eve, I mind hit fu' a mighty
  gloomy day—
Bofe de weathah an' de people—not a one of us
  was gay;
Cose you 'll t'ink dat 's mighty funny 'twell I try
  to mek hit cleah,
Fu' a da'ky 's allus happy when de holidays is
  neah.

But we was n't, fu' dat mo'nin' Mastah 'd tol' us
  we mus' go,
He'd been payin' us sence freedom, but he could
  n't pay no mo';
He wa'n't nevah used to plannin' 'fo' he got so po'
  an' ol',
So he gwine to give up tryin', an' de homestead
  mus' be sol'.

I kin see him stan'in' now erpon de step ez cleah
  ez day,
Wid de win' a-kind o'fondlin' thoo his haih all thin
  an' gray;
An' I 'membah how he trimbled when he said,
  "It 's ha'd fu' me,
Not to make yo Chrismus brightah, but I 'low it
  wa'n't to be."

All de women was a-cryin', an' de men, too, on de
  sly,

An' I noticed somep'n shinin' even in ol' Mastah's
   eye.
But we all stood still to listen ez ol' Ben come
   f'om de crowd
An' spoke up, a-try'n' to steady down his voice and
   mek it loud:—

"Look hyeah, Mastah, I 's been servin' you' fu' lo!
   dese many yeahs,
An' now, sence we 's got freedom an' you 's kind
   o' po', hit 'pears
Dat you want us all to leave you 'cause you don't
   t'ink you can pay.
Ef my membry has n't fooled me, seem dat whut I
   hyead you say.

"Er in othah wo'ds, you wants us to fu'git dat you
   's been kin',
An' ez soon ez you is he'pless, we 's to leave you
   hyeah behin'.
Well, ef dat 's de way dis freedom ac's on people,
   white er black,
You kin jes' tell Mistah Lincum fu' to tek his
   freedom back.

"We gwine wo'k dis ol' plantation fu' whatevah
   we kin git,
Fu' I know hit did suppo't us, an' de place kin do
   it yit.
Now de land is yo's, de hands is ouahs, an' I
   reckon we 'll be brave,
An' we 'll bah ez much ez you do w'en we has to
   scrape an' save."

Ol' Mastah stood dah trimblin', but a-smilin' thoo
   his teahs,

An' den hit seemed jes' nachullike, de place fah
   rung wid cheahs,
An' soon ez dey was quiet, some one sta'ted sof'
   an' low:
"Praise God," an' den we all jined in, "from
   whom all blessin's flow!"

Well, dey was n't no use tryin', ouah min's was sot
   to stay,
An' po' ol' Mastah could n't plead ner baig, ner
   drive us 'way,
An' all at once, hit seemed to us, de day was bright
   agin,
So evahone was gay dat night, an' watched de
   Chrismus in.

ANNER 'LIZER'S STUMBLIN' BLOCK

It was winter. The gray old mansion of Mr. Robert Selfridge, of Fayette County, Kentucky, was wrapped in its
usual mantle of winter somberness, and the ample plantation stretching in every direction thereabout was one
level plain of unflecked whiteness. At a distance from
the house the cabins of the Negroes stretched away in a
long, broken black line that stood out in bold relief
against the extreme whiteness of their surroundings.

About the center of the line, as dark and uninviting
as the rest, with its wide chimney of scrap limestone
turning clouds of dense smoke into the air, stood a
cabin.

There was nothing in its appearance to distinguish it
from the other huts clustered about. The logs that

formed its sides were just as seamy, the timbers of the roof had just the same abashed, brow-beaten look; and the keenest eye could not have detected the slightest shade of difference between its front and the bare, un-white-washed fronts of its scores of fellows. Indeed, it would not have been mentioned at all, but for the fact that within its confines lived and thrived the heroine of this story.

Of all the girls of the Selfridge estate, black, brown, or yellow, Anner 'Lizer was, without dispute, conceded to be the belle. Her black eyes were like glowing coals in their sparkling brightness; her teeth were like twin rows of shining ivories; her brown skin was as smooth and soft as silk, and the full lips that enclosed her gay and flexile tongue were tempting enough to make the heart of any dusky swain throb and his mouth water.

Was it any wonder, then, that Sam Merritt—strapping, big Sam, than whom there was not a more popular man on the place—should pay devoted court to her?

Do not gather from this that it was Sam alone who paid his *devoirs* to this brown beauty. Oh, no! Anner 'Lizer was the "bright particular star" of that plantation, and the most desired of all blessings by the young men thereabout. But Sam, with his smooth but fearless ways, Sam with his lightsome foot, so airy in the dance, Sam, handsome Sam, was the all-preferred. If there was a dance to go to, a corn-husking to attend, a social at the rude little log church, Sam was always the lucky man who was alert and *able* to possess himself of Anner 'Lizer's "comp'ny." And so, naturally, people began to connect their names, and the rumor went forth, as rumors will, that the two were engaged; and, as far as engagements went among the slaves in those days, I suppose it was true. Sam had never exactly prostrated himself at his sweetheart's feet and openly declared his passion; nor had she modestly snickered behind her fan and murmured Yes in the approved fashion of the present. But he had looked his feelings, and she had looked hers, while numerous little attentions bestowed on each other, too subtle to be detailed, and the attraction which kept them constantly together, were earnests of their intentions more weighty than words could give. And so, let me say, without further explanation, that Sam and Anner 'Lizer were engaged. But when did the course of true love ever run smooth?

There was never a time but there were some rocks in its channel around which the little stream had to glide or over which it had to bound and bubble; and thus it was with the loves of our young friends. But in this case the crystal stream seemed destined neither to bound over nor glide by the obstacle in its path, but rather to let its merry course be checked thereby.

It may, at first, seem a strange thing to say, but it was nevertheless true, that the whole sweep and torrent of the trouble had rise in the great religious revival that was being enthusiastically carried on at the little Baptist meeting-house. Interest, or perhaps, more correctly speaking, excitement ran high, and regularly as night came round, all the hands on the neighboring plantations flocked to the scene of their devotions.

There was no more regular attendant at these meetings, nor more deeply interested listener to the pastor's inflammatory exhortations, than Anner 'Lizer. The weirdness of the scene and the touch of mysticism in the services—though, of course, she did not analyze it thus—reached her emotional nature and stirred her being to its depths. Night after night found her in her pew, the third bench from the rude pulpit, her large eyes, dilated to their fullest capacity, following the minister through every motion, seeming at times in their steadiness to look him through and beyond to the regions he was describing—the harp-ringing heaven of bliss or the fire-filled home of the damned.

Now Sam, on the other hand, could not be induced to attend these meetings; and when his fellow-servants were at the little church praying, singing, and shouting, he was to be found sitting in one corner of his cabin, picking his banjo, or scouring the woods, carrying ax and taper, and, with a dog trotting at his heels, hunting for that venison of the Negro palate—'coon.

Of course this utter irreverence on the part of her lover shocked Anner 'Lizer; but she had not entered far enough into the regions of the ecstasy to be a proselyte; so she let Sam go his way, albeit with reluctance, while she went to church unattended. But she thought of Sam; and many a time when she secretly prayed to get religion she added a prayer that she might retain Sam.

He, the rogue, was an unconscious but pronounced skeptic; and day by day, as Anner 'Lizer became more and more possessed by religious fervor, the breach between them widened; still widening gradually until the one span that connected the two hearts was suddenly snapped asunder on the night when Anner 'Lizer went to the mourners' bench.

She had not gone to church with that intention; indeed not, although she had long been deeply moved by a consciousness of her lost estate. But that night, when the preacher had pictured the boundless joys of heaven, and then, leaning over the pulpit and stretching out his arms before him, had said in his softest tone, ''Now come, won't you, sinnahs? De Lawd is jes' on de othah side; jes' one step away, waitin' to receibe you. Won't you come to him? Won't you tek de chance o' be-comin' j'int 'ars o' dat beautiful city whar de streets is gol' an' de gates is pearl? Won't you come to him, sin-nah? Don't you see de pityin' look he's a-givin' you, a-sayin' Come, come?'' she lost herself. Some irresistible power seemed dominating her, and she rose and went forward, dropping at the altar amid a great shouting and clapping of hands and cries of ''Bless de Lawd, one mo' recruit fu' de Gospel ahmy.''

Someone started the hymn, ''We'll bow around the altar,'' and the refrain was taken up by the congregation with a fervor that made the rafters of the little edifice ring again.

The conquest of Anner 'Lizer, the belle of that sec-tion of Kentucky, was an event of great moment; and, in spite of the concentration of the worshipers' minds on their devotions, the unexpected occurrence called forth a deal of discussion among the brothers and sis-ters. Aunt Hannah remarked to Aunt Maria, over the back of the seat, that she ''nevah knowed de gal was unner c'nviction.'' And Aunt Maria answered solemnly, ''You know, sistah, de Lawd wuks in a myste'ious way his wondahs to pu'fo'm.''

Meanwhile the hymn went on, and above it rose the voice of the minister: ''We want all de Christuns in de house to draw up aroun' de altah, whar de fiah is bu'nin': you know in de wintah time when hit's col' you crowds up clost to de fiahplace; so now, ef you wants to git spi'tually wa'm, you mus' be up whar de fiah is.'' There was a great scrambling and shuffling of feet as the members rose with one accord to crowd, singing, around the altar.

Two of the rude benches had been placed end to end before the pulpit, so that they extended nearly the full width of the little church; and at these knelt a dozen or more mourners, swaying and writhing under the burden of their sins.

The song being ended, the preacher said: "Br'er Adams, please tek up de cross." During the momentary lull that intervened between the end of the song and the prayer, the wails and supplications of the mourners sounded out with weird effect. Then Br'er Adams, a white-haired patriarch, knelt and "took up the cross."

Earnestly he besought the divine mercy in behalf of "de po' sinnahs, a-rollin' an' a-tossin' in de tempes' of dere sins." "Lawd," he prayed, "come down dis evenin' in Sperit's powah to seek an' to save-ah; let us heah de rumblin' of yo' cha'iot wheels-ah lak de thundah from Mount Sinai-ah; oh, Lawd'ah, convert mou'-nahs an' convict sinnahs-ah; show 'em dat dey mus' die an' cain't lib an' atter death to judg-a-ment; tu'n 'em aroun' befo' it is evahlastin' an' eternally too late." Then, warming more and more, and swaying his form back and forth, as he pounded the seat in emphasis, he began to wail out in a sort of indescribable monotone: "O Lawd, save de mou'nah!"

"Save de mou'nah!" came the response from all over the church.

"He'p 'em out of de miah an' quicksan's of dere sins!"

"He'p, Lawd!"

"And place deir feet upon de evahlastin' an' eternal rock-ah!"

"Do, Lawd."

"O Lawd-ah, shake a dyin' sinnah ovah hell an'
fo'bid his mighty fall-ah!"

"O Lawd, shake 'em!" came from the congregation.

By this time everyone was worked up to a high state
of excitement, and the prayer came to an end amid great
commotion. Then a rich, mellow voice led out with:

> "Sabe de mou'nah jes' now,
> Sabe de mou'nah jes' now,
> Sabe de mou'nah jes' now,
> Only trust Him jes' now,
> Only trust Him jes' now,
> He'p de sinnah jes' now;"

and so to indefinite length the mournful minor melody
ran along like a sad brook flowing through autumn
woods, trying to laugh and ripple through tears.

Every now and then some mourner would spring half
up, with a shriek, and then sink down again trembling
and jerking spasmodically. "He's a-doubtin', he's a-
doubtin'!" the cry would fly around; "but I tell you he
purt' nigh had it that time."

Finally the slender form of Anner 'Lizer began to
sway backward and forward, like a sapling in the wind,
and she began to mourn and weep aloud.

"Praise de Lawd!" shouted Aunt Hannah, "de po'
soul's gittin' de evidence: keep on, honey, de Lawd
ain't fa' off." The sudden change attracted considerable
attention, and in a moment a dozen or more zealous al-
tar-workers gathered around Anner 'Lizer and began to
clap and sing with all their might, keeping time to the

melodious cadence of their music with heavy foot-pats on the resounding floor.

> "Git on boa'd-ah, little childering,
>   Git on boa'd-ah, little childering,
>   Git on boa'd-ah, little childering,
>   Dere's room fo' many mo'.

> "De gospel ship is sailin',
>   It's loaded down wid souls.
>   If you want to mek heab'n yo' happy home,
>   You mus' ketch it fo' it goes.
>   Git on boa'd, etc.

> "King Jesus at de hellum,
>   Fu' to guide de ship erright.
>   We gwine fu' to put into heab'n's po't
>   Wid ouah sails all shinin' white.
>   Git on boa'd," etc.

With a long dwell on the last word of the chorus, the mellow cadence of the song died away.

"Let us bow down fu' a season of silent praar," said the minister.

"Lawd, he'p us to pray," responded Uncle Eben Adams.

The silence that ensued was continually broken by the wavering wail of the mourners. Suddenly one of them, a stalwart young man, near the opening of the aisle, began to writhe and twist himself into every possible contortion, crying, "O Lawd, de devil's a-ridin' me; tek him off—tek him off!"

"Tek him off, Lawd!" shouted the congregation.

Then suddenly, without warning, the mourner rose

straight up into the air, shouting, "Hallelujah, hallelujah, hallelujah!"

"He's got it—he's got it!" cried a dozen eager worshipers, leaping to their feet and crowding around the happy convert; "bless de Lawd, he's got it." A voice was raised, and soon the church was ringing with

> "Loose him and let him go,
> Let him shout to glory."

On went the man, shouting "Hallelujah," shaking hands, and bounding over seats in the ecstasy of his bliss.

His conversion kindled the flame of the meeting and set the fire going. You have seen corn in the popper when the first kernel springs up and flares open, how quickly the rest follow, keeping up the steady pop, pop, pop; well, just so it was after this first conversion. The mourners popped up quickly and steadily as the strength of the spiritual fire seemed to reach their swelling souls. One by one they left the bench on which, figuratively speaking, they may be said to have laid down their sins and proclaimed themselves possessors of religion; until, finally, there was but one left, and that one—Anner 'Lizer. She had ceased from her violent activity, and seemed perfectly passive now.

The efforts of all were soon concentrated on her, and such stamping and clapping and singing was never heard before. Such cries of "Jes' look up, sistah, don't you see Him at yo' side? Jes' reach out yo' han' an' tech de hem of His ga'ment. Jes' listen, sistah, don't you heah de angels singin'? Don't you heah de rumblin'

of de cha'iot wheels? He's a-comin', He's a-comin',
He's a-comin'!''

But Anner 'Lizer was immovable; with her face lying
against the hard bench, she moaned and prayed softly to
herself. The congregation redoubled its exertions, but all
to no effect; Anner 'Lizer wouldn't ''come thoo.''

It was a strange case.

Aunt Maria whispered to her bosom friend: ''You
min' me, Sistah Hannah, dere's sump'n' on dat gal's
min'.'' And Aunt Hannah answered, ''I believe you.''

Josephine, or more commonly Phiny, a former belle
whom Anner 'Lizer's superior charms had deposed,
could not lose this opportunity to have a fling at her
successful rival. Of course such cases of vindictiveness
in women are rare, and Phiny was exceptional when she
whispered to her fellow-servant, Lucy: ''I reckon she'd
git 'ligion if Sam Me'itt was heah to see her.'' Lucy
snickered, as in duty bound, and whispered back, ''I
wisht you'd heish.''

Well, after all their singing, in spite of all their efforts, the time came for closing the meeting, and Anner
'Lizer had not yet made a profession.

She was lifted tenderly up from the mourners' bench
by a couple of solicitous sisters, and, after listening to
the preacher's exhortation to ''pray constantly, thoo de
day an' thoo de night, in de highways an' de byways
an' in yo' secret closet,'' she went home praying in her
soul, leaving the rest of the congregation to loiter along
the way and gossip over the night's events.

All the next day Anner 'Lizer, erstwhile so cheerful,
went about her work sad and silent, every now and then
stopping in the midst of her labors and burying her face
in her heat white apron to sob violently. It was true, as

Aunt Hannah expressed, that "de Sperit had sholy tuk holt of dat gal wid a powahful han'."

All of her fellow-servants knew that she was a mourner, and, with that characteristic reverence for religion which is common to all their race, and not lacking even in the most hardened sinner among them, they respected her feelings. Phiny alone, when she met her, tossed her head and giggled openly. But Phiny's actions never troubled Anner 'Lizer, for she felt herself so far above her. Once though, in the course of the day, she had been somewhat disturbed, when she had suddenly come upon her rival, standing in the springhouse talking and laughing with Sam. She noticed, too, with a pang, that Phiny had tied a bow of red ribbon on her hair. She shut her lips and only prayed the harder. But an hour later, somehow, a ribbon as red as Phiny's had miraculously attached itself to her thick black plaits. Was the temporal creeping in with the spiritual in Anner 'Lizer's mind? Who can tell? Perhaps she thought that, while cultivating the one, she need not utterly neglect the other; and who says but that she was right?

Uncle Eben, however, did not take this view of the matter when he came hobbling up in the afternoon to exhort her a little. He found Anner 'Lizer in the kitchen washing dishes. Engrossed in the contemplation of her spiritual state, or praying for deliverance from the same, through the whole day she had gone about without speaking to anyone. But with Uncle Eben it was, of course, different, for he was a man held in high respect by all the Negroes and, next to the minister, the greatest oracle in those parts; so Anner 'Lizer spoke to him.

"Howdy, Uncl' Eben," she said, in a lugubrious

tone, as the old man hobbled in and settled down in a convenient corner.

"Howdy, honey, howdy," he replied, crossing one leg over the other, as he unwound his long bandanna, placed it in his hat, and then deposited his heavy cane on the white floor. "I jes' thought I'd drap in to ax you how do you do today?"

"Po' enough, Uncl' Eben, fu' sho'."

"Ain't foun' no res' fu' yo' soul yit?"

"No res' yit," answered Anner 'Lizer, again applying the apron to her already swollen eyes.

"Um-m," sighed the old man, meditatively tapping his foot; and then the gay flash of Anner 'Lizer's ribbon caught his eye and he gasped: "Bless de Lawd, Sis 'Lizer; you don't mean to tell me dat you's gwine 'bout heah seekin' wid yo' har tied up in ribbon? Whut! tek it off, honey, tek if off; ef yo' wants yo' soul saved, tek it off!"

Anner 'Lizer hesitated, and raised her eyes in momentary protest, but they met the horrified gaze of the old man, and she lowered them again as her hand went reluctantly up to her head to remove the offending bit of finery.

"You see, honey," Uncle Eben went on, "when you sta'ts out on de Christian jou'ney, you's got to lay aside ev'ry weight dat doth so easy beset you an' keeps you f'om pergressin'; y' ain't got to think nothin' 'bout pussunal 'dornment; you's jes' got to shet yo' eyes an' open yo' hea't an' say, Lawd, come; you mustn't wait fu' to go to chu'ch to pray, nuther, you mus' pray anywhar an' ev'ry whar. Why, when I was seekin', I ust to go 'way off up in de big woods to pray, an' dere's whar de Lawd answered me, an' I'm a-rejoicin' today in

de powah of de same salvation. Honey, you's got to
pray, I tell you. You's got to brek de backbone of yo'
pride an' pray in earnes'; an' ef you does dat, you'll git
he'p, fu' de Lawd is a praar-heahin' Lawd an' plenteous
in mussy.''

Anner 'Lizer listened attentively to the exhortation
and evidently profited by it, for soon after Uncle Eben's
departure she changed her natty little dress for one less
pretentious, and her dainty, frilled white muslin apron
gave way to a broad dark calico one. If grace was to be
found by self-abnegation in the matter of dress, Anner
'Lizer was bound to have it at any price.

As afternoon waned and night came on, she grew
more and more serious, and more frequent recourse was
had to the corner of her apron. She even failed to see
Phiny when that enterprising young person passed her,
decked out in the whitest of white cuffs and collars setting off in pleasant contrast her neat dark dress. Phiny
giggled again and put up her hand, ostensibly to brush
some imaginary dust from her bosom but really to show
her pretty white cuffs with their big bone buttons. But it
was all lost on Anner 'Lizer; her gaze was downcast
and her thoughts far away. If anyone was ever
''seekin' '' in earnest, this girl was.

Night came, and with it the usual services. Anner
'Lizer was one of the earliest of the congregation to arrive, and she went immediately to the mourners' bench.
In the language of the congregation, ''Eldah Johnsing
sholy did preach a powahful sermon'' that night. More
sinners were convicted and brought to their knees, and,
as before, these recruits were converted and Anner
'Lizer left. What was the matter?

That was the question which everyone asked, but

there were none found who could answer it. The circumstance was all the more astounding from the fact
that this unsuccessful mourner had not been a very
wicked girl. Indeed, it was to have been expected that
she might shake her sins from her shoulders as she
would discard a mantle, and step over on the Lord's
side. But it was not so.

But when a third night came and passed with the
same result, it became the talk of three plantations. To
be sure, cases were not lacking where people had
"mourned" a week, two weeks, or even a month; but
they were woeful sinners and those were times of less
spiritual interest; but under circumstances so favorable
as were now presented, that one could long refrain from
"gittin' religion" was the wonder of all. So, after the
third night, everybody wondered and talked, and not a
few began to lean to Phiny's explanation, that "de ole
snek in de grass had been a'goin' on doin' all her dev'-
ment on de sly, so's *people* wouldn't know it; but de
Lawd he did, an' he payin' her up fu' it now."

Sam Merritt alone did not talk, and seemed perfectly
indifferent to all that was said. When he was in Phiny's
company and she rallied him about the actions of his
"gal," he remained silent.

On the fourth night of Anner 'Lizer's mourning, the
congregation gathered as usual at the church. For the
first half-hour all went on as usual, and the fact that Anner 'Lizer was absent caused no remark, for everyone
thought she would come in later. But time passed and
she did not come. "Eldah Johnsing's" flock became ag-
itated. Of course there were other mourners, but the one
particular one was absent; hence the dissatisfaction.
Every head in the house was turned toward the door,

whenever it was opened by some late comer; and
around flew the whisper, "I wunner ef she's quit
mou'nin'; you aint' heerd of her gittin' 'ligion, have
you?" No one had.

Meanwhile the object of their solicitude was praying
just the same, but in a far different place. Grasping, as
she was, at everything that seemed to give her promise
of relief, somehow Uncle Eben's words had had a deep
effect upon her. So, when night fell and her work was
over, she had gone up into the woods to pray. She had
prayed long without success, and now she was crying
aloud from the very fullness of her heart, "O Lawd,
sen' de light—sen' de light!" Suddenly, as if in answer
to her prayer, a light appeared before her some distance
away.

The sudden attainment of one's desires often shocks
one; so with our mourner. For a moment her heart stood
still and the thought came to her to flee, but her mind
flashed back over the words of one of the hymns she
had heard down at church, "Let us walk in de light,"
and she knew that before she walked in the light she
must walk toward it. So she rose and started in the direction of the light. How it flickered and flared, disappeared and reappeared, rose and fell, even as her spirits,
as she stumbled and groped her way over fallen logs
and through briers! Her limbs were bruised and her
dress torn by the thorns. But she heeded it not; she had
fixed her eye—physical and spiritual—on the light before her. It drew her with an irresistible fascination.
Suddenly she stopped. An idea had occurred to her.
Maybe this light was a Jack-o'-lantern! For a moment
she hesitated, then promptly turned her pocket wrong
side out, murmuring, "De Lawd'll tek keer o' me." On

she started; but lo! the light had disappeared! What! had the turning of the pocket indeed worked so potent a charm?

But no! it reappeared as she got beyond the intervention of a brush pile which had obscured it. The light grew brighter as she grew fainter; but she clasped her hands and raised her eyes in unwavering faith, for she found that the beacon did not recede, but glowed with a steady and stationary flame.

As she drew near, the sound of sharp strokes came to her ears, and she wondered. Then, as she slipped into the narrow circle of light, she saw that it was made by a taper which was set on a log. The strokes came from a man who was chopping down a tree in which a 'coon seemed to have taken refuge. It needed no second glance at the stalwart shoulders to tell her that the man was—Sam. Her step attracted his attention, and he turned.

"Sam!"

"Anner 'Lizer!"

And then they both stood still, too amazed to speak. Finally she walked across to where he was standing, and said: "Sam, I didn't come out heah to fin' you, but de Lawd has 'p'inted it so, 'ca'se he knowed I orter speak to you." Sam leaned hopelessly on his ax; he thought she was going to exhort him.

Anner 'Lizer went on: "Sam, you's my stumblin' block in de high-road to salvation. I's been tryin' to git 'ligion fu' fo' nights, an' I cain't do it jes' on you' 'count. I prays an' I prays, an' jes as I's a'mos' got it, jes as I begin to heah de cha'iot wheels a-rollin', yo' face comes right in 'tween an' drives it all away. Tell me now, Sam, so's to put me out of my 'spense, does

you want to ma'y me, er is you goin' to ma'y Phiny? I
jes' wants you to tell me, not dat I keers pussonally, but
so's my min' kin be at res' spi'tu'lly, an' I kin git 'ligion. Jes' say yes er no; I wants to be settled one way
er t' other.''

"Anner 'Lizer," said Sam, reproachfully, "you know
I wants to ma'y you jes' ez soon ez Mas' Rob'll let
me.''

"Dere now," said Anner 'Lizer, "bless de Lawd!"
And somehow Sam had dropped the ax and was holding
her in his arms.

It boots not whether the 'coon was caught that night
or not, but it is a fact that Anner 'Lizer set the whole
place afire by getting religion at home early the next
morning. And the same night the minister announced
that ''de Lawd had foun' out de sistah's stumblin' block
an' removed it f'om de path.''